Twelve Months of Sundays

Life Lessons from Spirit-filled teaching

Miss Nan

xulon
PRESS

Kristen,

It has been my privilege to walk beside you and watch Jackson become your home.

You are a special lady who is precious to me, but more so to our Lord. Keep looking up!

In Him,
Miss Nan

Praise for "Twelve Months of Sundays"

(From her former Colonial Heights pastors)

Every pastor needs a Miss Nan in his church! She has a passionate commitment to Jesus Christ and His church. She teaches God's Word with truth, clarity, and practical application. She has been a godly example and mentor to so many women in the church and has been an encouragement to me personally. The daily devotions written in this book come from her teachings over the years. They are inspirational as well as practical and have blessed so many. I am absolutely confident God will use this devotional book to encourage and inspire you.

Mark Anderson, Senior Pastor
Lynwood Baptist Church
Cape Girardeau, MO

I've had the privilege of knowing thousands of believers across the years. There is only one "Miss Nan." Her faithful, loyal, self-sacrificing spirit has made an indelible imprint on my soul. She is perhaps the truest, purest, most consistent example of a totally sold-out woman of God I have ever known. Her teaching is captivating, her conversations are stimulating, and her writings are anointed.

Read this devotional book and be blessed by a woman with an unde-niable agenda—to glorify God and exalt her Savior, Jesus Christ. This book will bless you.
Richard A. Powell, Senior Pastor
McGregor Baptist Church
Ft. Myers, Florida

Miss Nan is a woman of extraordinary faith with an uncompromising commitment to the Lord Jesus Christ. For decades she has saturated her soul with the Word of God and has taught it with remarkable understanding. Furthermore, she has lived out her faith in such an exemplary way that her lessons are full of life and credibility. Few teachers have ever endeared themselves to their students as has Miss Nan. Her Bible-based teaching ministry has truly edified the church and undergirded the ministry and effectiveness of her pastors to the glory of God.
J. Gerald Harris, Editor
The Christian Index
Atlanta, Georgia

I remember with fondness when Nan joined Colonial Heights and began her teaching ministry. Her hunger for the Word of God and her in-depth study have led her to become one of the finest Bible teachers that I have ever known. This book should serve as a great encouragement and source of inspiration to all Christians.
Len Turner
Len Turner Ministries, Inc.
Woodstock, Georgia

Dedication

To Terri, who encouraged the writing; to Janice, who compiled the writing; and to Macy, who imitates the writing. All three are dear friends and supporters.

Foreword

I believe church is the place that you will find your best friends. That's where I met my best friend, "Miss Nan," as we call her. Apart from my wife, children, and family, she is the most influential person in my life; and many in our church will say the same thing. There are many reasons for her influence to be so powerful, but I think this is the main one – I cannot think of Miss Nan without thinking of Jesus. If you hear her speak, teach, or pray, you will immediately understand how close she is to our Lord, how much she loves Him, and how great her desire is for Him to be glorified in the lives of those around her and in the church. Such people leave a lasting impression on your life.

This book is a compilation of what she has consistently taught and lived out before us for over thirty years. These daily lessons are scriptural truth aimed at getting us closer to Jesus in love and obedience and closer to one another, particularly in the church. The topics touch our relationship to the Lord in areas where we all need help and encouragement from time to time. Her teaching is always focused on our personal walk with the Lord and how we can bring love and unity to the church. One of her consistent quotes is, "We don't have to go to church; we get to go to church!" No one loves the church more than Miss Nan.

I believe this book is the direct result of the ministry the Lord has given Miss Nan, which is to learn and then teach Biblical truth. Her life ministry verses bear this out. Psalm 71:18: *"Now also, when I am old and gray headed, O God, do not forsake me, until I declare*

Your strength to this generation, Your power to everyone who is to come." Psalm 71:23-24: *"My lips shall greatly rejoice when I sing to You, and my soul, which You have redeemed. My tongue also shall talk of Your righteousness all the day long."* As you read these daily teachings, I believe you will get a greater understanding of righteous living and find yourself praising the Lord for His love, power, righteousness, and obedience, all of which will result in glory to Him.

Anointed teaching will always have a testimony, which you will see as you read the testimonies of people who have applied these teachings and her counsel to issues in their lives. These are only a few of the many lives that have grown in faith and in their walk as the Lord has used these teachings to draw them to His truth, His purpose, and His will.

I'm glad you are going to have a chance to meet and be taught by my best friend Miss Nan through this book, and I am certain that you will see through these pages our Very Best Friend, the Lord Jesus Christ.

Jack Jackson
Colonial Heights Baptist Church

Preface

One book, the first "Month of Sundays" was all I intended to write, but the Lord had other plans; thus one month, over time, became twelve. Some of my friends took the twelve and put them into this one book, which we have called, "Twelve Months of Sundays." May our Lord use these messages to minister to your heart.

January

A few years ago the church I attend was engaged in forty days of prayer and fasting for the future of the church. The church provided us with a little booklet to use as a guide.

One day my friend Terri called to say, "I have a suggestion. Why don't you write a similar booklet on all the principles you teach?" I agreed to pray about her request and asked her and another friend, Marsha, to pray with me. After praying, all three of us felt God leading me to write. The question was, "Where do I begin?"

My thoughts went immediately to a piece of paper that I keep in my Bible. It contains a list that Rhonda, a member at the time of the Sunday School class that I teach gave me. She made this statement in class one day: "Miss Nan teaches about six things, and most of her teaching is mainly expanding on these themes (which we need)." She had a point.

She handed me a piece of paper that listed the following six things:

"1. Armor of God – before you get out of bed –
2. Daily quiet time – whether you feel like it or not –
3. Fruit of the Spirit – you set the tone in your home –
4. Local church service – use your gifts in your church –
5. Pastoral authority – he is to feed the flock and be an example to the people-
6. No murmuring/complaining – get in on what God is doing."

All of these subjects are dear to my heart, so I began to write.

I. ARMOR OF GOD –
Before You Get Out of Bed

"Put on the whole armor of God, that ye may be able to stand against the wiles (schemes) of the devil" (Ephesians 6:11).
As Christians, we must understand that Satan carefully devises schemes and tactics against us. What do we do?

JANUARY 1   STAND!
Key Verse: *"...that ye may be able to stand against the wiles of the devil" (Ephesians 6:11). "...and having done all, to stand" (Ephesians 6:13). "Stand therefore..." (Ephesians 6:14a).*

Message: The late Bill Washburn took a class with me on spiritual warfare. Bill was a great soul winner. He told me of this experience he had in Oklahoma. He was standing on a street corner with a hostile man. Bill asked him about his personal relationship with the Lord. The answer he got was a string of curse words. Bill said that he started to turn and walk away, but he heard my voice in his ear repeating, "Stand," over and over, so he stood there until the man calmed down. Then Bill asked him about his family. At that point the man broke down and cried and asked Jesus into his heart. Stand!

This I know, folks. I am weak; Satan is strong; Jesus is stronger. Therefore, you and I can have victory, no matter what our circumstances. We are not to turn and run. Our Lord provides no armor for our backsides. Tell the Lord that you will stand in His strength, come what may.

JANUARY 2   THE BELT OF TRUTH
Key Verse: *"Stand therefore, having your loins girt about with truth..." (Ephesians 6:14).*

Message: What is truth? Read these two verses: *"Jesus saith unto him (Thomas), I am the way, the <u>truth</u>, and the life..." (John 14:6).* In Jesus' prayer to the Father for His own, He prayed, *"...thy word is truth" (John 17:17).*

14

The belt of truth holds our uniforms together as we operate in this world now in the hands of Satan. This world has no truth. Look for truth in no place—not in the philosophies of man nor in the wiles of the devil—but in our Lord and His Word.

JANUARY 3   THE BREASTPLATE OF RIGHTEOUSNESS

Key Verse: *"...and having on the breastplate of righteousness" (Ephesians 6:14a).*

Message: This is what was attached to you the day you got saved. *"For as many of you as have been baptized into Christ have put on Christ" (Galatians 3:27).* This means that Jesus imputed His righteousness to you. He covered you with Himself. Now read this verse that Jesus spoke concerning the Holy Spirit: *"...Ye know him for he dwelleth with you and shall be in you" (John 14:17).* This means that Jesus imparted His righteousness to you. The Holy Spirit lives in you. You have a new nature. Unfortunately, because of the "fall," you still have the old nature, the sin nature. Which one you follow must be an act of your will.

Thank the Lord that you are covered with Him. That is the only way you can go to the Father because He cannot look at sin. Pray that you will not take our Lord any place that He would not feel comfortable. Thank Him that the Holy Spirit lives in you and pray that you will be so filled with the Holy Spirit that you cannot hear that old sin nature talking.

JANUARY 4   MORE ON RIGHTEOUSNESS

Key Verse: *"Trust in the Lord with all thine heart; and lean not unto thine own understanding. In all thy ways acknowledge him, and he shall direct thy paths" (Proverbs 3:5-6).*

Message: Bob Spring asked me to say a word to the pastor search committee at our first meeting. I told them that we faced a monumental task and that the church had entrusted us to locate God's man for Colonial Heights Baptist Church. I stressed that in order for us to succeed, we had to be living where God answers prayer. I pointed out that we would have to trust Jesus and not try to seek a pastor based on our desires. Then I said, "If we want the Lord to '*direct our paths*,' we are going to have to constantly practice '*in all thy ways acknowledge him.*' We are going to have to be so right with God at home, at work, at church, at play—so right that He could trust us to find God's man." Do you need God's direction in your life? Then practice "*in all thy ways acknowledge him.*"

Acknowledge the Lord in all you do. Walk right straight toward Him. Do not veer to the right or to the left. Always remember that it is easy to get off the path of righteousness. When you do, ask the Lord to forgive you. Then get back on the straight path.

JANUARY 5   EVEN MORE ON RIGHTEOUSNESS

Key Verse: *"For the eyes of the Lord are over the righteous, and his ears are open unto their prayers..." (1 Peter 3:12). "...The Lord loveth the righteous" (Psalm 146:8). "For the righteous Lord loveth righteousness: his countenance doth behold the upright" (Psalm 11:7). "Therefore hath the Lord recompensed me according to my righteousness, according to the cleanness of my hands in his eyesight" (Psalm 18:24). "...The prayer of the upright is his delight" (Proverbs 15:8).*

Message: Ponder these verses. Blessings come to the righteous. Be sure that you are right with the Lord.

Don't you want our Lord's ears open to your prayers? Don't you want His face to shine on you? Don't you want to have your hands clean in His eyesight? Don't you want to experience His love? Don't you want to be His delight? If so, tell the Lord that you want to walk so close to Him that He will give you the desires of your heart.

JANUARY 6   SHOES THAT ADVANCE AGAINST THE ENEMY

Key Verse: *"And your feet shod with the preparation of the gospel of peace" (Ephesians 6:15).*

Message: What kind of peace do you have to have in order to announce the Good News? To advance against the enemy?

a. Peace with God: *"Therefore being justified by faith, we have peace with God through our Lord Jesus Christ" (Romans 5:1).* You must be sure of your salvation. That is what brings peace with God.

b. Peace within: *"And we know that all things work together for good to them that love God..." (Romans 8:28).* Our Lord is working all things together for good to them that love Him.

c. Peace with others: *"When a man's ways please the Lord, he maketh even his enemies to be at peace with him" (Proverbs 16:7).* When your ways please the Lord, He will act. The best way to be at peace with your enemy is to make sure your ways please the Lord. Peace with God! Peace within! Peace with others! Wear these shoes and you will advance against the enemy, even as you stand still.

We have peace with God through our Lord Jesus Christ. We have peace within when can say and really mean that He works out everything for our good and His glory. We have peace with others when our ways are pleasing to our Lord. Pray for these kinds of peace.

JANUARY 7 THE SHIELD OF FAITH
Key Verse: *"Above all, taking the shield of faith, wherewith ye shall be able to quench all the fiery darts of the wicked (one)" (Ephesians 6:16).*

Message: Satan will throw a fiery dart at you wherever and whenever he can. What can you do? Put up the shield of faith! What is it? Believing God's Word and using it against the devil! *"Every word of God is pure; he is a shield unto those who put their trust in him" (Proverbs 30:5).*

Faith means believing God's Word. Faith means trusting Him. Faith means obeying His Word. As we believe and trust and obey, His Word will be a shield for us against the fiery darts of the evil one. Always remember these words: *"But without faith it is impossible to please God" (Hebrews 11:6).* Pray that your faith will be strong.

JANUARY 8   THE HELMET OF SALVATION
Key Verse: *"And take the helmet of salvation..." (Ephesians 6:17).*

Message: The helmet of salvation is not about getting saved. You are not in the army unless you are saved. It is about eternal security that is a result of your salvation. That cap on your head is to remind you that at one point in your life you were saved from the penalty of sin. Today, you are being saved from the power of sin. When Jesus comes again, you will be saved from the presence of sin. *"We shall be like him..." (1 John 3:2).*

The Lord put the helmet of salvation on our heads when He saved our souls. Picture His nail-pierced hands holding it so tightly that no one can pry it off. Thank Him for saving your soul and keeping you saved. When you are tempted to give in to sin, picture that helmet and know that sin does not have to have power over you because *"...greater is he that is in you than he that is in the world" (1 John 4:4).*

JANUARY 9   THE SWORD OF THE SPIRIT
Key Verse: *"...and the sword of the Spirit, which is the word of God" (Ephesians 6:17b).*

Message: God's Holy Word! We use this weapon to cause Satan to retreat. James 4:7 says this: *"Resist the devil, and he will flee from you."* Now, I don't resist him by speaking to him. He is too powerful for me. How should we resist him? We must use the "sword of the Spirit." To use it, we have to know it. Memorize Scripture. However, memorizing isn't enough. Anyone can do that. Our verse says that the sword is the "sword of the Spirit." In other words, Paul is saying, "Take up the sword which the Holy Spirit provides for you which is the Bible." I believe this means that when you have God's Word in your heart, the Holy Spirit within you will bring a Scripture to your mind to use against the devil.

Every believer should desire to know God's Word. Ask the Holy Spirit to point you to the Scripture you need when Satan is after you just as He did when Satan was after Jesus. Matthew 4:1 says, *"Then was Jesus led up of the Spirit into the wilderness to be tempted of the devil.*" Because our Lord was filled with the Spirit, He was able to point a sword at Satan that said, *"It is written..." (Matthew 4:4).* Pray that you will be able to do likewise.

Note: I actually put on the "whole armor of God" before I get out of bed every morning, no exception. But I also like to concentrate on one piece at a time in my quiet time. Follow the pattern best for you. Just be sure to get the armor on. Why would anyone leave the house in the morning to face a world run by Satan without wearing his uniform for the battles of the day???

II. DAILY QUIET TIME –
Whether You Feel Like It or Not

Emotion is an important part of a believer's life, but discipline, not feelings, must be a mark of your Christian life. There is no substitute for that daily disciplined walk that includes having a quiet time every day, whether you feel like it or not.

JANUARY 10   GET ALONE WITH GOD
Key Verse: *"Thy word is a lamp unto my feet, and a light unto my path" (Psalm 119:105).*

Message: If this is true of you, and I pray that it is, the Word can only be your lamp and your light if you get alone with our Lord every day. My experience is that He speaks to me through His Word and sometimes in that "still small voice." So how can I hear Him if I am not in His Word? I speak to Him in prayer. How can He hear from me if I don't spend time alone with Him? My walk with the Lord took a step upward when I made this one of my "absolutes." I will get alone with God every day, no exception. And when I get alone with Him, I always begin by praying Psalm 119:18: *"Open thou mine eyes, that I may behold wondrous things out of thy law."*

Ask the Lord to make your time alone with Him a special time. Ask Him to bring to light Scripture that you will need for today. Ask Him to bring to light things you should pray for today. Then put into practice what He teaches you.

JANUARY 11   THE BEST TIME FOR A QUIET TIME

Key Verse: *"My voice shalt thou hear in the morning, O Lord; in the morning will I direct my prayer unto thee, and will look up"* *(Psalm 5:3).*

Message: I guess you can tell by this verse that I believe the morning is the best time to get alone with our Lord. Some people do so at night. Of course, this is personal preference; but think of this. In the morning you are going out to face a hostile world. At night you are going to sleep. When would a word from God help you the most?

David prayed this prayer: *"Cause me to hear thy loving kindness in the morning; for in thee do I trust; cause me to know the way wherein I should walk; for I lift up my soul unto thee." (Psalm 143:8).* Make this your prayer today.

JANUARY 12   WHAT IF I DON'T HAVE TIME?

Key Verse: *"And that, knowing the time that now it is high time to awake out of sleep; for now is our salvation nearer than when we first believed"* (Romans 13:11).

Message: Now, I do believe that we should wake up and take notice of our walk because time is short. However, I want to take a little liberty with part of this verse… *"it is high time to awake out of sleep…."* Some of you will need to get out of bed a little earlier in order to have a good morning quiet time. Some of you, for some reason or other, won't do that. You will have yours later. But I am a firm believer that you should speak to God and let Him speak to you before you speak to anyone else in your home. How can you do this? Well, to be a bit "earthy," I know you probably go to the bathroom when you first get out of bed. So, put some verses on 3x5" index cards and keep them in the bathroom. Grab one and read it; then whisper a prayer. Your morning with your family will go better if you do.

It is my privilege to say, "Good morning, Dear Father; good morning, Dear Jesus; good morning, Dear Holy Spirit," as I sit on the side of my bed each morning. It is also my privilege to have a lengthy quiet time on my blue couch (on most mornings). I may not be able to spend a long time every day, but I will spend some alone with our Lord each morning, no matter what. Tell the Lord that you will do likewise. Make it an absolute.

JANUARY 13   QUIET TIME ESSENTIALS

Key Verse: *"Praise ye the Lord. O give thanks unto the Lord..."* *(Psalm 106:1). "Let us come before his presence with thanksgiving..." (Psalm 95:2). "...daily shall he be praised" (Psalm 72:15).*

Message: So often we come to the Lord with our petitions, and we should. In fact, we can come to Him with anything; but I believe we should start each prayer with praise and thanksgiving. We should praise our Lord Jesus for who He is—the sinless Son of God, precious Lamb of Calvary, King of Kings and Lord of Lords, the One whose name is above every name. We should thank Him for loving us enough to exchange His throne for a cross. Praise! Thank! Be sure you remember that you are to thank Him for who He is. This is not the time to thank Him for your spouse or your child or Spot the dog. This can come after you thank Him for who He is.

    David prayed, *"I will praise thee, my God, O king; and I will bless thy name forever and ever. Every day will I praise thee... (Psalm 145:1-2).* Why don't you do as David did? Praise the Lord every day; thank Him every day. Thank Him that He stepped out of the portals of glory to come down here to suffer and bleed and die for us. Thank Him for praying for us. Thank Him for the assurance that He is coming again to receive us to Himself. Praise His Holy Name!!!!

JANUARY 14   ANOTHER WAY TO PRAISE

Key Verse: *"Seven times a day do I praise thee..." (Psalm 119:164).*

Message: How many times a day to you praise the Lord? It is not always easy to find the time during the day to sit down and read your Bible and pray. But I tell you what you can do. You can sing praises. The Psalmist says, *"I will sing of thy power; yea, I will* *sing aloud of thy mercy in the morning...*" *(Psalm 59:16)*. There's that "in the morning" again. As soon as I say good morning to the Trinity of heaven, I make up my bed (which I don't like to do) and sing a praise song. I often sing during my quiet time or when I am driving down the road. Sing, folks. Don't use that excuse that you can't sing. Everyone can obey this command: "*Make a joyful noise unto the Lord, all the earth; make a loud noise, and rejoice, and sing praise*" *(Psalm 98:4)*. You can make a joyful noise, a loud noise. Your singing might not sound like much to you, but it will be sweet music to the ears of our Lord. So, get in the shower and rev it up.

Over and over in the Psalms we hear these words: "*Sing praises to God, sing praises unto our king, sing praises*" *(Psalm 47:6)*. The Psalmist also says, "*...Sing ye praises with understanding*" *(Psalm 47:7)*. As you pray today, tell the Lord that you want to understand what you sing and mean what you sing. Don't sing, "*I'll go where you want me to go,*" if you are not willing to go.

Note: You will notice that I often use Scripture in my prayers. A wise pastor once said to me, "You can't pray out of the will of God when you pray the Word of God."

JANUARY 15   YET ANOTHER WAY TO PRAISE

Key Verse: "*...one of his disciples said unto him, 'Lord, teach us to pray.' And he said unto them, 'When ye pray, say, Our Father which art in heaven, hallowed be thy name...'*" *(Luke 11:1-2)*.

Message: Several years ago my friend Terri called me from the hospital where she was with her younger son who was in a life-threatening situation. She asked me how she should pray. I thought for a moment. How did Jesus begin the model prayer? With praise! "Hallowed be thy name...." I said to her, "Put Timothy into the hands of the Lord; you then pick up your Bible. Go through the Psalms and offer to God the first verse or two of each one that has to do with praise." Timothy recovered and is a fine healthy boy today, but Terri hasn't. She still goes through the Psalms and prays the praise verses to the Lord. She also reads a Psalm each day in her quiet time. So do I! Make this the best way to begin your prayer, no matter what situation you face.

Sometimes you don't know how to pray. That is the time to ask the Lord to lead you to praise verses in His Word. Always praise before you pray for anything else. Psalm 118:28 is a good place to begin: *"Thou art my God, and I will praise thee; thou art my God, and I will exalt thee."*

JANUARY 16   I COULDN'T PRAY
Key Verse: *"...but I forsook not thy precepts" (Psalm 119:87).*

Message: Often I have people say to me, "I can't pray or read my Bible because I hurt too much." I respond in various ways. Sometimes I say, "I know you can't right now, but I can. I'll pray for you." At other times I say, "Do it anyway. Force yourself even if you read one verse and just say 'Jesus' over and over." Sometimes I say, "Just sit at Jesus' feet and hold on to the hem of His garment." One day a woman who had been sick for twelve years *"...came behind Jesus and touched the hem of his garment. For she said within herself, if I may but touch his garment, I shall be whole....Thy faith had made thee whole" (Matthew 9:20-22).*

What made her well? Her faith! I want to make the application to a trial rather than an illness. The same principle applies. Let's say that you are in the midst of a trial. What are you to do? Hold on to the hem of His garment; have faith that He will deliver you. He will, in His way and in His time. Have faith and hold on for dear life. And when you are healed, praise the Lord and minister to someone who is in the midst of a trial. *"Thou hast turned for me my mourning into dancing; thou has put off my sackcloth, and girded me with gladness. To the end that my soul may sing praise to thee, and not be silent..." (Psalm 30:11-12).*

One day Jesus went to a place called Gennesaret. The men there went out and gathered the sick and brought them to Him. The sick prayed, *"...that they might only touch the hem of his garment; and as many as touched were made perfectly whole" (Matthew 14:36).* There is healing in the hem of His garment. That is the reason why it is so important for us to hold on to it. Psalm 133:2 says that the oil poured on Aaron's head *"went down to the edge of his garments."* The Lord Jesus is our high priest. There is oil in the hem of His robe.

Sit at Jesus' feet when you can't pray and hold on for dear life. Ask Him to let that oil flow into you for strength for today.

III. FRUIT OF THE SPIRIT – You Set the Tone in Your Home

Before I get to the fruit of the Spirit, I want to comment on "You set the tone in your home." I am speaking about the ladies. I often tell my girls that they set the tone in their homes, and often it isn't a good one. They sometimes blame their behavior on PMS. I tell them that those letters really stand for "Please keep your mouth shut." To do so is hard for women. We have to have help. That is the place where the Holy Spirit comes in.

JANUARY 17   THE HOLY SPIRIT

Key Verse: In John 16:14, Jesus said of the Holy Spirit: *"He shall glorify me, for he shall receive what is mine and shall declare it unto you."*

Message: When the Holy Spirit came to live in you, He brought with Him every attribute of Jesus. You have everything in you that you need to live a Spirit-filled life. And you have a special gift that Jesus gave to the Holy Spirit to give to you. That gift is found in Galatians 5:22-23. You will notice that I said, "gift," not "gifts." There is one gift with several parts. You have the whole gift—every part—in you. Here is the list: *"But the fruit of the Spirit is love, joy, peace, patience, kindness, goodness, faithfulness, gentleness, self-control."* These parts are all yours, but you have to claim them. If you are living where God answers prayer, you can. The Holy Spirit will produce them through you. Now in this section, I will cover several of these.

Remember this! Because you are saved, you have a new nature. The Holy Spirit lives in you. John 14:16 says of Him: *"He will abide with you forever."* John 14:17 says *"That he shall be in you."* Live so close to the Lord that the Holy Spirit in you can have the freedom to produce the fruit of the Spirit through you.

JANUARY 18   PATIENCE

Key Verse: *"But the fruit of the Spirit is…patience."(Galatians 5:22).*

Message: Have you ever said or heard someone say, "I don't pray for patience because I'm afraid I would find myself having to produce it"? Well, there are really two false premises in this statement. First of all, you do not need to ask for something you already have. Patience is part of the gift you have in you that the Holy Spirit is holding. Second, you can't produce patience. Patience is not part of your old nature.

Only the Holy Spirit can produce patience. Since this is true, don't pray, "Lord, help me to be patient." Instead, ask the Holy Spirit to produce it through you. You may get up one morning and say, "I am going to be patient with my child and my spouse." You might be for a while, until one of them pushes the wrong button. You will only have patience in the face of irritation if you allow the Holy Spirit to produce it through you.

You have to keep reminding yourself that our Lord has given the Holy Spirit within you the gift of patience to give to you. Ask the Holy Spirit to produce patience through you today if you face an irritable clerk or child or spouse or boss or co-worker or stranger on the street, or if you have to stand in line for a while at a restaurant or if a waiter messes up your order or if you drive beside an unruly driver. If you start to react in the flesh, remember these words: It is never all right for a Christian to be ugly to another Christian, and it's doubly not all right for a Christian to be ugly to a non-Christian.

JANUARY 19   KINDNESS

Key Verse: *"But the fruit of the Spirit is…kindness…" (Galatians 5:22).*

Message: I often make this statement: I believe kindness is a lost art in the home. I wish this were not true, but it is. Paul said to the Corinthians and to us: *"And be ye kind one to another…" (Ephesians 4:32).* Men, ponder this verse: *"What is desired in a man is kindness…" (Proverbs 19:22).* Ladies, ponder this verse about the "Proverbs 31" lady: *"...on her tongue is the law of kindness" (Proverbs 31:26).* Folks, meditate on these three verses. What would your home be like if these were true of you?

You know, these words just stuck in my mind: *"...on her tongue is the law of kindness."* That had to be an act of the "Proverbs 31" lady's will, for James 3:8 says, *"But the tongue can no man tame...."* Since this is true, she would have had to be yielded to our Lord. So must we. We need to heed David's words, *"I will keep my mouth with a bridle..." (Psalm 39:1).* When you are tempted to be unkind, ask the Lord to put a bridle over your mouth. You might ask the Holy Spirit to speak through your mouth as you bite your tongue.

JANUARY 20 GOODNESS

Key Verse: *"But the fruit of the Spirit is...goodness..." (Galatians 5:22).*

Message: When discussing someone who has just passed away, people who do not know the person's spiritual condition often say, "He was a good man." If he is lost, his goodness will count for nothing eternal. If he is saved, his goodness may have eternal reward. One of my favorite Bible characters is Barnabas. Acts 11:24 says of him, *"He was a good man, and full of the Holy Ghost and of faith; and much people was added unto the Lord."* "Goodness" was part of his life-style evangelism that led people to the Lord. His goodness had eternal value. How about yours? And let me repeat this: You will only have goodness in the face of temptation if you allow the Holy Spirit to produce it through you. (By the way, I tell people one of the reasons I never married is that Barnabas was born much too early. Ha!)

Paul said to the Romans: *"Now I, myself, am confident concerning you, my brethren, that you also are full of goodness" (Romans 15:14).* But he also said this to them: *"For I know that in me,(that is, in my flesh,) dwelleth no good thing" (Romans 7:18.)* Since this is true of us also, the only way we can be full of goodness is to be full of the Holy Spirit. Ask Him to fill you and to have the freedom to produce goodness through you

JANUARY 21   SELF-CONTROL

Key Verse: *"But the fruit of the Spirit is...self-control" (Galatians 5:23).*

Message: Self-control, used here, means the ability to harness and control one's passions and appetites. Today, we deal with issues we never dreamed could be such a stronghold. One is pornography. Once there were adult magazines; now there are the Internet, TV, movies, lots of magazines, etc. I wish I had good advice on this issue, but I don't. I do suggest that if you have a problem in this area or have a spouse who does that you put this verse on a card and put it on the bathroom mirror: *"I will set no wicked thing before mine eyes." (Psalm 101:3).*

I have a prayer that I pray for anyone who is addicted to pornography or anyone on his way to being addicted. Here it is: "Lord, I pray that whenever a brother starts to look at anything pornographic that your Word will appear before his eyes and block his vision." Many people into this want out. They get out for a while, but the lure is so great. They lack self-control. Therefore, I say again, you will only have self-control in the face of temptation if you allow the Holy Spirit to produce it through you.

I know how hard it is for people to control their passions and appetites—whether they be for pornography or gambling or alcohol or food or unhealthy relationships or anything that has a stronghold over them. If you see yourself here, get on your face before our Lord in repentance and ask the Holy Spirit within you to produce self-control through you.

IV. LOCAL CHURCH SERVICE – Use Your Gifts in Your Church

"I was glad when they said unto me. 'Let us go into the house of the Lord'" (Psalm 122:1). I love to go to the house of the Lord. Nothing makes me happier. How about you?

JANUARY 22   GO!

Key Verse: *"Not forsaking the assembling of ourselves together..."* *(Hebrews 10:25).*

Message: You have already heard me say that I believe in absolutes. It should be a "given" in your home that everybody gets to, not has to, go to church on Sunday. "Do we?" "Don't we?" These questions should never be asked. Going or not going should never come up for discussion. Being out late or being tired or being behind in housework or being a good host or being lazy should never even be talked about as a reason for missing church. Parents, do you wonder why your children do not attend church regularly when they go off to college? Could it possibly be that they didn't grow up with this as an absolute in your home? There is a special promise in Psalm 92:13-14a for parents who "plant" their children in the house of God: *"Those that be planted in the house of the Lord shall flourish in the courts of our God. They shall still bring forth fruit in old age."* Parents, I believe I would "plant" my children in God's house.

And by the way, I do not believe Sunday morning attendance is enough. We need to meet when the family meets. At Colonial Heights, the family meets on Sunday morning, Sunday night, and Wednesday night. We need to be there. We need to be there to encourage and strengthen one another. There is just something special about the ministry of your presence. You have no idea how your presence encourages your pastor. If meeting when the family meets is not an absolute in your home, why not make it one? May I add this verse as a personal testimony? *"One thing I have desired of the Lord, that will I seek after, that I may dwell in the house of the Lord all the days of my life..." (Psalm 27:4).*

Do you love to go to God's house? Can you sincerely pray with David: *"Lord, I have loved the habitation of thy house, the place where thy glory dwelleth" (Psalm 27:8)?* His glory is present every time we assemble because our Lord promised, *"where two or three are gathered together in my name, there am I in the midst of them" (Matthew 18:20).* Thank Him for this wonderful promise.

JANUARY 23   PARTICIPATE

Key Verse: *"...Since you are eager for spiritual gifts, let it be for the building up of the church..." (1 Corinthians 14:12).*

Message: When the Lord brought us into this world, He equipped us with a spiritual gift or gifts. When He saved our souls, He expected us to find out what they were and to use them to build up the local church, which I believe is God's instrument for this hour. No one was saved just to occupy a pew. No one was saved to use his gift to edify himself. All were saved to participate in the work of the church. And I believe that all of us are to participate in the worship service. God knows what He wants to happen each time we congregate for worship. Whether it is accomplished may depend in part on us.

Here is what I believe is our part. We are to *"enter into his gates with thanksgiving and into his courts with praise; be thankful unto him and bless his name" (Psalm 100:4).* We are to *"sing praises with understanding" (Psalm 47:7).* We are to know the meaning of the song we are singing and mean what we are singing. We are to repeat silently what someone is praying aloud so that one unified prayer can go to the throne of grace. We are to participate when the offering place comes by us by planting an offering as an act of worship. We are to participate by letting the Holy Spirit speak to our hearts through the message presented by our pastor. We are to participate in the invitation time. Some are to sing; some are to pray. No one is to leave, unless absolutely necessary. I'll be honest with you; I pray that anyone moving will have his feet stuck to the floor unless he is coming to the front to make a decision known. Folks, at this time, lives are hanging in the balance. Let's not cause them to miss heaven by our moving around. Let's do our part to accomplish God's purpose. Let's leave saying, "It was good to have been in the house of the Lord." Discipline yourself to participate. You will be amazed at how your worship experience will become more special.

Remember, you have been given a spiritual gift of gifts, not for self, but for the church. Tell the Lord that you will use yours to edify the church. Then lift up Psalm 111:1 to Him: *"...I will praise you Lord with my whole heart, in the assembly of the upright and in the congregation."*

V. PASTORAL AUTHORITY –
He is to Feed the Flock And Be
an Example to the People

Peter summed up what the ministry of the pastor is to be. He is to feed the flock (1 Peter 5:2) and be an example to the people (5:3). When a pastor meets these qualifications, God's Word teaches the following truths.

JANUARY 24   PROMISES CONCERNING THE PASTOR

Key Verse: *"And I will give you pastors according to mine heart, which shall feed you with knowledge and understanding" (Jeremiah 3:15).*

Message: These words were spoken to Israel, but they are a promise to believers today. Just knowing that we have a pastor after God's own heart should make us want to love him and encourage him and follow him. But God knew that some people in the church would not do so. Therefore, He gave the pastor some promises. God knew that some people would not listen to him, so He gave the same promise to the pastor that He gave to Jeremiah: *"...Thou shalt go to all that I send thee, and whatsoever I command thee thou shalt speak. Be not afraid of their faces....And they shall fight against thee; for I am with thee, saith the Lord, to deliver thee" (Jeremiah 1:7b, 8, 19).* God also knew that some people would rise up against the pastor, so He gave this promise to His servant: *"No weapon that is formed against thee shall prosper; and every tongue that shall rise against thee in judgment thou shalt condemn. This is the heritage of the* *servants of the Lord..."* (*Isaiah 54:17*). These verses tell me that the Lord is on the pastor's side, so I will be too. How about you?

I am so grateful that the Lord has given me a pastor after His own heart. It is a privilege to serve under his ministry. Folks, let's don't try to tell him how to lead the church. Let's leave that up to our Lord. If the pastor needs correcting, our Lord will do it because he is His chosen servant. That gives us great freedom; All we need to do is to hear God's word for the church from our pastor and then get in on what God wants done.

JANUARY 23   THE PASTOR AND PRIESTHOOD OF THE BELIEVER

Key Verse: *"But ye are a chosen generation, a royal priesthood..."* (*1Peter 2:9*).

Message: Some people today say that the priesthood of the believer means that all believers are equal, even the pastor. That is true because the real meaning of priesthood of the believer is that we all have access to the throne of grace. We do not have to go through a mediator. It does not mean that the pastor is just one of us. He is different in the role assigned to him. Let me give you an example. Some men decided to rise up against Moses and Aaron. They said to Moses and Aaron: *"Ye take too much upon you, seeing all the congregation are holy, every one of them, and the Lord is among them: wherefore then lift ye up yourselves above the congregation of the Lord"* (*Numbers 16:3*)? Here is the end result of their rebellion: *"And the earth opened her mouth and swallowed them up, and their houses...and all their goods"* (*Numbers 16:32*). They would have done well to have listened to these words: *"Touch not mine anointed, and do my prophets no harm"* (*Psalm 105:15*). So would we!

Now we know that the priesthood of the believer means that we can come to our Lord, as can every believer, including the pastor. But we must understand our role and His. On one occasion David had the perfect opportunity to kill Saul, but he didn't. Instead he said to Abishai: *"...Destroy him not, for who can stretch forth his hand against the Lord's anointed and be guiltless"* (*1 Samuel 26:9*)? David went on to say: *"The Lord forbid that I should stretch forth mine hand against the Lord's anointed..."* *(1 Samuel 26:11).* Ask the Lord to remind you of David's words if you are tempted to lift a hand against your pastor.

JANUARY 26   MORE ABOUT THE PASTOR'S ROLE

Key Verse: *"...do I seek to please men? For if I pleased men, I should not be the servant of Christ" (Galatians 1:10).*

Message: I said earlier that the pastor is to feed the flock and be an example to the people. He is to lead, not dictate. Let's get even more specific. As this verse says, the pastor is to listen to and please God, not us. You know, I do not know of one instance in the New Testament in which the Lord gave a message for the church to a layperson. Someone might say, "The head of the church is the Lord Jesus, not the pastor," That is true, but the Lord has given the message for the church to the under-shepherd, the pastor.

Remember the Jerusalem conference recorded in Acts 15? Barnabas gave a report about the salvation of many Gentiles. There was rejoicing, but some Pharisees stood up and said that these converts needed to be circumcised. Well, the apostles and elders had a private discussion in which much disputing took place.

Then Peter stood up. When he spoke, *"Then all the multitude kept silence..." (Acts 15:12).* But notice what happened when Pastor James spoke, He said, *"Men and brethren, harken unto me" (Acts 15:13),* and they did. Verse 22 says, *"Then it pleased the apostles and elders, with all the whole church...."* to do exactly what Pastor James said to do. These folks knew his role. And you know, so does Jesus.

In the Revelation, the Lord Jesus gave John a specific message to seven churches—churches that represent all churches during the church age. Each message is addressed to *"the angel of the church."* Here angel means "messenger." I believe it means "pastor." Some say that the letters are addressed to actual angels, but I can't see this. Have you ever heard an angel preach a sermon? Have you ever seen an example of God's giving a message to a human to give to an angel? I haven't. I believe the message to these seven churches and all churches is to be given to the pastor to be given to us.

The Lord has placed His minister over the congregation to do His bidding. According to Paul, he is here *"For the equipping of the saints, for the work of the ministry, for the edifying of the body of Christ" (Ephesians 4:12).* Tell the Lord that you will support him as he follows Paul's words.

JANUARY 27   OBEY

Key Verse: *"Obey them that have the rule over you, and submit yourselves: for they watch for your souls, as they that must give account, that they may do it with joy, and not with grief: for that is unprofitable for you" (Hebrews 13:17).*

Message: Did you get past the first word in the verse: obey? Some people have trouble submitting to authority and even more trouble submitting to the authority of the pastor. If so, I suggest that you read the rest of the verse very carefully. I believe this verse says that the one who watches over your soul will one day stand before the Lord Jesus and give an account of how you have served the Lord under his ministry.

Please study the last words of the verse very carefully: *"As they that must give account, that they may do it with joy, and not grief: for that is unprofitable for you."* Have you ever been guilty of saying, or even thinking such things as, "I can't teach Sunday School any more because I don't like the direction the pastor is leading the church, etc."? I suggest that you drop the "I don't like" statements from your vocabulary and serve the Lord faithfully under the leadership of the pastor. That would be profitable to you.

You know, it is so easy to say, "I don't like." Sometimes we speak before we think. Ask the Lord to call Hebrews 13:7 to mind when you start to state your opinion about how the church should be run: *"Remember them which have the rule over you, who have spoken unto you the Word of God, whose faith follow...."*

JANUARY 28   REWARD

Key Verse: *"And when the chief Shepherd shall appear, ye shall receive a crown of glory that fadeth not away" (1 Peter 5:4).*

Message: Peter had just told the pastors to feed the flock; be an example; and lead, not dictate. Then he said that when Jesus hands out rewards at the Judgment Seat of Christ, He will give a special reward—a crown of glory to the faithful pastor. Let me give you some good news: *"Whoever welcomes God's messenger because he is God's messenger, will share in his reward..." (Matthew 10:41 GN).* We share in the pastor's reward, his crown, if we willingly support his ministry. I may not get any other reward, but I plan to share this one because I will *"...welcome God's messenger because he is God's messenger."*

Be sure that you stand by your pastor on the day that our Lord hands the crown of glory to Him, and share in his reward. You can do so if you support him because he is God's messenger. Tell the Lord that you will do so.

Note: I realize that I have devoted a lot of space in this book to the pastor. I did so for two reasons:

1. Pastors cannot actually preach pastoral authority. Lay people must practice it and teach it. Sunday School teachers, please lead your people by example and by your teaching how important pastoral authority is to the local church.

2. I believe one of the reasons many churches have no power with God today is that lay people do not yield to the pastor's authority. Who knows what would happen in the fellowship if the people heard God's message to the church through the pastor and did as the church at Jerusalem did when they heard Pastor James speak: *"Then pleased it the apostles and elders, with the whole church" (Acts 15:22)* to do as he said.

VI. NO MURMURING/COMPLAINING
– Get in on What God is Doing

I am not going to devote a day to this because I have covered this in other sections. I would remind you that last in the list of things God hates is this: *"...He that soweth discord among brethren" (Proverbs 6:19),* and let me assure you that murmuring and complaining do just this. Pray with David: *"...I am purposed that my mouth shall not transgress" (Psalm 17:3).*

VII. PROPHECY –
Why is There a Number Seven?

I asked my class members if they had anything to add to the original list. Several replied, "You have to add prophecy." I will devote two days to this: one on what happens to saved people when Jesus comes for the church and one on what happens to lost people when Jesus departs from them. In both cases Jesus will be the judge. John 5:22 says, *"For the Father judgeth no man, but hath committed all judgment to the Son."*

JANUARY 29   JUDGMENT SEAT OF CHRIST
Key Verse: *"...We shall all stand before the judgment seat of Christ" (Romans 14:10).*

Message: One day, on God's timetable, all of the people saved during the Church Age will stand before Jesus the Judge. Only saved people will appear at this judgment. What will be judged? Our works! Our service record down here! Why? To determine our rewards in heaven! In 1 Corinthians 3:8 Paul says that *"every man shall receive his own reward according to his own labor."* Psalm 62:12 says, *"Thou rewardeth to every man according to his work."* Jesus will look at all the work we have done in His name.

In 1 Corinthians 3:11, Paul says that Jesus Christ has to be the foundation for our service. In 3:14 Paul says, *"If any man's work endures which he has built thereupon, he shall receive a reward."* If Jesus is the foundation of our service – if we serve Him because we love Him, He will call those deeds *"gold, silver or precious stone"* deeds. We will keep these deeds and take them with us when He says, *"Step into my heaven."* Now those deeds we have done for any other reason will be called *"wood, hay and stubble"* deeds. They will not go with us to heaven. Those deeds will be burned up.

But get this! Every person will be happy whether he has few rewards or many for two reasons: (1) because he will know that he is being judged by a just judge, and he will know that his reward is what he has earned, (2) because he will ever be with Jesus. *"And if I go and prepare a place for you, I will come again, and receive you unto myself; that where I am, there ye may be also" (John 14:3)*. Paul said, *"...and so shall we ever be with the Lord" (1Thessalonians 4:17)*.

Please be sure that you know that works do not save. In Ephesians 2:8-9, Paul says, *"For by grace are ye saved through faith, and that not of yourselves; it is the gift of God, not of works, lest any man should boast."* Paul goes on to say in verse 10 that *"we are his (God's) workmanship, created in Christ Jesus for good works."* Works don't save, but the saved work. How long? For as long as you can! Remember, it is always too early to quit. Ask the Lord for strength to stay in the battle.

JANUARY 30   WHITE THRONE

Key Verse: *"And I saw a great white throne...and I saw the dead... (lost people) stand before God..." (Revelation 20:11-12)*.

Message: A thousand years and a little longer after our works judgment on our way to heaven, God will strip the earth bare. All that will be visible will be a great white throne. Jesus the Judge will sit on the throne and will call the lost of all ages to stand before Him. He will use the same pattern to judge the lost, but oh how different the results! According to Revelation 20:13b, Jesus will *"judge every (lost) man according to his works."* Please note that the purpose of this judgment will not be to determine who will go to the Lake of Fire. That matter will have been settled and sealed by each lost person before his physical death.

Every person at the white throne will spend eternity in the Lake of Fire. How will he get there? He will stop by the white throne so that Jesus can determine his reward (actually the degree of his punishment) in the Lake of Fire. Luke 12:47-48 tells us that some will be beaten with more stripes than others. In Matthew 11:22 when Jesus began to upbraid the cities that had seen Him at work but had not repented, He said, *"It shall be more tolerable for Tyre and Sidon at the day of judgment than for you."* How will Jesus determine the degree of the lost person's punishment? He will take a book and books into His hand. According to Revelation 20:12, the books contain the service record of the lost person. Jesus will look at his works and will note that none will have Him as the foundation. He will then pick up His book, examine it carefully, then turn to the lost person and say, "Sorry, your name is not in my book, so step into the Lake of Fire where *you 'shall be tormented day and night for ever and ever'" (Revelation 20:10). "...where the fire shall never be quenched" (Mark 9:43).* The worst thing about hell is that Jesus will not be there.

Our Lord never intended for any person to go to the Lake of Fire. According to Matthew 25:41, it was *"prepared for the devil and his angels."* What a terrible place this must be! In verse 42 Jesus said that there *"shall be wailing and gnashing of teeth."* 2 Peter 3:9 says that our Lord Jesus is *"not willing that any should perish, but that all should come to repentance."* As you pray today, tell the Lord that you will do your best to keep people from perishing.

VIII. ANOTHER PERSON'S VIEW

JANUARY 31   FROM THE PEN OF LISA LUCAS

Key Verse: *"...I am come that they might have life, and that they might have it more abundantly" (John 10:10).*

Message: Lisa wrote the introduction to my Sunday School class booklet. She summed up what I have written. I will quote her words: "What do you learn as a part of this class...? Here are a few things you can count on hearing repeatedly. You could call

these the basics for living the abundant life Jesus promises in John
10:10. Here they are:

1. You must have a daily quiet time. It needs to be first thing in
    the morning. It must be every day. You do not need to speak
    to anyone until you have spoken to the Lord and He to you.
2. You need to be in church on Sunday mornings, Sunday nights,
    and Wednesday nights to worship with other believers. There
    are no excuses.
3. You must give a tithe and an offering. The tithe belongs to
    God, so give it to Him. The offering is extra for Him to work
    with. You will be blessed beyond what you can imagine
    when you become a faithful steward.
4. You already have all you need in you to live a fruitful life
    once you become a Christian, but you must ask the Holy
    Spirit to produce those things through you.

I thank the Lord for teaching me these truths and for teaching
them through me. My prayer is that those who read this book will
allow the Holy Spirit to produce them in their lives, but my main
prayer is, *"Not unto us, O Lord, not unto us, but unto thy name give
glory..." (Psalm 115:1).*

February

OBEDIENCE BRINGS BLESSINGS

One day we believers will participate in a wonderful praise service in heaven. We will cast our crowns at Jesus' feet and sing with the heavenly choir: *"Thou are worthy, O Lord, to receive glory and honor and power; for thou hast created all things, and for thy pleasure they are and were created" (Revelation 4:11).*

How often does it enter your mind that you have been created for our Lord's pleasure? Most of the time we are so concerned about our own pleasure that we miss the blessings which come from pleasing our Lord. Obedience brings blessings.

In the second month we will concentrate on what does not please the Lord, what does please Him, and the blessings that come when we please Him.

I will include in this month something that the Lord has recently revealed to me. I praise Him that He is still trusting this seventy-seven-year-old lady with fresh insight.

FEBRUARY 1   WHEN A MAN'S WAYS PLEASE

Key Verse: *"When a man's ways please the Lord, he maketh even his enemies to be at peace with him" (Proverbs 16:7).*

Message: This is a verse I have claimed for several people during the last few years. The key to this verse is "pleasing the Lord." I want us to concentrate first on the first part of the verse: *"When a man's ways please the Lord...."*

I asked myself, "What does it take to please the Lord?" I began to search the Scripture. Here is one truth that I discovered: *"Such as are upright in their way are his delight" (Proverbs 11:20).*

You know, Jesus didn't have much to smile about when He was down here, but He has a lot to smile about when He looks down and sees one of His own living the upright life—the righteous life.

Perhaps I should define righteousness. It means conforming to God's will in one's thinking and acting. When we do this, we please our Lord.

Note: I decided to spend some time on things that do not please the Lord. I did so because these are some areas that give us trouble and will have to be addressed as we strive to live the righteous life that pleases our Lord.

FEBRUARY 2   IN THE FLESH

Key Verse: *"...they that are in the flesh cannot please the Lord" (Romans 8:8).*

Message: In Romans 8:5-8, Paul is making it clear that lost people— those in the flesh—cannot please God. Saved people are to abandon the flesh and walk in the Spirit.

However, after they are saved, many believers continue to walk after the flesh. They don't grow because their minds are so full of self and the world that there is no room for the things of the Spirit.

In 1 Corinthians 3:3, Paul tells the believers that they are carnal, meaning "after the flesh." Then he gets specific: *"For whereas there is among you envying, and strife (dissensions), and divisions, are ye not carnal and walk as men (meaning after the flesh)?"*

Examine yourself in the light of this verse. If you see yourself, you are not pleasing God. Ask Him to deliver you. Then follow Him down the path of righteousness.

FEBRUARY 3 BACKSLIDING

Key Verse: *"...If a man draw back, my soul shall have no pleasure in him" (Hebrews 10:38).*

Message: Here the writer of Hebrews warns these believers (and us) of the dreadful consequences of backsliding. *"If any should draw back"* (or backslide), then *"God would have no pleasure in him."*

God surely had no pleasure in Judah at one time. In Jeremiah 3:13, He told the people that they had given their love to other gods and had not obeyed His commands. In verse 14, He made this plea: *"Turn, O backsliding children."* They did not. Disobedience has consequences. God showed His displeasure by sending the people of Judah into Babylonian captivity.

Are you giving your love to other gods? Before you say that you are not, remember that other gods are anything you put before the Lord. If you are, you are drawing back and not pleasing Him. Are you obeying His commands? He sent you down here for a specific purpose. Are you fulfilling that purpose? If not, you are not pleasing Him.

Take a little inventory. Are you closer to the Lord today than you have ever been? If not, you are not going forward. That means you must be going backward. You are going one way or the other because you don't stand still in your Christian journey.

Ask the Lord to help you keep your feet moving toward Him so that you might be pleasant in His sight.

FEBRUARY 4   GOD'S HATE LIST
Key Verse: *"These six things doth the Lord hate: yea, seven are an abomination unto him....He that soweth discord among brethren"* *(Proverbs 6:16-18).*

Message: Number seven on God's hate list is *"he that soweth discord among brethren."* "Hate" as used here does not mean what we usually think of when we use the word. To us it means "despise."

But here the word means "to reject from one's fellowship." When we sow discord among the brethren, we certainly are not pleasing the Lord. He won't even fellowship with us at that point. Sometimes we don't realize how seriously the Lord takes what comes out of our mouths.

Let me give you an example. Let's say that the church leadership has recommended that we relocate. Would you ever go to anyone and say something like this? "I don't want to leave this location."—"It would cost too much money."—"The building we have now is plenty big."

If you would say anything like this, you would be causing discord in the body, and the Lord would not be pleased with you. Be careful what comes out of your mouth.

When Jeremiah protested God's call, notice what happened: *"Then the Lord put forth his hand, and touched my mouth. And the Lord said unto me, Behold, I have put my words in thy mouth" (Jeremiah 1:9).* When you start to protest something the body is led to do, picture God's hand on your mouth, and let His words come forth.

Perhaps a good prayer for today would be, *"Let the words of my mouth, and the meditation of my heart, be acceptable in thy sight, O Lord, my strength and my redeemer" (Psalm 20:14).*

FEBRUARY 5   PERFECT, PERMISSIVE
Key Verse: *"...Thou shalt not go..." (Numbers 22:12)....Go with them..." (Numbers 22:20).*

Message: These instructions are confusing at first glance. Let me explain. Balaam went to God and said, "Balak has asked me to curse Israel for him so that he can drive them out of the land." In His answer we see God's perfect will: *"Do not go with these men, and do not put a curse on the people of Israel, because they have my blessing" (Numbers 22:12).*

Well, Balaam went back to God to be sure he had received the right message. It angered God that Balaam did not accept His first answer. When he came to God the second time, we see an example of God's permissive will.

He said to Balaam, *"Go on, but say only what I tell you to say..." (Numbers 22:25).* Let me tell you that Balaam's trip wasn't smooth sailing. God sent him on a wild donkey ride before using him to warn Balak: *"Whoever blesses Israel will be blessed, and whoever curses Israel will be cursed" (Numbers 24:9).*

At this point it seems that Balaam was in perfect harmony with God. But remember, he could only speak what God said.

What happened to this man who angered God after he finished this assignment? Lured by money, he *"taught Balak how to lead the people of Israel into sin by persuading them to eat food that had been offered to idols and to practice sexual immorality" (Revelation 2:14).* He couldn't curse Israel, but he did lead them into sin.

The story of Balaam reminds me of how God responded to the complaining, murmuring Israelites in the wilderness: *"And he gave them their request; but sent leanness into their soul" (Psalm 106:15).*

Beware if you know God's perfect will for your life but are living under His permissive will. He just might send you on a wild donkey ride to get your attention and send leanness into your soul. If you continue to live in His permissive will, He will not be pleased with you.

I leave you today with the best way I know to find God's perfect will: *"Trust in the Lord with all thine heart, and lean not to thine own understanding. In all thy ways acknowledge him, and he shall direct thy path" (Proverbs 3:5-6).* God's will is a day-by-day process.

FEBRUARY 6   PROMISES

Key Verse: *"When thou vowest a vow unto God, delay not to pay it; for he hath no pleasure in fools: Pay that which thou hast vowed" (Ecclesiastes 5:4).*

Message: Listen to the way the Good News states this verse: *"When you make a promise to God, keep it as quickly as possible. He has no use for a fool. Do what you promise to do."* Then in verse 6 the writer asks, *"Why make God angry with you?"*

What promises have you made to the Lord? To tithe? To give an offering? To plant a seed of faith? To give to the building fund? Have you been faithful to obey? If not, God has no pleasure in you.

To teach a Sunday School class or serve in some other way? Are you faithful to do so, or do you think nothing of being absent from duty when you are tired or when company comes or when you have something else you had rather do? If so, God has no pleasure in you.

Have you ever prayed, "Lord, if you will deliver me from this situation"—or—"Lord, if you will heal me"—or—"Lord, if you will save my marriage, etc. I'll be faithful to serve you," only to forget that vow when the calamity had passed?

If so, verse 5 has a message for you: *"Better not to promise at all than to make a promise and not keep it."* I can assure you of this: You cannot promise something to God, fail to keep it, and expect Him to find pleasure with you.

Avoid God's displeasure by heeding Psalm 66:13-14: *"I will go into thy house with burnt offerings. I will pay thee my promised deeds, which my lips have uttered, and my mouth hath spoken, when I was in trouble."*

As you pray today, you would do well to tell the Lord that you will honor the promises you have made to Him.

FEBRUARY 7   BUT WITHOUT FAITH

Key Verse: *"But without faith it is impossible to please him..."* *(Hebrews 11:6).*

Message: I'll admit that this verse scares me. When I start reading *"without faith it is impossible to please him...,"* I think of how often my faith has been too small.

But when I read the rest of the verse, I got a better idea of the meaning here. *"...for he who comes to God must believe that he is...."* The first thing a person must do to please Him is to believe that He is the only God—the God of the Bible. That is the beginning point.

"...and he a rewarder of those who seek him." Now it is not enough to simply believe that the God of the Bible exists. In order to please Him, we must believe that He is a loving, gracious God to *"those who seek him."* In order to please Him, we must believe that He rewards those who come to Him.

The greatest reward God gives us is our salvation. *"For God so loved the world, that he gave his only begotten son, that whosoever believeth in him should not perish, but have everlasting life"* *(John 3:16).*

One day our Lord will reward us for the work we have done since the day we were saved. In 1 Corinthians 3:8, Paul told those believers that at the Judgment Seat of Christ, *"every man shall receive his own reward according to his own labor.*

I believe the message here is that without faith to believe that God is the only God, that He is a rewarder of those who seek Him through Jesus Christ His Son, and that He is going to be a rewarder to us at the Judgment Seat of Christ—it is impossible to please Him.

I am sure you believe in one God—the God of the Bible and that you have been rewarded with salvation. But how about the rewards He will hand out? How much reward will you get for your own labor? The more He can give you, the more pleased He will be with you!

Ask the Lord to reveal to you how He wants you to labor for Him.

FEBRUARY 8   LEARN BY EXAMPLE

Key Verse: *"But with many of them God was not well pleased..."* *(1 Corinthians 10:5).*

Message: In 1 Corinthians 10, Paul reminded the believers that the Israelites, who followed Moses were under the protection of the cloud, passed unhurt through the Red Sea, and ate bread from heaven. They had it made.

However, *"with many of them God was not well pleased."* As a result many of them died in the wilderness. What did they do wrong? They lusted after evil things; they bowed down to idols; they turned their feasts into drunken orgies; they were guilty of sexual immorality; they tested God; they murmured (1 Corinthians 10:6-10).

These same verses tell us their fate. In one day twenty-three thousand of them died; many were killed by snakes; many were destroyed by the Angel of Death. Paul warned the Corinthians not to be like the Israelites. Then he told them his purpose in relating the wilderness events: *"All these things happened to them as examples for others, and they were written down (by Moses) as a warning for us"* *(1Corinthians 10:11 GN).*

The *us* includes you and me. If you are tempted to do any of these things, even to murmur, remember that you have been warned that God will not be well pleased with you.

And always remember, the more light you have, the more responsible you are. Jesus said in Matthew 11:23-24: *"And thou Capernaum, which are exalted unto heaven, shalt be brought down to Hades; for if the mighty works, which have been done in thee, had been done in Sodom, it would have remained until this day. But I say unto you, that it shall be more tolerable for the land of Sodom in the day of judgment, than for thee."*

Pray that the Lord will have no reason to be displeased with you in these areas.

Note: Now that we have looked at some things that do not please the Lord, we will look at some things and people that do please Him.

FEBRUARY 9   BE RIGHTEOUS

Key Verse: *"Such as are upright (righteous) in their way are his delight" (Proverbs 11:20).*

Message: I used this verse earlier to answer the question, "What does it take to please the Lord?" Here are some other verses that also answer the question. Ponder them.

1. Proverbs 15:8-9: *"...The prayer of the upright is his delight.... He loveth him that followeth after righteousness."*
2. Psalm 11:7: *"For the righteous Lord loveth righteousness; his countenance doth behold the upright."*
3. Psalm 33:5: *"For the Lord loveth righteousness...."*
4. Psalm 147:11: *"The Lord taketh pleasure in them that fear him...."*
5. 1 Peter 3:12: *"For the eyes of the Lord are over the righteous, and his ears are open unto their prayers...."*

We learn from these verses that the way to please the Lord is to live a life of righteousness. At the beginning of the month, I described righteousness. It means conforming to God's will in one's thinking and acting. When we do this, we please the Lord.

Examine yourself in light of this definition, and ask God to steer you down the path of righteousness.

FEBRUARY 10   OBEYING PLEASES GOD

Key Verse: *"...to obey is better than sacrifice..." (1 Samuel 15:22).*

Message: King Saul was summoned to a meeting with Samuel, who said to him, "Saul, God made you king and sent you to destroy all the people of Amalek. Why didn't you obey Him?"

"Oh, I did," replied Saul. "I killed all the Amalekites. I did bring back their king, and my men kept some of the best sheep and cattle and brought them here to offer as a sacrifice to God."

Listen to the answer Saul received: *"And Samuel said, hath the Lord as great delight in burnt offerings and sacrifices, as in obeying the voice of the Lord? Behold, to obey is better than sacrifice, and* to hearken than the fat of rams" (1 Samuel 15:22). God demanded total obedience. He does the same with us.

When you obey, He will accept your sacrifice. Let me tell you about a couple of sacrifices that please God: *"But to do good and to share forget not: For with such sacrifices God is well pleased" (Hebrews 13:16).* Do you "do good and share"?

When you obey Him, He will receive your offering, and you will be happy to give it. You will be the person Paul describes in 2 Corinthians 9:7: *"Every man according as he purposeth in his heart, so let him give; not grudgingly, or of necessity; for God loveth a cheerful (hilarious) giver."*

Tell the Lord that you understand that partial obedience is disobedience and that you want to be totally obedient and qualify as a hilarious giver.

FEBRUARY 11   GLORY IN HIM
Key Verse: *"...for in these I delight" (Jeremiah 9:24).*

Message: In what does our Lord delight? He starts off by stating some things that might delight you, but not Him. In Jeremiah 9:23, we read, *"This is what the Lord says, Let not the wise man boast of his wisdom or the strong man boast of his strength or the rich man boast of his riches...."*

You might be able to boast about your vast education, mighty power, great wealth; but the Lord is not impressed with that kind of boasting.

Well, what kind of boasting delights Him? *"...but let him who boasts boast about this: that he understands and knows me, that I am the Lord, who exercises kindness, justice, and righteousness on earth, for in these things I delight, declares the Lord" (Jeremiah 9:24).*

In essence God is saying that this is what pleases Him—things of which you can boast—that you know Him, that you know that He is kind and does what is just and right down here on earth. Can you say, "I do," to all of the above? If so, you are a delight to our Lord.

Pray that you will glory in nothing except our Lord. Also pray with the Psalmist: *"Let my mouth be filled with thy praise and with thy glory all the day long" (Psalm 71:8).*

FEBRUARY 12   JESUS OUR EXAMPLE

Key Verse: *"And lo a voice from heaven saying, This is my beloved son, in whom I am well pleased" (Matthew 3:17).*

Message: When Jesus came up out of the baptismal waters, the Father gave verbal approval to the ministry of His *"beloved Son."* That beloved Son was never a disappointment to Him. In John 8:29 Jesus said, *"I do always those things that please the Father."* In John 5:30, He said, *"I seek not mine own will, but the will of the Father which hath sent me."* In John 6:38, He said, *"I came down from heaven, not to do mine own will, but the will of him that sent me."*

On one occasion Jesus took Peter and James and John to a high mountain where He temporarily appeared in His glorified body before them—in the body He has today.

This was a foreshadowing of Jesus' body when His work on earth was done. What did the Father have to say about His Son then? Hear Peter's testimony: *"For he received from God the Father honor and glory, when there came such a voice to him from the excellent glory, This is my beloved Son, in whom I am well pleased" (2 Peter 1:17-18).*

Oh, that I had this approval of the Father! Oh, that I had the testimony of Jesus! Oh, that I would do only what pleases our Lord!

One day we will stand before Him in our glorified bodies. Wouldn't it be wonderful to hear Him say, "Well done thou good and faithful servant"? It could happen if you do only those things that please the Father. Pray to that end.

FEBRUARY 13   MARY

Key Verse: *"...thou...art highly favored..." (Luke 1:28).*

Message: The angel of the Lord came to Mary and proclaimed, *"Rejoice, thou that are highly <u>favored</u>. The Lord is with thee...."* Mary was deeply troubled and began to wonder to herself what the angel meant. He soon made it clear: *"And the angel said unto her, fear not, Mary; for thou hast found <u>favor</u> with God" (Luke 1:30).*

Here was a young girl, not yet married, an ordinary person; but God chose her to be the mother of Jesus. I have often wondered why

He did so. I believe one reason could be that, when she understood the message of the angel, she didn't put up a string of arguments. She simply agreed to obey. *"Behold the maidservant of the Lord, be it unto me according to thy word..." (Luke 1:38).*

I believe another reason why she was highly favored could be that she knew when it was time to release Jesus to do His Father's work; and she did so at the wedding at Cana when she said, *"Whatsoever he saith unto you, do it" (John 2:5).*

We see the yieldedness of Mary in these, her last recorded words in the Bible. Is it any wonder that she found favor with God? You can too if you heed her words: *"Whatsoever he saith unto you, do it."*

Put yourself into a position where you can hear His direction. The best place I know to do this is in your quiet time every morning alone with Him and His Word. Pray that your quiet time will be a daily "absolute." If it is and if you obey our Lord, you will find favor with Him.

FEBRUARY 14   SOLOMON
Key Verse: *"...ask what I shall give thee" (1 Kings 3:6).*

Message: On one occasion God appeared to Solomon in a dream and asked, "What would you like me to give you?"

Solomon began his answer by saying, "You always showed great love for my father David, and you have continued to show him your love by giving him a son who now rules in his place. Lord, you have let me succeed my father, even though I am inexperienced and do not know how to rule."

Then Solomon made his request: *"So give me wisdom I need to rule your people with justice and to know the difference between good and evil..." (1 Kings 3:9 GN).*

Verse 10 says that his answer *"pleased the Lord...."* Because his answer pleased the Lord, He gave Solomon wisdom, plus things he didn't ask for such as wealth and honor.

Why the added favor? God said in essence, "I added these favors because you didn't pray a selfish prayer for long life and wealth and death of your enemies."

You see, folks, God had sent Solomon to earth for this purpose: to be king. Solomon knew that he could not accomplish the task without wisdom from God. You too have been sent to earth for a purpose. Only you and the Lord know what it is.

Suppose the Lord appeared to you today and asked you the question, "What would you like me to give you?" Would you, like Solomon, ask for wisdom to know how to fulfill your purpose — or would you ask for selfish things?

Who knows what God might give you if you pray Solomon's prayer! After all, He *"is able to do exceeding abundantly above all that we ask or think..." (Ephesians 3:20).*

You just have to pray for the right things. For what did you pray this morning? Was it a Solomon prayer? If not, pray it tomorrow and mean what you pray. If you do, you will please the Lord.

FEBRUARY 15   ENOCH

Key Verse: *"...He (Enoch) had this testimony, that he pleased God" (Hebrews 11:5).*

Message: *"That he pleased God"* was a wonderful testimony to have. What did Enoch do to please God? Very simply put, *"He walked with God."*

When Enoch was sixty-five years old, his son Methuselah was born. Genesis 5:22 says, *"And Enoch walked with God after he begat Methuselah three hundred years."* Enoch walked with God every day that he spent on earth. He didn't say, "I'm an old man now. It's time for the younger folks to take over." No; he walked! The word "walked" indicates that he kept his feet moving.

What was Enoch's reward for faithfulness to the end? In verse 24, these words were repeated: *"And Enoch walked with God."* Then we see the reward in the next part of the verse: *"...and he was not, for God took him."* Enoch didn't die. He disappeared into the heavens because God took him.

Why did God let Enoch just walk out of this world into his heavenly home? Hebrews 11:5 has the answer: *"...for before the translation he had the testimony, that he pleased God."*

Sometimes the Lord puts things in His Word to show us a picture of a future event. Did you know that if you please the Lord (and you can only do so if you have been saved by the blood of the Lamb) and are alive when Jesus comes for His bride, you will have the same experience that Enoch had?

Corinthians 15:23 says that when Jesus appears in the air, believers who are alive will get their glorified bodies *"in the twinkling of an eye."*

1 Thessalonians 4:17 says, *"We which are alive shall be caught up…in the clouds, to meet the Lord in the air, and so shall we ever be with the Lord."*

This will happen to you if you please the Lord, and you please Him by walking with Him all the days of your life. Remember! It is always too early to quit! Ask the Lord to remind you of this when you are tempted to retire to your easy chair.

FEBRUARY 16   EVEN OUR ENEMIES

Key Verse: *"When a man's ways please the Lord, he maketh even his enemies to be at peace with him" (Proverbs 16:7).*

Message: We have learned that the way to please the Lord is to live uprightly before Him. Here is what the Lord has taught me recently. When we please Him, He will favor us and cause others to favor us, even our enemies.

One day as I was flipping through the TV channels, I paused long enough to hear a preacher mention the word "favor." Something he said caught my attention. I turned off the TV and began to research the word in the Word of God.

What I found led me to discover a new way to deal with relatives who do not speak to one another, spouses that do not honor their spouses, children that are disrespectful to their parents, and others who are at odds with one another.

As I looked into God's Word, the Holy Spirit led me to look at some of God's servants who were cast into the presence of people who were potential enemies, but did not turn out to be. Because these servants found favor with God, they also found favor with their potential enemies. We will look at some of them.

FEBRUARY 17 JOSEPH

Key Verse: *"And we know that all things work together for good to them that love God, to them who are called according to his purpose"* *(Romans 8:28).*

Message: If anyone was a living testimony of this verse, Joseph was. Things happened to him that looked as if they would not be to his good, but they turned out to be. Why? Because *"...God gave him favor..." (Acts 7:10).*

Let's look at the first example. Joseph's brothers hated him. They hated him because he was his father's favorite. They hated him even more because he told them that in a dream he saw them bowing down to him.

One day they saw an opportunity to get rid of him. The boys' father sent Joseph to check on his brothers. When they saw him coming, *"they conspired against him to slay him" (Genesis 37:18).* But they did not succeed! Why not? The real reason was that *"God gave him favor...."*

Oh, his brothers still hated Joseph. They couldn't kill him, but they vowed to get rid of him. Acts 7:9 says, *"And Jacob's sons, moved with envy, sold Joseph into Egypt, but God was with him."*

This seventeen-year-old young man, his father's favorite son, was now a slave in a foreign land. Things looked bad for Joseph. *"All things work together for good to them that love God, to them who are the called according to His purpose"???* *Let's see!*

FEBRUARY 18 JOSEPH AND POTIPHAR

Key Verse: *"...and Joseph found grace in his sight..." (Genesis 39:4).*

Message: *"And Joseph was brought down to Egypt, and Potiphar, an officer of Pharaoh, captain of the guard, an Egyptian, bought him..." (Genesis 39:1).*

Joseph was sold to a pagan high official in Pharaoh's court, who could have treated him as the lowest of slaves; but he didn't. Why not? Because *"the Lord was with Joseph and made him successful..." (Genesis 39:2).*

53

Now Potiphar, this pagan, saw that the Lord was with Joseph. (Can a pagan see that the Lord is with you?) *"And Joseph found grace in his (Potiphar's) sight...and he made him overseer over his house, and all that he had, he put into his hand" (Genesis 39:4).*

Because Joseph found favor in God's sight, God caused him to find favor in Potiphar's sight. This official made Joseph *"overseer in his house and over all that he had..." (Genesis 39:5).*

"All things work together for good to them that love God...." We have before us a good example of this truth. Joseph went from being a slave in Potiphar's house to overseer of the whole house. The reason? *"The Lord was with Joseph...."*

We began February 1 with this verse: *"When a man's ways please the Lord, he maketh even his enemies to be at peace with him" (Proverbs 16:7).* Joseph's ways were so pleasing to the Lord that He not only made Joseph's potential enemy to be at peace with him but also to favor him.

Pray that your ways will please our Lord.

FEBRUARY 19   JOSEPH AND THE JAILER
Key Verse: *"But the Lord was with Joseph..." (Genesis 39:21).*

Message: Have you ever said, or heard your children say, "That's not fair"? Well, if anyone had cause to say that, Joseph did—but he didn't.

He refused to have an affair with Potiphar's wife. He did what Paul told the Corinthians to do: *"Flee immorality" (1Corinthians 6:18).* Joseph took off running, but Potiphar's wife grabbed his coat. After this evil woman told lies about Joseph, her husband *"...took him, and put him in prison..." (Genesis 39:20).*

Surely this time Joseph could have said, "This isn't fair. I've been put in prison for something I did not do"—but he didn't. So what happened to Joseph in prison? *"The Lord was with Joseph and gave him favor in the sight of the keeper of the prison" (Genesis 39:21).*

Joseph was still in God's favor, even as a prisoner. The keeper could have done him great harm, but God gave Joseph favor in the jailer's eyes. This jailer put Joseph over all the prison. Genesis

39:23 says, *"The jailer did not have to look after anything for which Joseph was responsible...."* Why was the keeper able to trust Joseph with running the prison? The next statement gives the answer: It was *"...because the Lord was with Joseph and made him succeed in everything he did."*

Truly, Joseph was as faithful in running the prison as he was in running Potiphar's house. Why was this so? *"Because the Lord was with Joseph and made him succeed in everything he did."*

Are you beginning to grasp the idea of the value of pleasing the Lord, no matter where you are? Joseph could echo Paul's testimony: *"I have learned, in whatsoever state I am, therewith to be content"* *(Philippians 4:11)*. Can you? If so, your ways can be pleasing to the Lord. Pray 1Timothy 6:6. "Lord, I know that *'godliness with content- ment is great gain.'"* I pray that this might describe your life.

FEBRUARY 20   JOSEPH, WAITING
Key Verse: *"And it came to pass at the end of two full years..."* *(Genesis 41:1)*.

Message: The Pharaoh's chief baker and butler were in prison with Joseph. One day he came to them and asked why they were so sad. Their reply was, *"Each of us has had a dream, and there is no one here to explain what the dreams mean..."* *(Genesis 40:8)*.

Joseph didn't say, "I can interpret them." Rather, he said, *"It is God who gives the ability to interpret dreams. Tell me your dreams"* *(Genesis 40:8)*. In essence Joseph said that the dreams meant that both would be released from prison in three days and that the butler would live and the baker would be killed. It happened just as Joseph said it would.

Now, before the butler left, Joseph made a request of him. Basically he said, "Please put in a good word for me with the Pharaoh and help me get out of here. I didn't do anything to deserve being put in prison." (You don't get the idea that there was any bitterness or anger in his voice.) The butler agreed to do so but promptly forgot when he got out of prison.

Well, two full years went by. Two long years before Joseph would see the favor of God that would release him from prison!

The point I want to make here is that favor does not always come on our timetable. One of the hardest things for us to do is what David said in Psalm 37:7: *"Rest in the Lord and wait patiently for him...."* Joseph did, and two years later the favor came.

The Pharaoh had a dream that no one could interpret. The butler suddenly remembered Joseph the dream interpreter. He was brought from prison and interpreted the dream—that there would be seven years of plenty followed by seven years of famine.

Then Joseph presented the king a plan that would keep food on the tables of all the people during the famine. Pharaoh liked the plan. In Genesis 41:39-40, he said, *"Forasmuch as God hath showed thee all these things...only in the throne will I be greater than thou."*

At the end of two years, Joseph went from being a prisoner to being the number two man in all of Egypt. Paul's words in 1 Timothy 6:6 describe Joseph's life: *"Godliness with contentment is great gain."*

God's favor led him from a pit to a seat next to the throne. Why? Because his ways pleased the Lord! Pray that God will lead you from where you are right now to a higher plane.

FEBRUARY 21　　　THE CHILDREN OF ISRAEL

Key Verse: *"I will give this people favor..."* (Exodus 3:21).

Message: When the children of Israel were in bondage in Egypt, they had a hard time. Exodus 1:14 says that the Egyptians *"made their lives miserable by forcing them into cruel slavery....They had no pity on them."*

After the children of Israel had suffered enough in the eyes of God, God said to Moses: *"I have heard their cry to be delivered from their taskmasters...and I am come down to deliver them out of the hand of the Egyptians..."* (Exodus 3:7, 8).

Truly these folks had to go through some tough times before they felt God's favor, but they kept crying out to Him. They didn't give up, and God delivered. When He decided it was time for the children of Israel to leave Egypt, God changed the enemy Egyptian task masters.

In Exodus 3:21, God made this promise to Moses: *"I will give this people favor in the sight of the Egyptians."* Psalm 105:37 says, *"He brought them forth with silver and gold; and there was not one feeble person among their tribes."*

The children of Israel who had been mistreated in Egypt had to wait a while, but they came into God's good favor. The enemy became the helper and piled jewels and silver and gold on them. They came out of bondage—out of Egypt—rich and healthy because God had caused the children of Israel to find favor with the enemy Egyptians.

You may have to go through some tough times before you receive God's favor, but hang on. Deliverance will come. Pray for the ability to weather the storm.

FEBRUARY 22 DANIEL
Key Verse: *"But Daniel purposed in his heart..."* (Daniel1:8).

Message: These words are perhaps the words most used in connection with Daniel. What made him utter these words? Let's look at the story.

Daniel 1:3 says that Daniel was *"of the king's seed."* He was of royal blood. He was a fine-looking, healthy, intelligent, eighteen-year-old young prince who had been taken into captivity in Babylon.

King Nebuchadnezzar of Babylon was looking for a few such young men, and Daniel made the list. The king's purpose was to brainwash him and turn him into a Chaldean (Babylonian). He would begin by serving Daniel the best food and wine from his own table.

You know, the king could plan all day, but my Bible says *"People may plan all kinds of things, but the Lord's will is going to be done"* *(Proverbs 19:21 GN).* And it was!

Daniel didn't take the first step—the second is a lot easier—into being a Chaldean. He didn't say, "I'm a captive; I'd better do as the king says." Compromise was not a word in Daniel's vocabulary.

Well, the king's meat and wine were not on Daniel's diet. So what did he do? *"But Daniel purposed in his heart that he would not defile himself with the portion of the king's meat, nor with the wine which he drank,"* so he went to the chief eunuch and asked to eat his regular diet.

Notice verse 9: *"Now God had brought Daniel into <u>favor</u>...with the prince of the eunuchs."* The head eunuch could have made it hard on Daniel, but he didn't. He let Daniel's immediate supervisor make the decision. He allowed Daniel to follow his diet. The result? At the end of a ten-day trial, Daniel and his friends were head and shoulders above those who ate the king's food.

Daniel experienced God's favor. Why? Because he passed the very first test put before him!!! He purposed in his heart, not in his head. Purpose to serve God in your heart. Ask the Lord to get your obedience to Him from your head to your heart. Obedience brings blessings. It did to Daniel, and it can to you too.

FEBRUARY 23　　　　　　DANIEL IN A CRISIS

Key Verse: *"...and the king was angry and furious and commanded to destroy all the wise men of Babylon" (Daniel 2:12).*

Message: King Nebuchadnezzar had a dream. He was furious because his wise men could not interpret it. As a result, he sent out a decree *"that the wise men should be slain, and they sought Daniel and his friends to be slain" (Daniel 2:13).*

Daniel went to the king and said, "If you will give me time, I will show you the interpretation." The king could have had Daniel killed right then, but he didn't because Daniel had favor with God.

Daniel had a real crisis. His life was on the line. What did he do? He went to his friends Shadrach, Meshach, and Abednego and asked them to pray with him that God would reveal the meaning of the dream.

May I say this to you very sincerely. When you face a crisis, pray; but don't pray alone. Ask your friends to pray with you. You may hurt so badly that you cannot pray as you ought, but your friends can. Don't hesitate to ask them.

Well, in a night vision Daniel received the interpretation. He immediately broke out in praise: *"Blessed be the name of God for ever and ever..." (Daniel 2:21).* Daniel went back to the king with the message that God in heaven had revealed to him what the dream meant.

This king who had earlier sent out a decree to have Daniel killed now made him *"ruler over the whole province of Babylon" (Daniel 2:48).* Because God was with Daniel, He made this captive—who had purposed in his heart not to defile himself—to find favor with the king who made Daniel the number two man in the country.

As a young man, Daniel determined to live by God's law even as a captive, and God always rewarded him. He turned potential enemies into great admirers. This can happen to you if your ways please the Lord. Pray that they do.

FEBRUARY 24   ESTHER
Key Verse: *"If I have found favor…" (Esther 7:3).*

Message: Esther was an orphan Jewish girl in a pagan court. (No one knew she was Jewish.) When King Xerxes, king of Persia, wanted a new wife, he had a lot of fair maidens brought before him. Esther was one of them.

The people responsible for her did everything they could to enhance her beauty. Esther 2:15 says that Esther *"obtained favor in the sight of all them that looked upon her."*

One by one the maidens passed by the king. Esther caught his eye, and he made her his queen. Verse 17 says that *"The king loved Esther above all women, and she obtained…favor in his sight."*

There was a wicked man in the king's court, and his name was Haman. He convinced the king to sign a decree to have all Jews killed. Who could save them? Esther's uncle Mordecai uttered these immortal words to her: *"…who knoweth whether thou art come to the kingdom for such a time as this" (Esther 4:14)?*

Esther knew the danger of going to the king; but she went, saying, *"If I perish, I perish" (Esther 4:16).* She went to the king and made her request. In 7:3, she said, *"If I have found favor in thy sight, O king, and if it please the king, let my life be given me at my petition, and my people at my request."*

Until this point, the king did not know that Esther was Jewish. He could have done away with her right then, but he didn't. Instead, he showed her favor. He found a way to save her and her people. God had a mission for Esther: to save her people. Because she had favor with God, she had favor with the court and with the king.

God has a mission for you. Do you know what it is? If you do, ask God to fulfill it through you. If you don't, ask Him to reveal it to you. Then get busy fulfilling it.

FEBRUARY 25   EVEN OUR ENEMIES

Key Verse: *"...In all thy ways acknowledge him..." (Proverbs 3:6).*

Message: Everything I have written so far has been leading up to what God has recently showed me. I have mentioned some things that do not please God. Don't do them! I have mentioned some things that do please Him. Do them! Pleasing Him is the key to what I am about to say.

Let me mention this verse again: *"When a man's ways please the Lord he maketh even his enemies to be at peace with him" (Proverbs 16:7).*

The last four people I have mentioned—Joseph, the Israelites, Daniel, Esther—were in the presence of people who were their potential enemies. However, they did not become real enemies because these Bible characters found favor with God, and He changed their potential enemies.

What does this mean to you? Whom do you need to favor you? A spouse? A parent? A child? A sibling? A friend? A teacher? An employer?

Now, I am not necessarily saying that the person from whom you need favor is an enemy, but I am saying that if you are not being favored by that person, there is an "enemy" element in your relationship.

The "natural" side of you wants to tell that person what it would take to please you and how to go about doing so. I am sure you have tried this method. It didn't work, did it? Running that person down or trying to change him does little good and much harm. So, you ask, "What should I do?" Read on!

FEBRUARY 26   LIVE RIGHT! THEN PRAY!
Key Verse: *"...In all thy ways acknowledge him..." (Proverbs 3:6).*

Message: The first thing you must do, if you want this person to favor you, is to be sure you are living a life that is right with God.

I used Proverbs 3:6 again because it perfectly illustrates how to live a righteous life: *"...In all thy ways acknowledge him...." "In all thy ways...."* This means wherever you are—at home, at work, at play, at school, at church—that you are living a life that would cause our Lord to favor you. Our Bible characters did, and God favored them.

Now the second thing you must do, if you want this person to favor you, is to pray a certain prayer. (I want to caution you that the effectiveness of your prayer will depend on your right standing before the Lord.)

Here is the prayer: "Lord, if I have found favor with you, and I pray that I have, please cause _____ to favor me." Pray this prayer over and over and over, any time and anywhere.

Do not add to the prayer. Do not complain. Do not give God a list of what it would take for this person to please you. Let our Lord make this decision; let Him handle the details. I have seen this prayer work. Read on to see how!

FEBRUARY 27   TESTIMONIES
Key Verse: *"For the eyes of the Lord are over the righteous..." (1 Peter 3:12).*

Message: When the Lord gave me this principle, I was scheduled to teach the pre-school teachers for a month. I wanted to teach this lesson, but I needed to see what would happen if people prayed, "Lord, if I have found favor with you, and I pray that I have, please cause _____ to favor me."

I asked several people to pray this prayer. I want to tell you about two of them. I chose these two because I could check with them on a regular basis to see the results. For obvious reasons, I cannot reveal names; but I will tell you that one needed to be favored by a spouse; one, by a child.

I said to each one, "I want you to pray this prayer over and over. Don't add to it. Don't give God a list of wants. Just pray the prayer." I have talked with each of them several times since then. Their response was and has continued to be, "Things are much better."

Now, why is this prayer working for these two? Very simply put, they are living the Spirit-filled life, the life that pleases the Lord. They are not perfect by any means, but they are traveling down the path of righteousness.

I know they are faithful supporters of the local church and its leaders; I know they are storehouse tithers; I know that they do not murmur; I know that they have a quiet time of prayer and Bible study every morning.

As a result, 1 Peter 3:12 describes them: *"For the eyes of the Lord are over the righteous, and his ears are open unto their prayers."*

This verse can describe you also if you, as an act of your will, live a Spirit-filled life—a life that pleases our Lord. Tell Him that you want to please Him and set about doing so. Obedience brings blessings.

FEBRUARY 28   OBEY AND PLEASE

Key Verse: *"And whatsoever we ask, we receive of him..."* (1 John 3:22).

Message: Wouldn't we like for this statement to be all of the verse? However, it isn't. There are conditions to this promise, as we see in the rest of the verse: *"And whatsoever we ask, we receive of him because we keep his commandments, and do those things that are pleasing in his sight."*

"...we keep his commandments...." I don't know any better reference than 1 Samuel 15:22: *"And Samuel said, hath the Lord as great delight in burnt offerings and sacrifices, as in obeying the voice of the Lord? Behold, to obey is better than sacrifice, and to hearken than fat of rams."*

"...(we) do those things that are pleasing in his sight." (1 John 3:22). The ultimate evidence of our pleasing our Lord is that we do what He requires of us. Micah 6:8 (GN) says, *"...what he requires*

of us is this: to do what is just, to show constant love, and to live in humble fellowship with our God."

Folks, there is no short cut. To have your prayers answered, you must live to obey and please our Lord. My King James Study Bible has this quotation: "Right living is an important part of successful praying."

FEBRUARY 29   OBEDIENCE EQUALS BLESSINGS

Key Verse: *"...walk in the light..." (1 John 1:7).*

Message: I close this month by going back to the title: "Obedience Brings Blessings." I believe we can look at several statements in 1 John concerning obedience.

First of all, we must *"walk in the light."* We must know the Light of the World as our personal Savior and walk with Him. Second, we must realize that *"the blood of Jesus Christ his Son cleanseth us from all sin."* Now, we are cleansed from the penalty of sin, but that doesn't mean that we do not sin anymore. In this verse John did not say that the blood cleansed the believer; he said that it *"cleanseth"* us. It goes on cleansing. That leads to the third point. We must confess our sins. *"If we confess our sins, He is faithful and just to forgive our sins, and to cleanse us of all unrighteousness" (1 John 1: 7, 9).* We must stay prayed up.

Of course, we will face obstacles. That is the reason Paul tells us to take *"the shield of faith wherewith ye shall be able to quench all the fiery darts of the wicked one" (Ephesians 6:16).* I believe Paul is indicating that we are to take *"the shield of faith"* in Jesus' blood to quench those fiery darts that come at us.

Let me give you an example. I seem to see more and more anger between spouses that results in mental abuse and physical abuse. (True also in parents, children, etc.!) We talk about anger management, but see few results.

Here is what the Lord impressed on my heart. The abused spouse usually cannot control the abuser. So what can? Putting up the shield! Putting up the blood!

You see, Jesus' blood covers all sin known to man. I tell someone who is being abused, "Draw that shield as a blood line around that abuser's head and pray this way, 'Lord, my spouse has the sin of anger in his heart. Your blood covers anger. Please do not let that anger come from his mouth or his fist and cross that shield blood line and get to me.'" I also pray this prayer for several people.

If you are really walking in the Light, our Lord just might not let that anger cross the blood line and attack you. Much depends on your obedience. Pray the bloodline prayer every day and "walk in the Light."

Truly, obedience brings blessings!

March

GLEANINGS FROM SELECTED PSALMS

In 1 Chronicles 16:4, David appointed the Levites "... *to record, and to thank and praise the Lord God. ...*" We see the results in the Psalms. This book is a record of petitions, praise, and thanksgiving to God by His people. As such, it has been a source of encouragement, comfort, and blessing to God's children throughout the ages. It has been just that to me. As a result, I decided to share with you in this month what I have gleaned from selected Psalms.

I. PSALM 73

"Truly God is good. . . ." *(Psalm 73:1).* The first four words of this Psalm comprise one of the absolutes that every believer must accept: *"Truly God is good. . . ."* We see this repeated often in the Psalms. In 25:8, we read, *"Good and upright is the Lord. . . ."* In Psalm 52:1, we read, *"The goodness of God endureth continually."* In Psalm 86:5, the Psalmist prayed, *"For thou, Lord, art good. . . ."* He can be no other way. This was the conclusion of the Psalmist in Psalm 73, but he didn't arrive at this conclusion over night. He had to go through a process. In the next few days, we will see the path he took to reach the conclusion that God is always good.

MARCH 1   HE LOOKED AT THE WICKED

Key Verse: *"Behold, these are the ungodly who prosper in the world; they increase in riches"*
(Psalm 73:12).

Message: The first thing the Psalmist did was to look at some people who were quite obviously ungodly. As he did so, he began to observe some things about them that he couldn't quite understand. In 73:5, he said, *"They are not in trouble as other men; neither are they plagued like other men."* In 73:7, he said, *"They have more than heart could wish."* At this point he had a big "why—it just doesn't seem fair"! Ever been there? Are you there now? If so, keep reading.

It is so easy to focus on the wicked who seem to have it all together, who are successful according to the world's standards. Ask the Lord to change the focus of your eyes and pray with the Psalmist: *"I will lift up mine eyes unto the hills from which cometh my help. My help cometh from the Lord, which made heaven and earth"* *(Psalm 121:1-2).*

MARCH 2   HE LOOKED AT HIMSELF

Key Verse: "Verily I have kept my heart pure in vain. . ." (Psalm 73:13).

Message: This man was having a very hard time. He was living the godly life. Yet, although he was doing so, he was having a great deal of trouble. He said to himself, "It seems that my effort has been in vain." In Psalm 73:14, he said, "All the day long have I been plagued. . . ." He does not tell us exactly what his trial was. It may have been illness or trouble in a relationship or a job or money woes. (Supply your own trial.) But whatever it was, it hurt; and it hurt even worse when he looked at what was happening to him and what was happening to the ungodly. Ever been there? Are you there now? If so, keep reading.

Have there been times when you had to confess that you didn't understand why a godly person had to suffer and an ungodly person didn't? The Lord brought to mind what a former pastor of mine once told me: "God deals with His own on a cash basis and with the wicked on a credit basis." There will be a payday for them, one we would not wish on anyone. Ask the Lord to keep your eyes on Him, not on the wicked and not on your trials, remembering His words: "In the world ye shall have tribulation; but be of good cheer; I have overcome the world" (John 16:33).

MARCH 3   HE LOOKED AT OTHER BELIEVERS
Key Verse: *"If I say, I will speak thus: Behold, I should offend against the generation of thy children" (Psalm 73:15).*

Message: This man tried using logic. He said to himself, "After all, I am living a godly life; and this is what is happening to me. Those wicked people are saying things that should never be thought, let alone said. They are prosperous; their children are doing well; they have more than heart could wish. Meanwhile, I am suffering the exact opposite."

He worked himself up to a point where he said, *"As for me, my feet were almost gone; my steps had well nigh slipped."* But on the way down, he caught himself. He forced himself not to say what was on the tip of his tongue. He still didn't have an answer to his dilemma, but he was very sure that it was wrong to be a stumbling block to God's children. He saw the consequences of what he was about to do and declared, "I will not open my mouth." When you are tempted to murmur or complain—even if you don't understand what is happening— do as the Psalmist did.

My mother often said, "If you can't say something good about a person, don't say anything at all." That is the advice this man followed and is good advice for us to follow. If you start to complain, ask the Lord to bring these verses to your mind: *"I will keep my mouth with a bridle" (Psalm 39:1). "If thou hast done foolishly in lifting up thyself...lay thy hand upon thy mouth" (Proverbs 30:32).*

MARCH 4   HE LOOKED TO THE RIGHT PLACE

Key Verse: *"Until I went into the sanctuary of God; then understood I their end" (Psalm 73:17).*

Message: This man said, "I tried to think this problem through, but it was too difficult for me. I needed help." What did he do? He went to the right place. He went to God's house. There he got the answer to his problem.

Folks, there are some things you can only learn at church where the Word is taught and preached. My friend, Ron, in a testimony before the church, said that he told a former pastor that he didn't need to go to church to be a Christian, but that he had learned the value of being involved in the local church. He took to heart Hebrews 10:25: *"Not forsaking the assembling of ourselves together, as the manner of some is; but encouraging one another. . . ."* Meeting when the family meets—Sunday morning, Sunday night, Wednesday night—is now an "absolute" in the Windom home.

By the way, when this is an absolute in your home, your children will get the message. Recently, my friend, Stephanie, told me that her son Matthew was scheduled to play his first baseball game on a Tuesday evening. The game got rained out and rescheduled for Wednesday night at 6 p.m. when Royal Ambassadors meet. Stephanie knew what had to be done, but she was torn. She hated for him to miss his first game. When she broke the news to Matthew, he simply said, "I can't play in that game." Being in God's house is an absolute in this home. That is all Matthew knows; therefore, he made the right decision, and I pray that you will too if faced with a similar situation.

When the man in the Psalm went to God's house, everything began to be clear to him. He was set right and began moving to the point where he could say, "God is always good." We must know that He is always good. Pray with the Psalmist: *"I love the house where you dwell, O Lord, the place where your glory dwells" (Psalm 26:8).*

MARCH 5   WHAT DID HE LEARN?

Key Verse: *"For, lo, they that are far from thee shall perish. . ." (Psalm 73:27).*

Message: The Psalmist learned beyond a shadow of doubt that the lost would spend eternity in a devil's hell, separated from God. When he realized their fate, he was so ashamed of his envy of them. I believe he just shut his eyes, expecting God to disown him; but that didn't happen. He opened his eyes and gave this wonderful testimony about our loving Lord: *"Nevertheless I am continually with thee: thou hast held me by my right hand. Thou shalt guide me with thy counsel, and afterward receive me to glory" (Psalm 73:23-24).* What joy it was for the Psalmist to know this! And the same is true for me. These are my life verses. I am so thankful that I know my Lord is always with me, that He holds me by my right hand, that he guides me with His Word, and that He will take me to glory when He is ready. I can truly say with the Psalmist that *"God is always good."*

When this man went to God's house, everything began to be clear to him. He was set right and began moving to the point where he could say, "God is always good. I know that He is always good. Do you? Pray with the Psalmist: *"I love the house where you dwell, O Lord, the place where your glory dwells" (Psalm 26:8 GN).*

MARCH 6   HIS CONCLUSION

Key Verse: *"Truly God is good . . . even to such as are of a clean heart" (Psalm 73:1).*

Message: This man started this Psalm with the conclusion he had reached at the end of it. He learned that it takes a clean heart for a person to be able to say, *"Truly God is good. . . ."* When he went into God's house, he didn't have a clean heart; when he came out, he did. He came out concluding that his happiness could only be found in a growing relationship with God. His testimony became, *"But as for me, how wonderful to be near God, to find protection with the Lord God and to proclaim all that he has done"(Psalm 73:28 GN).* This should be the testimony of every believer. Is it yours? I pray that it is.

We Christians only know true happiness when we are clean before the Lord. That awful sin of David's ultimately broke his heart. In repentance he cried out: *"Create in me a clean heart, O God; and renew a right spirit within me" (Psalm 51:10).* May we do likewise when we sin.

II. PSALM 23 THE LORD IS MY SHEPHERD

I believe David wrote this Psalm in the latter years of his life. It seems that he looked back over his life and saw the good times and the bad times. The conclusion of the king, who was once a shepherd boy, was that God was the source of his happiness—his source of supply—no matter what his circumstances were. He could honestly say, *"The Lord is my shepherd. . . ."* Let me ask you a question. At the point where you are right now in your life's journey, can you say this? You can if you live Psalm 23.

MARCH 7   I SHALL NOT WANT
Key Verse: *"The Lord is my shepherd; I shall not want" (Psalm 23:1).*

Message: What does the word "want" often mean to us? "I want a new car—house—boat—computer—washing machine—spouse—etc." But in Psalm 23: "want" means "I have everything I need." The key is "need." A former pastor, Brother Len, once said, "If gasoline is $10 a gallon and God's faithful children need gas, God will see that they get it." Truly, God takes care of His own. One of the verses I claim is Psalm 37:25: *"I have been young, and now am old; yet* *have I not seen the righteous* (the key to this verse) *forsaken, nor his seed begging bread."*

Sometimes we have trouble distinguishing between "want" and "need." To be honest, there are a lot of things we want; and it is so easy to get our eyes on these earthly things that have no eternal value. Pray that you will direct your eyes toward our Lord and depend on the promise in Philippians 4:19: *"But my God shall supply all your needs according to his riches in glory by Christ Jesus."*

MARCH 8   GREEN PASTURES AND STILL WATERS

Key Verse: *"He maketh me to lie down in green pastures; He leadeth me beside still waters" (Psalm 23:2).*

Message: This is a promise of God. The key to experiencing this promise is that you are following the Shepherd in your journey through life. David knew that, because the Lord was his shepherd, he could find an oasis right in the middle of the barren valley. You see, when we let the Lord lead us, we are led toward green pastures and still waters. But, when we get into the driver's seat, we often end up in the barren desert and in turbulent water. At one point in David's life, he was in turbulent water. He said, *"Oh, that I had wings like a dove! For then I would fly away and be at rest."* David just wanted to get out of town.

Have you ever wanted to get away from something: job? city? neighborhood? marriage? in-laws, etc.? David found that running away wouldn't help. I imagine the same would be true of you. David learned to put his trust in the Lord right where he was, and thus could say, *"He maketh me to lie down in green pastures; he leadeth me beside still waters" (Psalm 23:2).* Folks, when you let the Shepherd lead you, He may not change your circumstances; but He will guide you to a green oasis in the midst of the barren valley and to calm water in the midst of a roaring sea. It all depends on who is doing the leading: the Shepherd or you!

Our Lord can lead us to green pastures and still waters. Only He can lead us to a place of rest in the midst of the turbulent world in which we live. He said, *"Come unto me, all ye that labor and are heavy laden, and I will give you rest" (Matthew 11:28).* Thank Him for that promise.

MARCH 9 — HE BRINGS BACK HIS OWN

Key Verse: *"He restoreth my soul. . ." (Psalm 23:3).*

Message: David had wandered from the fold. He was not following the Shepherd. Thus, he fell into sin. He was away from God. I call this being in the far country. I believe there are several possibilities when a person is in the far country:

- If he is lost, he will not come back unless he gets saved.
- If he is saved, he probably will return to the fold at some time.

Remember the prodigal son? Because he was a son, he didn't like the pig pen. He came home. I often use Psalm 92:13-14 to encourage parents of children away from God—parents who planted their children in God's house: *"Those that be planted in the house of the Lord shall flourish in the courts of our God. They shall still bring forth fruit in old age. . ." (Psalm 92:13-14).* Parents, if you have planted your children in the house of God, I believe they will return. David did. Our Lord brought him back. I can add that He has done the same for me, and He probably has for you. Thank God that He is a God who restores His own!

Peter went to the far country, but our Lord didn't let him stay there. He said, *"Simon, Satan hath desired to have you, that he may sift you as wheat, but I have prayed for thee, that thy faith fail not..." (Luke 22:31-32).* I believe the Lord Jesus prays the same prayer for everyone in the far country: *"...that thy faith fail not...."* May we pray likewise.

MARCH 10 — HE LEADS

Key Verse: *". . . he leads me in the path of righteousness for his name's sake" (Psalm 23:3).*

Message: Our Lord leads us down the path of righteousness, but we have to choose to follow. I hope that you start each day by putting on the whole armor of God. One part we wear is the *"breastplate of righteousness" (Ephesians 6:14).* What does this mean? When you got saved, you got covered with Jesus. In Galatians 3:27, Paul said, *"For as many of you as have been baptized into Christ have put on Christ."* Now, as your covering, Jesus will point you toward the path of righteousness, but He will not force you down that path. It is your choice.

Also, when you got saved, a new person set up residence in your heart, the Holy Spirit. In John 14:17, Jesus says, *". . . he shall be in you."* However, when the new person came to live in you, the old didn't move out. Thus every believer has two natures: old and new. Which we follow is an act of our will. If we follow the old, we will not trod the path of righteousness. If we follow the old, we will take Jesus, who is our permanent covering, where He will not feel comfortable. But if we let the Holy Spirit in us take control, He will lead us with our Lord down the path of righteousness.

David prayed, *". . . lead me into the land of uprightness" (Psalm 143:10).* This also is my prayer, to be so filled with the Holy Spirit that I will let Him lead me down the path of righteousness. Will you make this your prayer today?

MARCH 11   IN THE VALLEY
Key Verse: *"Yea, though I walk through the valley of the shadow of death, I will fear no evil; for thou art with me" (Psalm 23:4).*

Message: Have you ever stared death in the face? Have you ever been in a trial that was so dark that you felt you were walking *"through the valley of the shadow of death"?* Did you immediately say to yourself, *"I will fear no evil"?* Probably not! Probably your first reaction was "fear."—"What am I going to do?"—"How am I going to make it?"—"Why did this happen?" Now, I won't say that we won't have fear. I have a hard time with it, but I draw comfort from these words of David. I may fear the unknown, but I don't fear evil. I don't have to fear Satan. Why not? Because my Lord is with me!

Today we are walking down the pathway of life in the shadow of death—not the real thing—but the shadow. This is the place we will stay until we reach the real thing. And when we do get there, we have no need to fear because our Lord is with us. Thank the Lord that He is always with you. Ask with Paul, *"O death, where is thy sting? O grave, where is thy victory"* *(1Corinthians 15:55)?*

MARCH 12   ROD AND STAFF
Key Verse: *"... thy rod and thy staff they comfort me"* *(Psalm 23:4).*

Message: When I think of a rod and a staff, my mind goes more to a hair brush or a switch off a tree or a fly swatter or wooden spoon than to "comfort." To understand, I had to look up how the shepherd used them. The rod was a short club that he used to fight off wild animals. Our Lord uses that rod to keep the enemy away from us as we travel down the path of righteousness. I don't believe we have any idea how often He uses that rod to protect us. Think of the "near misses" you have had. Those were times when our Lord was using that rod.

Then there was the staff. It was a long stick with a crook, used to keep the sheep from straying. Our Lord uses the staff to keep us on course as we travel down the path of righteousness. Sometimes we choose to get off course. When we do, our Lord hooks that crook around our ankles to get us back in line. When He has to do this, He will probably send us to His school. Psalm 25:12 says, *"What man is he that feareth the Lord? Him shall he teach in the way that he shall choose."* When He has to reach out that crook to pull us back into the fold, He will have a lesson for us, and He will decide how to teach us.

The Psalmist said, *"...lead me into the land of uprightness"* *(Psalm 143:10).* This is the direction that we believers should go. We can be thankful that His rod will always be with us to fight off the enemy and that His staff will always be with us to keep us on course as we travel down the path of righteousness. This knowledge brought comfort to David, and it should to us also. Thank Him for His rod and staff.

MARCH 13   A BANQUET TABLE

Key Verse: *"Thou preparest a table before me in the presence of mine enemies" (Psalm 23:5).*

Message: My! My! Here we see a guest at a banquet table with enemies all around the table. That guest is you; it is I; it is every believer. Someone might ask, "Can I be victorious down here, no matter what is going on around me? Can I keep on following the path of righteousness?" Yes! You can follow God's direction no matter what the circumstances. How? Well, let's go back to the table. You are sitting there, and you have before you a one-dish meal. In that dish are several ingredients. The meal is the fruit of the Spirit. The ingredients are *"love, joy, peace, patience, kindness, goodness, faithfulness, gentleness, self-control" (Galatians 5:22-23a).*

These are all attributes of Jesus. He has given them to the Holy Spirit within you as a gift for you. But you have to reach out and claim them. You have to ask the Holy Spirit to produce them through you. You are always sitting at that banquet table. When you let the Holy Spirit produce what you need—patience, kindness, self-control, etc.—through you, you can shine for Jesus even in the midst of your enemies.

Paul told the Philippians to shine as lights in the world *"...in the midst of a crooked and perverse generation" (Philippians 2:15).* May we always remember that we are always at the banquet table in the midst of an evil world. May we never be tempted to get up from the table. Ask the Lord to keep a picture of this table before you.

MARCH 14   GOODNESS AND MERCY

Key Verse: *"Surely goodness and mercy shall follow me all the days of my life. . ." (Psalm 23:6).*

Message: Someone goes before us and something comes behind us as we travel down the path of righteousness. The Shepherd goes before us. Two spiritual blessings come behind us. They are *"goodness"* and *"mercy."* Some translations call them *"goodness"* and *"lovingkindness."* I read that one minister calls them the Shepherd's twin angels. As we travel down the path of righteousness, they follow us. We don't have to look at our past. These twins are behind us to block our backward look. We can keep our eyes on the Shepherd and move forward.

Have you ever stopped to think where you would be today without our Lord's goodness and lovingkindness? Keep this picture in your mind: the Shepherd before you and the twin angels behind you. Knowing this, press on and thank the Lord for those twin angels, goodness and mercy (lovingkindness).

MARCH 15   I WILL DWELL!

Key Verse: *". . . and I will dwell in the house of the Lord forever"* *(Psalm 23:6).*

Message: What awaits us at the end of the journey? A happy eternity!! *"I will dwell. . . ."*

I wonder how many of us realize what we have in Jesus every day. In this Psalm we learn that He leads us toward home on a path of righteousness. He leads! He covers us and points us in the right direction. He indwells us. As an act of our will, we allow the Holy Spirit to control us. When we do, we move forward down the path of righteousness.

Every day of our lives, our Shepherd has in His hand a rod to protect us from the world and a staff to draw us back when we wander. Every day of our lives, our Shepherd prepares a banquet for us, even with our enemies all around us. Every day of our lives, we are followed by our Shepherd's twin angels: *goodness* and *lovingkindness*. One day our Shepherd will lead us home. O happy day! It will be a happy day indeed if we keep walking, no matter what our circumstances. *"I will dwell. . . ."* Stay the course, folks. We'll soon be going home!

Paul tells us in 1 Thessalonians 4:17 that one day we shall *"meet the Lord in the air and so shall we ever be with the Lord."* Thank Him that the time is coming when you will be with Him forever.

III. PSALM 1

"Blessed is the man. . ." (Psalm 1:1). This Psalm begins with the word *"Blessed,"* which means "happy." In the original it is not in the singular, but in the plural. Thus, this Psalm can begin with "Happy, Happy." I don't know about you, but I want to be doubly happy. Let's see what the happy person does. But, let's begin where the Psalmist began — with what the happy person does not do.

MARCH 16   HE WALKS NOT!

Key Verse: *"Blessed (Happy, Happy) is the man that walketh not in the counsel of the ungodly. . ." (Psalm 1:1).*

Message: The point here is that the happy person does not listen to ungodly people — to the *". . . counsel of the ungodly. . . ."* "Counsel" means "advice." The happy person does not seek the advice of the ungodly. Who are they? They are the ones who leave God out of their counseling. Folks, be very careful to whom you go for counseling. I am a firm believer that the first place to go is to the Word of God in your daily, consistent, quiet time. Then if you still need counseling, go to someone who will say, *"Thus saith the Lord."*

Unfortunately, sometimes we have a pet sin, and we seek the counsel of someone who will tell us our sin is all right. The "happy, happy" person will listen only to the counsel of God's Word and God's servant. If you need to talk with someone, seek out a "bond-slave of the Lord Jesus Christ" — a minister, a counselor, a lay person. Find a "Paul"; avoid a "Judas." Ladies, here is a word for you. Be careful about going to your mother and complaining about something your husband has done. You will get past the problem, but your mother might not.

Proverbs 4:14 tells us: *"Enter not into the path of the wicked...."* Do not do so. Instead, follow the advice in Proverbs 4:25-27: *"Let thine eyes look right on, and let thine eyelids look straight before thee. Ponder the path of thy feet...turn not to the right hand nor to the left...."* May we do just this, with our Lord as our destination.

MARCH 17   HE STANDETH NOT

Key Verse: *Blessed (Happy, Happy) is the man that . . . standeth not in the way of sinners. . ." (Psalm 1:1).*

Message: Now, I cannot tell you not to be friendly with lost people. You need to be in order to lead them to Jesus. But I can tell you not to participate in their sinful activities. Your contact with them should not be at some club. You might say, "It is all right for me to go there and dance. I don't drink." If you say this, you are on dangerous ground.

Remember Peter? He stood in the way of sinners when he warmed himself at the enemies' fire and consequently denied his Lord with curses. This could happen to you if you stand with these sinners. They will tell you it is all right to go certain places and do certain things. Proverbs 16:2 says, *"All the ways of a man are clean in his own eyes. . . ."*

If you stand with these sinners, you will most likely think that whatever they are doing is all right in your eyes too. Folks, we must do what is clean in the eyes of the Lord, not in the eyes of man.

Our Lord has a promise for those who stand in the way of the righteous, not in the way of sinners. It is found in 1 Peter 3:12: *"For the eyes of the Lord are over the righteous, and his ears are open unto their prayers...."* Pray that you will be standing where He can be clearly in your line of vision.

MARCH 18   HE SITTETH NOT

Key Verse: *"Blessed (Happy, Happy) is the man that . . . sitteth not in the seat of the scornful" (Psalm 1:1).*

Message: The scornful are scoffers who look with disdain at things in the Bible, such as the story of Jonah and the whale and the virgin birth. They also want to convince you that the Bible has errors. The "happy, happy" person must have absolutely nothing to do with these folks.

But being scornful also means something else. It means to reject something because you don't like it. Folks, it is easy to have a critical spirit. You get with people who criticize the church staff and church programs; and you will, if you are not careful, soon be as scornful as they. Do not sit with these folks. You want to know God's attitude toward scorners? Proverbs 3:33 tells us: *"Surely he (God) scorneth the scorners, (the scoffers). . . ."*

Please know that our Lord scorns the scoffers. Don't be with these folks. Be with the folks in the last part of verse 33: *"...but he giveth grace to the humble."* Pray for His grace. Live so that you can avoid His scorn.

Note: A good way to check your walk with the Lord is to take a good look at where you are walking, where you are standing, and where you are sitting. Notice the order: walking, standing, sitting. If you don't repent and get right with the Lord when you catch your- self in the walking stage, you will soon be sitting in a dangerous position.

Maybe you are saying, "I don't associate with these folks, but I can't say that I am really 'happy, happy.'" Well, maybe you should check out the source of your happiness. Some of us think that our happiness depends on our having a spouse (not I) or having one that is what we want him/her to be. Some of us think that happiness depends on our having children or having them that are what we want them to be. Folks, God's Word does not teach that any human being is the source of our happiness. Then what is? Look at March 19.

MARCH 19   HIS DELIGHT
Key Verse: *"But his delight is in the law of the Lord, and in his law doth he meditate day and night" (Psalm 1:2).*

Message: The "happy, happy" person finds his delight in meditating on God's Word. I am going to mention my friend Ron again because I so feel that he exemplifies this verse. He has walked farther and quicker down the road of Lordship than any other person I have known. He stays in the Word. He is also very faithful to hear the Word taught and preached. When he comes to my mind, the first thing I think of is how he delights in the Word.

Folks, how about you? What do you do in your quiet time? Do you use devotional material? That might be what you need. However, I suggest that you spend at least part of your quiet time simply reading God's Word and meditating on it. Let me say this to you. I don't believe you will ever experience all that God has for you until you learn to delight yourself in the Word of God.

Joshua told the people: *"This book of the law shall not depart out of thy mouth; but thou shalt meditate therein day and night, that thou mayest observe to do according to <u>all</u> that is written therein..."* *(Joshua 1:8).* Tell the Lord that you delight in His Word. Keep in mind that you will experience delight when you obey it.

MARCH 20   PLANTED
Key Verse: *"And he shall be like a tree planted by the rivers of water" (Psalm 1:3).*

Message: The *"rivers of water"* represent God's Holy Word. Jeremiah says, *"Blessed is the man that trusteth in the Lord ... for he shall be as a tree planted by the waters, that spreadeth out her roots by the river..."* *(Jeremiah 17:7-8).* Literally, the tree planted away from the water might dry up when the drought comes, but the tree planted by the water will stay green *(His leaf also shall not wither.)* Why is this so? Because those roots will reach out and drink from that water! As they do, they will keep the tree green and growing. This is the picture of *"the man that trusteth in the Lord."* He will be planted in the Word. He will drink deeply from the Word. As he does so, he will keep green and growing. Here is something I believe. The more you stay in the Word, the more you will grow.

Guys, I have to say this to you. Women, as a whole seem to have a deeper walk with the Lord than men. This should not be the case. Then why is it so? One reason might be the fact that women usually spend more time in the Word. I will say this about men. I know some who are really in the Word. They are spiritual leaders in the church and in the home. I like these folks. Men, the key word is *"planted."* You cannot be a sagebrush that blows away when a puff of wind comes along. You must be *"planted"* in the Word. What a church your church would be if all the men were *"planted"* trees!

Psalm 119 is all about God's wonderful Word. Verse 105 says that His *"word is a lamp unto my feet and a light unto my path."* Be so planted in it so that He will light your way straight toward Him.

MARCH 21   A TESTIMONY

Key Verse: *"Thy word have I hid in my heart. . ." (Psalm 119:11).*
"And these words which I command thee this day . . . thou shalt teach them diligently unto thy children" (Deuteronomy 6:6-7).

Message: Recently I had an interesting conversation with my friend Jimmy. He told me that his objective is to open God's Word and read at least one verse from it every morning, without fail, no matter how late he is in leaving the house. His desire is to feast on the Word, and he does when he has time. But if he can't have a feast, he at least has a snack to tide him over. Guys, you might try Jimmy's plan.

Also, Jimmy has a unique way of memorizing Scripture. He has learned and can quote a verse beginning with every letter in the alphabet. He learned these verses by putting them on a card and taping them to his bathroom mirror. I like his plan, but here is something I like even better. He has taught his daughter Elizabeth, who is nine years old, to do the same thing. She can quote verses for all twenty-six letters. Jimmy is working on J.T. He can quote about three verses, but he is only four. Dad, do you teach the Word to your children, or do you leave that to their mother??? Psalm 78:5 says, *"For He established a testimony in Jacob, and appointed a law in Israel, which he commanded our <u>fathers</u>, that they should make them known to their children."*

I pray that our Lord will raise up more men like Jimmy who love the Word, who learn the Word, and who teach the Word to their children. Please join me in this prayer.

MARCH 22   PROSPEROUS

Key Verse: *". . . and whatsoever he doeth shall prosper" (Psalm 1:3).*

Message: Perhaps you are wondering if I am teaching a health and wealth gospel. Does this verse mean that if I am "planted," I will be healthy and wealthy? It could, but not necessarily. The Old Testament teaches material blessings; the New Testament, spiritual. You might ask, "Then what does *'prosper'* mean to me?" Well, if you put Jesus first in your life and meditate in His Word and lead a

Spirit-filled, "planted" life, you will prosper. How? Everything in your life will be better—at home, at church, at work, at play.

Psalm 35:27 says that our Lord has *"...pleasure in the prosperity of His servant."* Rejoice with those whom He blesses materially; rejoice with those whom He blesses spiritually. Tell the Lord that you will do so.

Note: Psalm 1 ends this way: *"For the Lord knoweth the way of the righteous..." (Psalm 1:6).* Nahum 1:7 says that God *"knoweth them that trust in him."* Please know that our Lord sees us all, but the promise here is that He has a special relationship with those who are "planted." Try Him! Try putting Him first! Try the disciplined walk! Be an evergreen!

IV. PSALM 101

Why did David write this Psalm? One day he said, "I am going to bring the ark to Jerusalem." He tried to do so. He loaded it on a cart and started for home. Here David made a mistake. Oh, he was doing something good, but he forgot to consult God. Now, he couldn't say that he didn't know God's Word. He knew the Law, but he decided to do God's work his way. The Law said that the sons of Kohath should bear the ark upon their shoulders. It was not to ride on a cart. David and his party made other mistakes (2 Samuel 6). As you can imagine, the journey was a royal failure. When David saw what a mess he had made, he said, "How can I take the ark with me now?" So he went home without it. I believe he must have said to himself, "I've messed up again. I had good intentions, but I messed up."

Did this ever happen to you? Have you had good intentions concerning your daily quiet time, only to get off schedule? Have you had good intentions in your dealing with your family, only to lose it? Folks, I wish I didn't have to tell you this, but you are going to mess up. Are you going to throw up your hands and say, "What's the use? I'll just mess up again." If you are saved, you will not be able to bear having a broken relationship with our Lord for long. David couldn't. Three months later, he went back after the ark, but this time he would do things God's way. But before he went, he made a fresh beginning. In Psalm 101, he told the Lord what he would be and do so that the ark could dwell in Jerusalem. Do you need to make a fresh beginning? If so, listen to David to see what he did.

MARCH 23   PRAISE

Key Verse: *"I will sing of mercy and justice; unto thee, O Lord, will I sing praises" (Psalm 101:1).*

Message: David began with a praise song. He didn't start with excuses. He didn't start by talking about himself and his faults. He began by praising the Lord who is full of mercy and justice—the One who makes no mistakes. David was on the right track because his song was to the Lord—the only One worthy of praise. Folks, praise is the place to begin your prayer if you have messed up. Praise Him for His lovingkindness and His justice. When you mess up, the best way to begin to get your fellowship restored with the Lord is to praise Him for who He is. By the way, don't you need to do this every morning? I do!

Pray with David: *"O Lord, our Lord, how excellent is thy name in all the earth..." (Psalm 8:1).* Aren't you glad that our Lord has an excellent name, a name that is above every name? Bow before Him right now in praise and adoration.

MARCH 24   I WILL BEHAVE

Key Verse: *"I will behave myself wisely in a perfect way..." (Psalm 101:2).*

Message: David is saying, "Lord nothing in my personal behavior will create a situation in which I will be out of fellowship with You." *"I will behave myself wisely . . . I will walk within my house with a perfect heart"* (A heart without blemish). What a resolve! *"I will walk within my house with an unblemished heart."* David began with himself. Where would you begin? It is much easier to begin with your spouse. It is easier to say, "I could have the home David described if my spouse would only...."

This should not be your thinking. You should vow to walk in your home in such a way that the Lord could pop in at any time. David did. What would you run to do if you saw Jesus through the peephole in your front door? Turn off the TV? Hide the beer can? Stop the fighting? Change the radio station? Clean up your mouth? If you would have to do any of these things, you are not walking in your home with an unblemished heart. Change! Let the change begin with you.

Ladies, you set the tone in your home. God's Word supports this. In Titus 2:5, Paul says that women are to be *"keepers at home."* In 1 Timothy 5:14, Paul says that they are to manage the house. Pray that you will set the example of walking wisely in your home.

MARCH 25   SEE NO EVIL
Key Verse*: "I will set no wicked thing before mine eyes. . ." (Psalm 101:3).*

Message: I personally believe that the remote control is one of the worst inventions to come along in a while. Before I had remote control, I would turn on a ball game, and that was it. Now, when a commercial comes on or the game is boring, I start flipping those channels. I avoid certain channels, but sometimes my eyes catch something they should not see. I get off that channel as quickly as I can, but my eyes have caught a glimpse of something unhealthy. For that I am sorry. I do not deliberately let my eyes watch something that would not be all right for my pop-in guest to see.

What do your eyes watch? Folks, when your eyes are looking where they shouldn't, there are other eyes looking at you. *"The eyes of the Lord are in every place, beholding the evil and the good"* *(Proverbs 5:21).* *"...for mine eyes are upon all their ways; they are not hid from my face, neither is their iniquity hid from my eyes"* *(Jeremiah 16:17).* Be careful what your eyes behold.

God's Word says that *"...all things are naked and opened unto the eyes of him with whom we must give account" (Hebrews 4:13).* His eyes are on us; our eyes are to be on Him. If they are, you will follow the advice found in Proverbs 4:25: *"Let thine eyes look right on, and let thine eyelids look straight before thee."*

MARCH 26   TOUGH LOVE
Key Verse: *"He that worketh deceit shall not dwell within my house; he that telleth lies shall not tarry in my sight" (Psalm 101:7).*

Message: These verses lead me to believe that David resolved to practice tough love. He resolved to make his home a place where our Lord could feel at home. He said that he would not tolerate deceit and lies. His resolve was good. Too bad it broke down in practice! He forgot his resolve when he caught sight of Bathsheba and resorted to adultery and murder. He really messed up this time. But do you know what I can tell you? God forgave him and used him again. In Psalm 89:3-4, God said, *"I have made a covenant with my chosen. I have sworn unto David my servant. Thy seed will I establish forever. . . ."*

Folks, your responsibility is to provide a home where there is no deceit and lying—a home where Jesus would feel comfortable. If your child wants to go the way of the world and still live at home, be careful. He may deceive you; he may lie to you. Do not make excuses for him. Do not lower the standards in your home for him. You keep your home a place in which Jesus feels comfortable, even if it means having to practice tough love. Has your resolve ever broken down in practice? Have you messed up? Do you know what I can tell you? God will forgive you. Here is His promise: *"If we confess our sins, he is faithful and just to forgive our sins, and to cleanse us from all unrighteousness" (1 John 1:9).* When you mess up, repent and get back to your resolve.

MARCH 27   THE MOUTH
Key Verse: *". . . with my mouth will I make known. . ." (Psalm 89:1).*

Message: When David realized God's goodness to him, he proclaimed, *"I will sing of the mercies of the Lord forever; with my mouth will I make known thy faithfulness to all generations" (Psalm 89:1).* David said that with his mouth he would praise the Lord forever.

Folks, how much time do you spend using your mouth to praise the Lord? I don't have to tell you that your mouth will have a big impact on what kind of home you have? I don't have to tell you that the tongue is a fire and full of deadly poison. I am sure you have had first-hand experience. Your tongue is the best tool of your <u>old</u> nature. James says, *"Out of the same mouth proceedeth blessing and cursing. My brethren, these things ought not to be" (James 3:10).*

He is so right. It must be an act of your will to keep a godly tongue. David made this resolve: *"I will take heed to my ways that I sin not with my tongue: I will keep my mouth with a bridle. . ." (Psalm 39:1).* How many times have you said this in theory, only to have it break down in practice? How many times have you vowed not to nag or yell or snap at your spouse or child, only to do just that?

Folks, you cannot control your tongue, but I know someone who can. As part of your morning quiet time, why don't you pray this prayer of David? *"Set a watch O Lord, before my mouth; keep the door of my lips" (Psalm 141:3).* Ladies, let me speak to you. You set the tone in your home. When you have a yielded tongue, as queen of your home, you will be amazed at what will happen to the mouths of your queendom.

Make this prayer be yours: *"Let my mouth be filled with thy praise and with thy honor all the day" (Psalm 71:8).* This verse says that your mouth is to praise our Lord and honor Him all the time, no matter the circumstances. I pray that you will do just that.

V. PSALM 127

Solomon was given the task of building God's house. Oh, how David, his father, wanted to build it; but the Lord didn't allow him to do so because he was a man of war. David accepted God's will and said, *". . . to Solomon his son, be strong and of good courage and do it" (1 Chronicles 28:20).* And do it he did! He built a beautiful temple. But, actually, he didn't—as we shall see in Psalm 127.

MARCH 28   WHO BUILDS THE CHURCH?
Key Verse: *"Except the Lord build the house, they labor in vain that build it" (Psalm 127:1).*

Message: This truth applies as much to us as to Solomon. It applies to every local church—to every effort made down here to build God's house. You see, God's house is not going to be built by man; it is going to be built by the Holy Spirit—by Christ living in and working through believers.

Do you know how you can tell if the Lord has built the church? By what comes out of it! Psalm 118:15 says, *"The voice of rejoicing and salvation is in the tabernacles of the Righteous..."* This may not be the primary meaning, but here is what this verse says to me. It says that if God has built the house, the people will be right with Him and these things will happen in the worship center. There will be praise, not murmuring. There will be rejoicing, not complaining. But the major thing that will happen is that people will be saved. Praise and rejoicing and salvation are the marks of a church God has built.

Consider these questions: Is the church you attend a place of praise and rejoicing? Is salvation of souls causing the bells of heaven to ring? Our Lord's church is marked by praise and rejoicing and salvation. Ask yourself, "How much am I contributing to making sure that church is the house the Lord build?" Ask our Lord the same question.

MARCH 29   WHO BUILDS THE HOME?
Key Verse: *"Except the Lord build the house, they labor in vain that build it" (Psalm 127:1)*

Message: Do you know how you can tell if the Lord has built your house? By what comes out of it! Is your home a place of praise and rejoicing? Have you led your children to Jesus? Are you living a life of joy before your spouse and children? Is their salvation and spiritual growth the main priority in your home? It is so easy for it to be school or sports or clubs, etc.

Sit down tonight and take inventory of your day. Answer the questions I just posed. Do your answers give evidence that you are right with God and that praise and rejoicing and salvation and spiritual growth are the mainstays in your home? If not—???

If the Lord Jesus listened at the doors of our houses, what would He hear? Would He hear praise music, clean language, laughter, joyful noises, conversations about Jesus, complimentary words, kind tones, encouraging words? How many on this list describe your home? Not many? I hope not; but if so, ask the Holy Spirit to produce these things in your home.

MARCH 30   SLEEP
Key Verse: *". . . for he giveth his beloved sleep" (Psalm 127:2).*

Message: Sleep is a gift of God for His *"beloved."* Who are they? Paul tells us that through Jesus, we have been *"accepted in the beloved" (Ephesians 1:6).* That means that our Lord gives us sleep. I accept that gift. It restores my energy and soothes my nerves, but it does more that that. The New American Standard puts Psalm 127:2 this way: *". . . For he gives to his beloved even in his sleep."* He is not talking about dreams, but it is in sleep that an answer often comes.

I always had a policy at school to wait until the next day to make an important decision. Why? I wanted to pray about it and sleep on it. I would go to bed, commit the whole matter to our Lord, go to sleep, and wake up with a clearer picture of the solution. Ever had anyone say to you, "Sleep on it. Everything will look better in the morning"? That is Biblical. If you are His *beloved,* He will give to you sleep; and He will give to you in sleep. Remember! Sleep is God's gift to us.

Here is what I pray every night before I go to sleep: "Lord, Psalm 121:4 says that you *'neither slumber nor sleep.'* You watch over us while we do, and I thank you. Your Word also says that you *'give your beloved sleep.'* I ask for sleep, and I ask you to teach me while I sleep." Why not pray the same prayer?

MARCH 31   CHILDREN

Key Verse: *"Lo, children are a heritage of the Lord..." (Psalm 127:3).*

Message: When God sends a baby down here, He has a purpose for that baby. When He sent Jesus as a baby, He had a purpose for Him. It was to die on a cross so that we might live. When God sends a baby into your home, He has a purpose for that child. You are to bring that child *"... up in the nurture and admonition of the Lord" (Ephesians 6:4)* and thereby help him discover his purpose for being in this world.

Folks, the more "absolutes" he sees in your life, the more likely he is to discover and fulfill his purpose. And by the way, when God sent you down here, He had a purpose for your life. Are you fulfilling it?

Proverbs 22:6 says, *"Train up a child in the way he should go, and when he is old (mature), he will not depart from it."* Parents, help your children develop a taste for the things of God so that when they are mature, they will live their lives according to God's purpose for them. Pray for wisdom as you *"train up your child in the way he should go."*

April

FAITH

I could give you a scholarly definition of "faith," but I am not scholarly. Therefore, I will give you a short version. To me faith means believing God.

When I put on the whole armor of God each morning, I always pray, "Lord, your Word says I am to take the shield of faith with which I *'will be able to quench all the fiery darts of the evil one'* (*Ephesians 6:16*). Faith means that I believe you, and I do. *'I esteem all thy precepts concerning all things to be right...'*" (*Psalm 119:128*).

I am convinced that most of us believe the Lord and know that He makes no mistakes. We have heard faith verses from the Bible; but so often when we really need to exercise faith, we find that what we know in theory breaks down in practice.

In this month we will study "faith." Every day there will be a different message on faith. I believe if we concentrate on what the Bible says about faith, we will be better able to lead a faith-based walk.

APRIL 1   WHEN REMEMBERING HINDERS

Key Verse: *"In the day of my trouble, I sought the Lord..." (Psalm 77:2). "I have considered the days of old..." (Psalm 77:5). "Hath God forgotten to be gracious..." (Psalm 77:9)?*

Message: The Psalmist remembered God's goodness in the past, but remembering didn't help. He remembered how God had been faithful in the past, but he was sure God wouldn't help with his current problem.

Remembering should have increased his faith. Why didn't it? Because he got bogged down in the big "I" instead of having faith in the "Great I am"! Ever been there?

Consider the Psalmist's focus. Eighteen times in the first six verses, he refers to himself; only six to God. As a result of his focus, he felt that God would not help him at the present time. Ever been there?

Remembering God's goodness in the past should have increased his faith, but it didn't because he was focused on his problem, not on the one who could deliver him. Ever been there? However, the Psalmist woke up. Read on!

APRIL 2   WHEN REMEMBERING HELPS

Key Verse: *"And I said, this is my anguish, but I will remember the years of the right hand of the Most High" (Psalm 77:10).*

Message: When the Psalmist got to verse 10, he had a change of attitude about "remembering." Notice the shift: *"I will remember the works of the Lord; surely I will remember thy wonders of old. I will meditate also of all thy work, and talk of all thy doings" (Psalm 77: 11-12).*

The Psalmist began to get his focus right. He said that he would remember what God had done in the past, that he would meditate on God's Word, and that he would testify of our Lord's wonderful *"doings."* He no longer dwelt on his *"anguish."* Why not?

Because his faith was restored! His faith was restored when he remembered what God had done for him in the past. As a result, he chose to have faith in Him in the present. May we do likewise!

If you are going through a hard time right now, listen to these words from Dr. D. Martin Lloyd-Jones: "If the Lord has been with you and provided for your needs right up to this moment, do you think he will now turn His back on you and fail to provide for your current needs?" He won't.

As you pray today, *"Remember his marvelous works that he hath done..." (Psalm 105:5).*

APRIL 3   HEARING

Key Verse: *"Then faith cometh by hearing, and hearing by the Word of God" (Romans 10:17).*

Message: You know by now how much I believe in the power of the Written Word. I once heard an unusual testimony on television concerning the Word. I don't remember it all, but here is the message I got.

A minister pointed to his wife in the audience and noted that she was the picture of health. (I thought to myself, "He is about to tell us about a miraculous healing," but he didn't—exactly!)

Instead, he told that his wife had been very ill and had been sent home from the hospital to lie in bed and waste away.

This verse came to his mind: *"Faith cometh by hearing, and hearing by the Word of God."* He concluded that the only way that he and his wife could have the faith that God would heal her was to immerse themselves in the Word. This they did! As this lady lay in bed, she listened to the Word on tape. Her husband read it to her when he was at home. Every waking hour this lady had the Word flowing into her ears.

In essence her husband said this: "My wife's healing didn't happen at once. It took time. It was a slow process. But she was healed! It wasn't anything I did that caused her to be healed. Her healing came about because the Living Word used the Written Word to make her whole."

Maybe you need physical healing. I cannot promise what only God can grant. I can ask you to saturate yourself with the Word of God and see what happens. Perhaps you need other types of healing, healing for wounds caused by a broken relationship, for heartache from the loss of a loved one, for bondage to a sinful habit that has you in its throes.

Saturate yourself in the Word, trusting God's message in Isaiah 55:11: *"So shall my word be that goeth forth out of my mouth: it shall not return unto me void, but it shall accomplish that which I please, and it shall prosper in the thing whereto I sent it."*

Pray that you will have faith in the Written Word of the Living Word.

APRIL 4   I WILL TRUST

Key Verse: *What time I am afraid, I will trust in thee"* (Psalm 56:3).

Message: "Trust" is a synonym of "faith." Here David is saying that when he was afraid, he trusted God. He had faith in Him.

"Fear" is certainly not a stranger to us. We fear many things: losing a job or a mate or health or wealth. We may fear that a child is headed for the far country. We may fear being alone. We may even fear the dark.

We know we can have faith in the Lord in these situations, and we really want to; but we cannot get our minds off of what has caused our fear. Can we have victory over fear? Can we have the faith to believe that God will deliver us? Yes, we can! But how? We can do as David did. In Psalm 56:3, he said, *"What time I am afraid, I will put my trust in thee."* Then in the very next verse he began to praise: *"In God I will praise his word."* He repeats this twice in verse 10: *"In God will I praise his word, in the Lord will I praise his word."* The Good News puts it this way: *"...I know this; God is on my side, the Lord, whose promises I praise."*

Why did David praise the Word? Because it was in the Word that He learned that he need not be afraid! David could declare that God was on his side because he had praised the promises of the Lord. As a result he could say, *"In him I trust, and I will not be afraid..."* *(Psalm 56:11GN).*

It is a great thing to praise the promises of God in time of fear. It has been said that there are some thirty-thousand promises in the

Bible. Search for those that fit your need and have faith that God will make them come true.

Why not pray this prayer with David: *"O my God, I trust in thee..." (Psalm 25:2).* Have faith in God; have faith in His Word!

APRIL 5   THEIR FAITH

Key Verse: *"I say unto thee, arise, and take up thy bed..." (Mark 2:11).*

Message: Jesus had been traveling all over Galilee, preaching and healing. He made His way back to Capernaum. Word came that He was in a certain house, and people came to hear Him. The place was so crowded that there was not a place for one other person.

Well, four men had a paralyzed friend who needed to see Jesus. They carried him on a stretcher and got to the door. That was as far as they got, but they were determined to get their friend to Jesus. So what did they do? Mark 2:4 says that they *"uncovered the roof... and let down the bed wherein the sick of the palsy lay."* (Would we show as much perseverance in trying to bring a friend to Jesus? We could all take lessons from Jimmy Evans, one of the most consistent witnesses that I know.)

Verse 5 begins, *"When Jesus saw their faith, he said unto the sick of the palsy, Son, thy sins be forgiven thee."* Please understand that it was not the faith of these men that saved their paralyzed friend. It was their faith that brought him to Jesus—to the One who could heal him.

When, as a result of their faith, these men got their friend to Jesus, He took over and healed the paralyzed man spiritually and physically. *"...Thy sins be forgiven thee...arise, and take up thy bed and walk" (2:9).*

Put yourself in the paragraph I just read. "When, as a result of my faith, I got my friend to Jesus, He took over and healed...." Do you have this testimony? If not, pray for this kind of faith. If so, pray for more opportunities to exercise this kind of faith.

I want to make one more point before I leave this Scripture. The paralyzed man could not get to Jesus, but his friends could. Sometimes you may not be able to get to Jesus. You may be hurting so badly that you can't even pray, but your friends can. Don't hesitate to ask them to do so.

APRIL 6   RAIN

Key Verse: *"...and he said again, Go again seven times" (1Kings 18:43).*

Message: 1 Kings 16:30 says that *"Ahab did evil in the sight of the Lord, more than all that were before him."* For one thing, he married Jezebel; for another, he set up an altar for Baal. Verse 33 says that he *"did more to provoke the Lord...to anger than all the kings of Israel that were before him."*

Well, you know that judgment was coming. God sent Elijah to King Ahab with this message: "In the name of the Lord I tell you that there will be no rain until I say so." He was to *"say so"* (according to James 5:17) three years and six months later. As you can imagine, there was a great famine. 1Kings 18:1 says *that the word of the Lord came to Elijah in the third year, saying Go, show thyself unto Ahab; and I will send rain upon the earth."*

After the contest on Mount Carmel, Elijah went to Ahab and said to him, *"Get thee up, eat, and drink; for there is a sound of abundance of rain" (1 Kings 18:41).* But there was no rain immediately! Elijah bowed down to wait for the rain to fall. He told his servant to look toward the sea. The servant went, came back and reported, "I didn't see anything."

At this point I might have begun to question God and ask, "Did I get the right message from you?" I might even have given up, but Elijah didn't. He knew that what God promises, He delivers. He had the faith to believe that the rain would come.

Elijah had to send his servant out seven times before he came back with this message: *"I saw a little cloud no bigger than a man's hand coming up from the sea" (1 Kings 18:44 GN).* Verse 45 (GN) tells us that *"in a little while the sky was covered with dark clouds, the wind began to blow, and a heavy rain began to fall."*

Folks, if you believe the Lord has given you a word, start praying and walking toward it. Just keep praying and walking. If you are faithful to do so, God will either open the door wider or close it.

Pray that you will have the faith to keep praying and walking until the answer comes.

APRIL 7   DON'T QUIT

Key Verse: *"You should have struck five or six times..." (2 Kings 13:19 GN).*

Message: When Elisha was on his death bed, he received a visit from Joash, king of Israel. The king wept and said in essence, "You have been the great defender of Israel." I believe he wept because he didn't think that God would give him victory without Elisha's help. He did not have faith in God alone.

Elisha's reply was to tell the king to shoot an arrow through the window. He obeyed. Elisha said to him: *"You are the Lord's arrow, with which he will win victory over Syria..." (2 Kings 13:17 GN).*

Next Elisha told King Joash to take the rest of the arrows in the quiver and hit the ground with them. Here Joash showed that he was a man of little faith. He started shooting but quit before he used up all of the arrows. Why did he quit?

Dr. J. Vernon McGee made this statement: "Because King Joash didn't have the faith that God would give him deliverance, discouragement caused him to quit."

Could this be said of you when you have faced a crisis: "Because I didn't have the faith that God would give me deliverance, discouragement caused me to quit." If so, you might get the same message that King Joash received: *"Elisha said to him, you should have struck five or six times, and then you would have won complete victory over the Syrians; but now you will defeat them only three times" (2 Kings 13:19 GN).*

Joash's faith was small. Consequently, he received partial victory. Don't be like him. Have faith that our Lord will deliver you. Hold on to the hem of His garment in prayer until He does so. Don't give up in mid-stream. Who would want a partial victory? Pray for endurance even when you become discouraged or someone opposes you. **Note:** Partial obedience brings little satisfaction, because in God's eyes partial obedience is disobedience.

APRIL 8   START POURING

Key Verse: *"...Pour out into all those vessels..." (2 Kings 4:4).*

Message: A prophet's widow went to Elisha and said to him, "My husband has died. As you know, he feared the Lord. A man to whom he owed money has come to collect, and I can't pay. He is going to take my two sons as payment."

Elisha asked her, "What do you want me to do for you? What do you have in the house?" *"And she said, thine handmaid hath not anything in the house, save a pot of oil" (2 Kings 4:2).* Elisha told her to borrow every empty jar in the neighborhood and to shut herself and her sons up in their house. Now picture this: a mother, her two sons, and a room full of empty jars. Elisha gave an unusual request: *"Start pouring oil into the jars..." (2 Kings 4:4 GN).*

I might have asked, "How am I going to fill up all these jars if I only have one little one to begin with?"—But she didn't. She obeyed. There was just a room full of jars until she took a step of faith and started pouring. This widow didn't see how she and her sons could make it with only one jar of oil. But when she took a step of faith, God showed her that He was her source of supply.

One day my friend Ashley came to me and said that she really felt as if God wanted her to quit work and to stay at home with young Jack and to do it right away. She told me that she and her husband Crull had figured out that they would be able to manage her staying at home in a few months. Then she added, "But that wouldn't be acting on faith, would it?"

I replied, "No, it wouldn't be. If God has impressed on your heart that you are to quit work right now, do so. Take that step of faith. Remember! God is your source of supply." She did so.

I called her after she had been at home for a few months and asked her how things were going. Her reply was, "Just fine! It doesn't work out on paper, but we are making it." Crull and Ashley took that step of faith instead of waiting until they had worked out all the details by themselves, and God is blessing.

Do you need to take a faith venture? The temptation is to say, "I'm afraid I won't be able to make it." Replace "fear" with "faith," and let God lead you and be your source of supply.

You won't get the blessing until you start pouring. Ask the Lord to give you the courage to do so.

APRIL 9   FAITH AND ABRAHAM

Key Verse: *"By faith Abraham...obeyed..." (Hebrews 11:8).*

Message: There was a famine in Canaan, so Abram and Sarai went to Egypt. Abram said to her, "You are very beautiful. When the Egyptians look at you and realize that you are my wife, they will kill me and save you."

Notice what he asked her to do: *"Say, I pray thee, thou art my sister..." (Genesis 12:13).* This was not a one-time request. Notice what he said after he was saved and became Abraham: *"...at every place whither we shall come, say of me, he is my brother" (Genesis 20:13).*

Well, Sarai was Abraham's half-sister, but his statement was a lie. And we know how God feels about liars. *"A false witness that speaketh lies" (Proverbs 6:19)* is one of the seven deadly sins on God's hate list.

Abraham sinned but was forgiven and used by God in a mighty way. You see, God didn't remember Abraham's sin; He remembered his faith. We see this in Hebrews 11:8: *"By faith Abraham, when he was called to go out into a place which he should after receive for an inheritance, obeyed; and he went out, not knowing where he was going."*

Why didn't God remember Abraham's sins? Because what He forgives, He forgets! Psalm 103:12 says, *"As far as the east is from the west, so far hath he removed our transgressions from us."* Isaiah 38:17 says, *"...for thou hast cast all my sins behind thy back."* In Isaiah 43:25 God says, *"I, even I, am he that blotteth out thy transgressions, for mine own sake, and will not remember thy sins."*

Folks, don't let past sins keep you from stepping out in faith to obey the Lord. He has forgotten your confessed sin; do likewise. You may be like Abraham and not know where you are going. Just get your feet moving. Ask the Lord to direct your path.

APRIL 10   TOUCH THE HEM

Key Verse: *"...thy faith hath made thee whole..." (Matthew 9:22).*

Message: A woman who had had a flow of blood for twelve years was in the crowd that surrounded Jesus on one occasion. She said to herself: *"If I may but touch his garment, I shall be whole" (Matthew 9:21).* Verse 20 says that she *"touched the hem of his garment."* Jesus turned around, saw her, and said, *"Daughter, take courage; thy faith hath made thee whole..." (Matthew 9:22).*

Mark 6:56 says that wherever Jesus went, the sick were brought to Him *"that they might touch if it were but the border of his garment: and as many as touched him were made whole."*

What is special about touching the hem of His garment? Psalm 133:2 gives us a picture of the first high priest on earth: Aaron. When Moses anointed him with the precious oil, *"It ran down upon... Aaron's beard: that went down to the edge of his garments."* The oil gathered in the hem. We have a high priest in heaven, Jesus, and by faith we can touch the hem of His garment. Hebrews 4:14 says that *"We have a great high priest, that is passed into the heavens, Jesus the Son of God."* The writer goes on to say that Jesus knows our weaknesses and feels for us because He experienced everything we experience but did not sin.

Therefore, verse 16 says, *"Let us come boldly unto the throne of grace, that we may obtain mercy, and find grace in time of need."* You have the privilege of going into the throne room of God. Picture yourself bowing before our Lord in all His whiteness and brightness. Touch the hem of His garment.

Take whatever illness you have to Him: a broken walk with Him, a broken relationship, broken health, a broken job—and lay it at His feet and hold on to the hem in faith.

Pray that the oil from the hem of His garment will flow into your body to soothe and to heal whatever you have laid before Him—and have faith!

APRIL 11   THY FAITH
Key Verse: *"...thy faith hath saved thee" (Luke 19:42).*

Message: On several occasions when Jesus healed, He did so because of a person's faith. One day as Jesus was entering Jericho, he saw a blind man sitting by the wayside. Over and over and louder and louder the blind man cried, *"Jesus, thou Son of David, have mercy on me" (Luke 19:38).* Jesus' answer to him was, *"Receive thy sight; thy faith hath saved thee" (Luke 19:42).* On one occasion two blind men followed Jesus and cried, *"Thou Son of David, have mercy on us" (Matthew 9:27).* Jesus asked them a question: *"Believe ye that I am able to do this? They said unto him, Yea, Lord" (9:28).* Jesus touched their eyes and said, *"According to your faith be it unto you" (9:29).*

I want to call you attention to the question that Jesus asked these men: *"Believe ye that I am able to do this?"* I believe that every one of us would agree that Jesus is able to heal, but we are not sure how to pray. Do we pray for healing or for God's will to be done? Both! It is perfectly all right to pray for God to heal; it is certainly all right to pray for God's will to be done. Confused?

I was until the Lord settled this in my heart. I asked myself, "Do I have the faith to believe that our Lord will heal this seriously ill person for whom I am praying?"

Here is the answer I received in my Spirit, and I lifted it up in prayer: "Lord, I have faith that you will heal this believer. Whether it is in this life or the next is up to you. I leave the timing in your hands. I know you make no mistakes."

Since the Lord taught me to pray this way, I have perfect peace about how to pray for the sick. I'll admit that I do say to Him, "Lord, you know I want to see this person healed, but I want your will even more."

Ask God to speak to your heart about praying for the sick.

APRIL 12   HOW JESUS HEALS
Key Verse: *"Say a word..." (Luke 7:7).*

Message: Jesus used various methods to heal. He healed the blind man we met April 11 by speaking to him. He healed the two blind men we met in April 11 by touching their eyes. He healed a man blind from birth by applying clay to his eyes and sending him to the pool of Saloam to wash (John 9:11). He healed ten lepers while they were on a faith journey to see the priests (Luke 17:14).

Jesus again healed at a distance. A centurion had a dear servant who was sick and about to die. He sent a message to Jesus: *"Say a word, and my servant shall be healed" (Luke 7:7).* When the messengers got back to the house, *"they found the servant whole (healthy) that had been sick" (Luke 7:10).*

My point in giving all these examples is to show that Jesus can use any method He chooses to heal. He uses medicine; He uses our prayer; He uses miracles. I'll let Him decide. Whatever method He uses, it is never for show. It is for God's glory.

Folks, if you are healed, the reason is that God has something else for you to do. Pray that you will be faithful to obey.

APRIL 13   INCREASE OUR FAITH
Key Verse: *"And the apostles said unto the Lord, Increase our faith" (Luke 17:5).*

Message: On one occasion Jesus taught His apostles about forgiveness. In Luke 17:1, He said, *"Offenses will come."* He goes on to say that if someone offends you, you have to forgive him if he repents.

Perhaps the apostles could handle this command, but I believe Jesus' next words must have caused them much concern: *"And if he trespass against thee seven times in a day, and seven times in a day turn again to thee, saying, I repent; thou shalt forgive him" (Luke 17:4).* The magnitude of this command led the disciples to plead for help. They said, "Lord, increase our faith."

"Faith" as used here also means "faithfulness." This is a characteristic of Jesus. Hebrews 3:2 says that *"Jesus was faithful to him that appointed him."* Jesus was faithful in every situation. He was faithful to forgive. Even while hanging on the cross, He prayed, *"Father, forgive them; for they know not what they do" (Luke 23:34).*

Since Jesus was faithful to forgive, you can be too. How do I know this? I know because

Jesus gave everything of Himself to the Holy Spirit to give to us. All we have to do is claim it. Will you allow me to take a little liberty with Jesus' reply to His apostles? I believe the underlying message is, "Why ask for what you already have? You don't need more faith. Faith as a grain of mustard seed is all you will ever need."

Folks, Jesus was serious about forgiveness. When Peter asked Jesus how often one should forgive a brother who had sinned against him, Jesus' answer was *"seventy times seven" (Matthew 18:22).* You would never to able to do this on your own, so ask the Holy Spirit to forgive through you.

Before I leave this subject, I want to say a word to any of you who has the spirit of unforgiveness in you. 1 John 4:20 says this: *"If a man say, I love God, and hateth his brother, he is a liar; for he that loveth not his brother whom he hath seen, how can he love God whom he hath not seen?"* Also, check out Mark 11:25-26 and Ephesians 4:31-32.

If you take forgiveness as seriously as Jesus does, you will get busy forgiving. Pray that you will do what you need to do in order to be free of this burden.

APRIL 14   BELIEVING GOD

Key Verse: *"The Lord is on my side; I will not fear. What can man do to me" (Psalm 118:6)?*

Message: In the beginning of this month, I said that to me faith means believing God. In my quiet time this morning, I read Psalm 118. As I looked at verse 6, the thought hit me. "If I believe that faith means believing God, I will believe that *'the Lord is on my side';* thus I will not need to fear."

I checked out some other verses. In Psalm 27:1, David said, *"The Lord is my light and my salvation; whom shall I fear? The Lord is the strength of my life: of whom shall I be afraid?"*

He said in Psalm 56:9: *"When I cry unto thee, then shall mine enemies turn back. This I know; for God is for me."* Paul said in Romans 8:31: *"...if God be for us, who can be against us?"*

Ten of the spies came back and gave this report: "We can't take the land. There are too many giants there." To that Moses replied: *"...the Lord is with us; fear them not"* (Numbers 14:9).

Folks, the Lord is on our side. There is no need to fear. Believe God! When you are feeling that the world is against you, remind yourself that God is on your side and thank Him for that promise.

APRIL 15   WALK BY FAITH

Key Verse: *"For we walk by faith, not by sight"* (2 Corinthians 5:7).

Message: Romans 1:17, Galatians 3:11, and Hebrews 10:38 all say basically the same thing, *"The just shall live by faith."* All are saying that the Spirit-filled believer—the believer right with God—shall live by faith. Not easy! In 2 Corinthians 5:7, Paul says that we *"walk by faith, not by sight."*

If we are honest, we will admit that we walk more by sight than by faith. (For example; I don't see how I can tithe.) So how do I change? The key is in the word "walk." Paul says in Romans 1:17: *"For therein is the righteousness of God revealed from faith to faith: as it is written, the just shall live by faith."*

Walk by faith—from faith to faith. Start walking. Keep your feet moving. Your faith will increase as you start walking in trusting obedience; thus you go from "faith to faith."

The Good News Bible puts Romans 1:17 this way: *"For the Gospel reveals how God puts people right with himself: It is through faith from beginning to end."* (It is always too early to quit!)

Is there an area in which you need to take a faith journey? Tithing keeps coming to my mind. If you are not tithing, for whatever reason, put that first foot forward and start walking. Doing so will bless you and make you more qualified to be called a righteous person who walks by faith. Ask the Holy Spirit to produce walking faith through you.

APRIL 16   FAITH IN A STORM
Key Verse: *"Where is your faith" (Luke 8:25)?*

Message: Jesus had had a busy day. The multitudes were following Him. When evening came, He said to His disciples: *"Let us cross over to the other side" (Mark 4:35)*. They sent the multitude away and set sail. But soon a great wind storm arose. The waves beat against the ship, and it was filling up with water. The disciples were afraid.

"Where is Jesus? We need help!" Verse 38 says *"He was in the stern part of the ship, asleep on a pillow."* They woke Him up and said to Him: *"Master, carest thou not that we perish" (Mark 4:38)?*

Well, Jesus got up, silenced the wind, and said to the sea, *"Peace be still. And the wind ceased, and there was a great calm" (Mark 4:39)*. Now notice verse 40: *"And he said unto them, why are ye so fearful? How is it that ye have no faith?"*

Why did Jesus rebuke their faith? They forgot what He had told them. He had said, *"Let us cross over to the other side."* They should have known that He always means what He says. They obeyed at first and started out; but when the storm came, they forgot His words and felt that He had deserted them. Their faith failed in the middle of the storm.

Ever been like the disciples? Perhaps you had been sailing along on a smooth sea, walking with Jesus. Then a storm of life hit you and you felt that Jesus was asleep and had deserted you. He had not. He "neither slumbers nor sleeps." He is always in the boat with you. Pray for faith in the midst of the storm.

APRIL 17   LITTLE FAITH
Key Verse: *"O thou of little faith, wherefore didst thou doubt" (Matthew 14:31)?*

Message: After Jesus had fed the five thousand, He told His disciples to enter a boat and go to the other side of the Sea of Galilee while He sent the multitude away.

Then He went alone to a mountain to pray. The disciples were in the boat in the midst of the sea and in the midst of a mighty storm. They were afraid, but they were even more frightened when they saw Jesus walking on water toward them. They cried out, *"It is a ghost and they cried out for fear" (Matthew 14:26).*

Immediately Jesus said, *"Be of good cheer: it is I: be not afraid" (Matthew 14:27).* Immediately Peter said, "If you are my Lord, let me walk on water to you." Jesus replied, *"Come. And when Peter was come down out of the ship, he walked on water to go to Jesus" (Matthew 14:29).*

Let's talk about "faith" as it applies to this situation. First of all, the disciples should not have panicked when the storm came because Jesus had told them to go to the other side. They should have had faith to know they would make it because He means what He says.

Then there is Peter. Jesus addressed him as *"O thou of little faith."* He had enough faith to get out of the boat and start walking but not enough to make it to the other side. He got his eyes off of Jesus and onto the storm. But I will say this for Peter. At least he had enough faith to get out of the boat and start walking. The rest of the disciples stayed huddled together, afraid to move.

Do you see yourself anywhere in this situation? Are you afraid that when the storm comes, you won't make it to the other side? The disciples had our Lord's word. So do we. In Hebrews 13:5-6, we read, *"For he hath said, I will never leave thee, nor forsake thee, so that we may boldly say, the Lord is my helper, and I will not fear what man shall do unto me."*

Are you afraid that as you are walking toward Jesus, a storm of life might hit you and cause you to stumble? Remember: *"I will never leave thee, nor forsake thee."* Are you afraid to get out of the rocking boat and start walking toward Jesus? Remember: *"I will never leave thee, nor forsake thee."*

Pray that whatever storm comes, you will keep your eyes on Jesus and keep walking. You will get to the other side.

APRIL 18   NEVER FORSAKEN

Key Verse: *"For he hath said, I will never leave thee, nor forsake thee, so that we may boldly say, the Lord is my helper, and I will not fear what man shall do unto me" (Hebrews 13:5-6).*

Message: A few years ago I took a faith journey based on this verse. Let me tell you the story.

For twenty years I was president of a small private junior college that offered associate degrees. During the last ten years, we experienced a great deal of growth. This got the attention of the public sector because we were cutting into their market.

One day the director of higher education at that time called me, the president of another of our schools, and our owner to come to the conference room for a visit. We were dumbfounded by what we heard. In essence this man said to us, "You are not to issue another associate degree until you get our type of accreditation." (We had private school accreditation that authorized us to issue associate degrees.) He went on to say, "If you don't do as I say, I will smear you in every newspaper in the state." We were stunned!

The next day the three of us were on a conference call. They each said to me, "We will do what you suggest that we do." I said, "I am not going to tell a school full of students that they cannot receive the degree we have promised them that is perfectly legal for them to get. And besides, it would take several years to get the additional accreditation.

"We have no choice. We will have to go to court. I want us to go, based on these two verses that are found in Hebrews 13:5-6: '*For he hath said, I will never leave thee, nor forsake thee, so that we may boldly say, the Lord is my helper, and I will not fear what man shall do unto me.*'"

We went to court. That was a big faith venture. I realized what could have happened to my school, but I had to do what was right. I could not let fear of the possible consequences stop me. I knew that during this trying ordeal the Lord would never leave me. The final result was that we did not have to stop awarding associate degrees, and we did seek double accreditation.

This was the farthest my faith has ever been stretched, but the result was a wonderful way to watch the Lord at work. He specializes in things that seem impossible. Trust Him!

APRIL 19   JESUS PRAYS FOR YOU

Key Verse: *"But I have prayed for thee, that thy faith fail not..."* *(Luke 22:32).*

Message: In 1 Peter 5:8, Peter told the people: *"Be sober, be vigilant...."* Then he told them why: *"Because your adversary the devil, as a roaring lion, walketh about, seeking whom he may devour."*

Peter had heard about that roaring lion. On one occasion Jesus said to Peter: *"Satan hath desired to have you, that he may sift you as wheat" (Luke 22:31).* We know Peter's response: "I'm with you; I'll go to prison with you; I'll even die with you."

Jesus knew that Peter would deny Him; so before Peter's vow of faithfulness, Jesus said to him; *"But I have prayed for you, that your faith fail not..." (Luke 22:32).* Then He added, *"And when thou are converted (when you have turned)...."*

As I said, Jesus knew that Peter was going to deny Him—take a trip to the far country—but Jesus also knew that he would return. How did Jesus reveal that He knew this? By saying, *"I have prayed for you that your faith fail not..."*!

You see, when Jesus prays for His own who are away from Him, He prays that they will not lose their faith, and they won't. What Jesus prays comes true.

If you have a loved one in the far country who is saved, take heart; he will in all likelihood be back. How do I know this? I know this because Jesus is praying for him. Do likewise! Avoid the lectures; don't play the Holy Spirit; trust God—and pray.

I'll tell you why I said "in all likelihood." I did so because occasionally, when a saved person will not repent and get out of the far country, God takes that believer home early. 1 John 5:16 is referring to a "brother"—a believer. John says this: *"There is a sin unto death."* He is talking about the believer whom God takes home early.

Thank our Lord that you cannot lose your faith, and ask for guidance so that you will not go to the far country. And, incidentally, you can be in the far country right where you are. Examine your heart. Are you putting anyone or anything above Jesus? If so, repent and return.

APRIL 20   PRAYERS
Key Verse: *Accept, I beseech thee...." (Psalm 119:108).*

Message: As I was reading through the Psalms, I had this thought strike me: You can tell a person of faith by his prayers. How does he pray? I believe he would pray Psalm 119:108: *"Accept, I beseech thee the freewill offerings of my mouth..."*

And what are they? Hebrews 13:15 gives us a great example: *"By him therefore let us offer the sacrifice of praise to God continually, that is, the fruit of our lips giving thanks to his name."*

What two words that come from our lips stand out here? *"Praise"* and *"thanks"!* I believe that the person of faith spends a great deal of his prayer time just praising our Lord and thanking Him for who He is.

Pray the Scriptures.
* Psalm 63:3: *"Because thy loving-kindness is better than life, my lips shall praise thee."*
* Psalm 71:8: *"Let my mouth be filled with thy praise and with thy glory all the day."*
* Psalm 86:12: *"I will extol thee, O Lord my God, with all my heart, and I will glorify thy name for evermore."*
* Psalm 145:1-2: *"I will praise thee, my God, O king, and I will bless Thy name for ever and ever. Every day will I bless thee; and I will praise thy name for ever and ever."*

A person of faith praises and thanks. One of the best ways to do this is to pray the Scriptures. Remember! You can never pray outside the will of God if you pray the Word of God.

APRIL 21   EYES

Key Verse: *"I will lift up mine eyes..." (Psalm 121:1).*

Message: The direction of your eyes tells a lot about your faith. Think for a moment of a time when you were feeling low and deserted by God. Where did your eyes look? Down? Wrong direction!

What is the right direction? Up! Listen to some Psalms on the subject:

- 25:15: *"My eyes are ever toward the Lord; for he shall pluck my feet out of the net."*
- 121:1: *"I will lift up mine eyes unto the hills, from which cometh my help."*
- 123:1: *"unto thee lift I up mine eyes, O thou that dwellest in the heavens."*

The one who walks by faith will look up; and as he does, his eyes will come in contact with the eyes of the object of his faith. Psalm 33:18 says, *"Behold, the eye of the Lord is upon them that fear him, upon them that hope in his mercy."* Psalm 34:15 says, *"The eyes of the Lord are upon the righteous, and his ears are open unto their prayers."*

If you "fear" Him and are "righteous," your eyes will meet our Lord's eyes. And when you look into His wonderful face, you will know that you can trust Him to guide your every step.

Make this your prayer today: *"Mine eyes are unto thee, O God the Lord: in thee is my trust..." (Psalm 141:8).*

APRIL 22   THE CENTURION

Key Verse: *"...A centurion came to him asking for help" (Matthew 8:5).*

Message: I wrote about this Centurion earlier, but I want to spend more time on this Gentile. Matthew 8:5 says, *"When Jesus had entered Capernaum, a Centurion came to him, asking for help."* He had a serious problem that he could not solve, so he voiced it to Jesus: *"My servant lies at home paralyzed and in terrible suffering" (Matthew 8:6).*

You will notice that he did not ask Jesus for help. He just laid his need at Jesus' feet. This reminds me of the message Mary and Martha sent to Jesus when their brother Lazarus was ill; *"Lord, behold, he whom thou lovest is sick" (John 11:3).* (Sometimes this is the prayer I offer up for a brother or sister who is ill.)

Jesus' reply to the Centurion was, "I'll come home with you and heal him." To that the Centurion replied, *"Lord, I do not deserve to have you come under my roof. But just say the word, and my servant will be healed" (Matthew 8:8). –"Just say the word!"* What faith!

Verse 10 says, *"When Jesus heard this, he was astonished and said to those following Him, I tell you the truth, I have not found anyone in Israel with such great faith."*

I will now quote from a Sunday School lesson one of our adult teachers wrote.

"The faith of this Centurion surprised Jesus. Why was He surprised? Because this man demonstrated more genuine faith than anyone else He had found in Israel! There had been those who had believed in Jesus, but none with the depth of faith as this Gentile soldier.

"Would your faith surprise Jesus? Why or why not?

"When you face a difficulty in life, learn to practice the "turn and trust" more. 1) Turn immediately to Jesus with your problem. 2) Trust Him to take care of it. This will develop within you a faith that will astonish Jesus!"

APRIL 23   THE FAITH OF THE CHURCH

Key Verse: *"...your faith is spoken of throughout the whole world" (Romans 1:8).*

Message: In most of this month, I have talked about faith and individuals. I think we must also talk about faith and the church. What message is flowing from the local body into the community and around the world? I pray that it is a message we see in one of the early churches.

In his letter to the Roman church, Paul said, *"I thank my God through Jesus Christ for you all, that your faith is spoken of*

throughout the whole world" (Romans 1:8). In 16:19, he said, *"...
your obedience is reported abroad to all men...."*

Rome was a terrible place. All kinds of evil took place there. Yet,
at the risk of their lives, believers served the Lord faithfully. People
over the known world knew that this church had a reputation for
godliness.

Now why did the Roman church have this reputation? In Romans
1:12, Paul said that he and the believers had *"mutual faith."* They all
believed that they had been saved by the shed blood of Jesus and that
they served a risen Savior. They were all on the same page. And their
faith was manifested in obedience, in spite of their circumstances.

What kind of reputation does your church have? Are you known
in your community and around the world as a people of faith and
obedience? The answer is up to each member.

In Psalm 133:1, David said, *"Behold, how good and how
pleasant it is for brethren to dwell together in unity!"* Each of us
must be a person of faith and obedience. We must dwell together in
unity. (That means no murmuring, no bickering, no complaining, no
criticizing, no apathy, no being AWOL, etc.) If we are unified, we
will impact our community for Christ.

Pray that you will be one who will send a message of faith and
obedience from your body of believers.

APRIL 24   ACCESS

Key Verse: *"By whom also we have access by faith into this grace..."*
(Romans 5:2).

Message: Paul begins Romans 5 with these words: *"Therefore being
justified by faith...."* He is actually saying, "Because we have been
put right with God through faith, there are great results."

The first result is that *"We have peace with God through our
Lord Jesus Christ" (Romans 1:1).* Because of what Jesus did for us
and we accepted, we are no longer enemies with God. We have been
reconciled. In verse 10, Paul says that when we were enemies, we
were reconciled to God by the death of His Son.

The second result is that by Jesus *"we have access by faith...."* We have "access." This means that we can come directly into the presence of God and our Lord Jesus.

Let me give you a personal example. Before my morning quiet time prayer, I picture myself in the throne room of God. I begin my prayer something like this: "Father, I am so thankful that I can come before you and bow at your throne. I cannot see you, but I know you are there. I can see all those gem-like colors coming from your throne and that rainbow of green above it. I know I am here only because you let your Son die for me. I thank you."

"Lord Jesus, I can see you as I bow before you in all of your whiteness and brightness. I cannot see your face clearly, but I see you arrayed in all of your glory, King of Kings and Lord of Lords. I know I am here only because you willingly took my place on the cross. I thank you that you are my intercessor with my Father." I then continue my prayer time.

When I realized that I had "access" to heaven, my prayer life became more focused. Picturing myself there, bowing before the throne of God and before our Lord Jesus enhanced by prayer time. All of us who have been *"justified by faith"* have this privilege. Take an upward journey this morning.

APRIL 25   FAITH WORKS

Key Verse: *"For by grace are ye saved through faith and that not of yourselves; it is the gift of God, not of works, lest any man should boast"* (Ephesians 2: 8-9).

Message: Paul is saying that it is by God's unmerited favor that we have been saved through faith. Salvation is not the result of our works. It is God's gift. I believe we are all clear on this. We are not saved by works, <u>but</u> genuine faith results in works.

In verse 10, Paul says, *"For we are his workmanship, created in Christ Jesus unto (for) good works, which God hath ordained that we should walk in them."*

I like the way the Good News states this verse: *"God has made us what we are, and in our union with Christ Jesus, he has created us for a life of good deeds, which he has already prepared for us to do."*

When our Lord sent you down here, He sent you with the work you were intended to begin the day you got saved by faith. Let me ask you this: "Are you doing what He sent you to do?" If you are just a "pew sitter," you are not.

Ask the Lord to reveal His work plan for you and get busy. Remember what James said, *"...faith without works is dead" (James 2:26).* Folks, genuine faith works!

APRIL 26   WAIT
Key Verse: *"But they that wait upon the Lord..." (Isaiah 40:31).*

Message: In Psalm 25:2, David prayed, *"O my God, I trust in thee...."* If most of us were to start a prayer this way, we probably would have added, "I need your help now, etc."

We live in the day of "instant" things—instant coffee, instant breakfast, instant potatoes, instant healing, instant happiness. We want instant gratification. Young couples want a new house and all that goes with it as soon as they are married. We don't really like the word "wait."

We must learn that those who trust in the Lord must sometimes "wait" for the Lord to act. Do you know how David continued his prayer? He made his request. Then he said in verse 5: *"...on thee do I wait all the day."* In verse 21, he added, *"...for I wait on thee."* A note in my King James Study Bible puts in this way: *"For I wait in faith on thee."* In Psalm 3:34, he said, *"Wait on the Lord, and keep his way (commands)...."*

Good advice! Part of the hymn, "Have Faith in God" goes like this: "Wait on the Lord, trust His Word and be patient. Have faith in God. He'll answer yet."—and He will! There is always a reason for waiting on the Lord.

Isaiah 40:31 says that one reason is so that your strength to carry on will be renewed: *"But they that wait upon the Lord shall renew their strength; they shall mount up with wings as eagles; they shall run, and not be weary; they shall walk, and not faint."*

Remember! God always answers prayer. His answer may be "yes," "wait," or "I have something better for you." If you are in the waiting stage, wait in faith. "He'll answer yet."

APRIL 27   JEREMIAH

Key Verse: *"...I am with thee saith the Lord, to deliver thee" (Jeremiah 1:19).*

Message: When God called Jeremiah, He said to him in essence, "You are to preach to the people in Judah. They won't listen to a word you say; you will not have one convert. They will try to kill you, but I won't let them."

What a call! Would you have answered it? Probably not! But Jeremiah did. For over forty years he preached the Word of God without compromise. The Jews beat him; they tried to kill him; they threw him into prison.

As I thought about Jeremiah's prison experience, I was reminded of yesterday's message: "Wait on the Lord." I am going to read several verses to you from the Good News concerning Jeremiah's times in prison and the cells into which he was placed.

According to Jeremiah 37:21, his second prison was *"in the palace courtyard."* His next prison was a much worse cell: *"They took me and let me down by ropes into Prince Malchiah's well... there was no water in the well, only mud, and I sank down in it" (Jeremiah 38:6).*

An Old Testament Samaritan, Abedmelech, persuaded the king to let him take Jeremiah from the well. Putting some rags under his arms so that the ropes would not hurt him, Abedmelech and three helpers pulled him from the well.

What happened next? Was he set free? No! Verse 13 says, *"After that I was kept in the courtyard."* He was moved back to his second prison. His conditions were better; but he was still in prison, awaiting future deliverance.

Was he delivered? Yes! King Nebuchadnezzar of Babylon who captured Judah gave these orders: *"Go and find Jeremiah and...do for him whatever he wants" (Jeremiah 39:12).* Where did the guard find Jeremiah? In his prison in the palace courtyard! *"They had me brought from the palace courtyard..." (Jeremiah 39:13).*

Then what? *"Nebuchadnezzar turned him over to Gedaliah... to take him back to his home. So he remained among his own people" (Jeremiah 39:14).* Free at last! He had to wait, but he was delivered.

Here is my point. I believe that in the waiting period God often delivers in stages, a step at a time. That is what He did with Jeremiah, and He probably has with you also.

Think back. Was there a time when someone asked how you were doing, and you answered, "I'm a little better today," or "I'm getting better every day," or "I think I'm going to make it"? If so, you were progressing through your waiting period. Were you one day able to say, "I'm doing just fine"? If so, your waiting period ended in deliverance, just as it did for Jeremiah.

"Those that wait upon the Lord...." Be one of those. *"Wait in faith!"*

APRIL 28   GOD'S WALL
Key Verse: *"...speak unto the children of Israel, that they go forward" (Exodus 14:15).*

Message: Moses led the children of Israel out of Egypt. They camped by the Red Sea. Meanwhile, Pharaoh regretted having let them go, so he gathered over six hundred chariots and took off after them. Exodus 14:9 says that they *"overtook them camping by the sea...."*

Verse 10 says that the Israelites looked up and saw the Egyptians and were scared to death. Did they react in faith? No! They murmured! They said a lot of things, one of which was, *"For it had been better for us to serve the Egyptians than we should die in the wilderness" (Exodus 14:12).*

The people had no faith, but Moses did. He said to them in verse 13: *"Fear ye not. Stand still, and see the deliverance of the Lord...."* In essence he said, "Just be calm and watch the Lord deliver you completely from the Egyptians." (Great advice for us when a trial hits us!)

God's next instructions were "Go forward." Just imagine what those people must have said to themselves when they heard this command: "We have the Egyptian army behind us and the Red Sea in front of us and God says to move forward. Really now!"

But God had a way of escape. Verse 21 says that He used a strong east wind. It blew all night and divided the waters and *"made the sea dry land."* Verse 22 says that the *"waters were a wall unto them on their right hand, and on their left."* Think how high this wall was. When God turned the wall of water loose to cover the Egyptians, there was enough to cover those six hundred plus chariots. That was a mighty high wall.

If I had been one of the Israelites, I might have been afraid to put a foot on that dry ground for fear that the wall of water would come crashing down on me. But they weren't. Verse 29 says that they *"walked upon dry land in the midst of the sea; and the waters were a wall unto them on their right hand, and on their left."*

They took a step of faith, and God saw them safely through. Hebrews 11:29 says, *"By faith they passed through the Red Sea as by dry land...."*

Let me ask you this: "Are there any rivers that seem to be uncrossable? Are there any mountains you cannot tunnel through? God specializes in things that seem impossible. He knows a thousand ways to make a way for you." Sing this song and trust Him.

Pray for faith to put your toe in the water.

APRIL 29   A MAN OF FAITH

Key Verse: *"And they chose Stephen, A man full of faith and of the Holy Ghost..." (Acts 6:5).*

Message: When the apostles chose seven men to take over the service ministry, they selected Stephen as one of the seven. His listed qualifications were that he was *"a man full of faith and of the Holy Ghost..." (Acts 6:5).*

I am a firm believer in the fact that the church will only go as far as the men take us. Every leader in the church should have the qualifications that Stephen had. Let's talk about this special man.

Acts 6:8 says this: *"And Stephen, full of faith and power did great wonders and miracles among the people."*

As you can imagine, some Jewish officials started arguing with him. They didn't get to first base with this man who was full of faith and the Holy Spirit: *"But the Holy Spirit gave Stephen such wisdom that when he spoke, they could not refute him."* So what did they do to get him? They bribed some people to tell lies about Stephen—lies that stirred up the people. They seized him, took him to court, and brought in some more men to tell more lies about him. How did God answer these false charges? He answered through Stephen's face: *"And all that sat in the council, looking steadfastly on him, saw his face as it had been an angel" (Acts 6:15).*

When that crowd looked at Stephen, they didn't see an evil man; they saw a man with the glory of God on his face. No other man in the Bible, except Moses, had this privilege. Stephen had the glory of God shining on his face because he was *"full of faith and of the Holy Ghost."*

One day when Jesus comes for us, we will shine like Stephen. What about now? Paul says in 2 Corinthians 3:18 (GN): *"All of us reflect the glory of the Lord with uncovered faces; and that same glory, coming from the Lord, who is the Spirit, transforms us into his likeness in an ever greater degree of glory."*

Paul is saying that we are to go on day by day being transformed into the image of our Lord Jesus Christ. As we live the Spirit-filled life, we reflect the glory of the Lord in our faces more and more. *"When he shall appear, we shall be like him" (1 John 3:2).*

Ask the Lord to shine through your face more every day. The more we look like Him when He appears, the greater will be our reward!

APRIL 30   PRAYER AND FASTING

Key Verse: *"This kind (of faith) goeth not out but by prayer and fasting" (Matthew 17:21).*

Message: One day a "certain" man came to Jesus and said, *"Sir, have mercy on my son! He is an epileptic and has such terrible fits that he often falls into the fire or into water" (Matthew 17:14 GN).*

Then he added, *"I brought him to your disciples, but they could not heal him."* Jesus cast the demon out of the boy and healed him.

The disciples asked Jesus, *"Why could we not cast him out? And Jesus said unto them, because of your unbelief..." (Matthew 17:19-20).* The disciples didn't have mountain-moving faith. In Mark 11:23, Jesus was talking about this kind of faith, and He added, *"And shall not <u>doubt</u> in your heart...."* In Matthew 21:21, He said, *"If you have faith, and <u>doubt</u> not...."*

I'm sure you know how hard it is to have faith that God will move the mountain in your life and not have any doubts. Jesus said that there is only one way this kind of faith will come and that is *"by prayer and fasting."* I truly believe that some things can only come by prayer and fasting. In the "Watchman Prayer Guide," my pastor, Brother Mark lists several prayer requests. This one is always included: "Pray for revival and spiritual awakening."

It seems to me that his request will only happen if the church gets serious about its mission "to invite everyday people to experience Christ in every way." To get serious means to pray and fast.

Ask the Lord to guide you as you learn to pray and fast. I'm still learning. I pray that you will join me. I also pray that as you read this book, you will take a faith journey that will lead you to a deeper relationship with the Lord and renewed service to Him. Faith is the victory!

May

HEAVEN

The purpose of this month is to show you what awaits you when you depart this world that is not your home and enter your next home: heaven.

Now the only people who will live in this magnificent abode are people who have been saved by the blood of Jesus.

I took this excerpt from our church's Sunday bulletin:

"How to Become a Christian:

1. Admit that you are a sinner and you need God's forgiveness.
2. Turn from your sins.
3. Believe that Jesus died on the Cross and arose from the grave for you.
4. Invite Jesus Christ to come in and control your life."

This is the only passport to the home Jesus is preparing for us right now. In John 14:2-3, He promised, *"In my Father's house are many mansions....I go to prepare a place for you, and if I go to prepare a place for you, I will come again and receive you unto myself; that where I am, there ye may be also."*

MAY 1   GETTING READY TO GO

Key Verse: *"...whosoever liveth and believeth in me shall never die" (John 11:26).*

Message: One day we will experience physical death, if Jesus tarries; but we will not die. In John 11:26, Jesus promised: *"...whosoever liveth and believeth in me shall never die."* In John 3:15 He promised: *"That whosoever believeth in him should not perish, but have eternal life."*

Maybe your question might be, "What in me will live forever?" We find the answer in Genesis 2:7: *"And the Lord God formed man in the dust of the ground, and breathed into his nostrils the breath of life; and man became a living soul."* The eternal part of every person is the soul. The soul is what you are. The soul is a rational being that will live forever.

The soul of every believer has a different look in this world, in heaven, and in eternity.

MAY 2   THE SOUL TODAY

Key Verse: *"...absent from the body is to be present with the Lord" (2 Corinthians 5:8).*

Message: In this world the soul of the believer is housed in a corrupt covering. I am sure you are aware of the flaws in your own body. As long as a believer lives down here, his soul will be covered by a corrupt body.

When a person experiences physical death, the body goes to the grave. The grave may be in the ground or in the sea or in an urn, but according to Ecclesiastes 3:20: *"All go unto one place; and all are of the dust, and all return to dust again."* No matter where the body is put to rest, it will return to dust.

What happens to the soul at the physical death? Paul says that to be *"absent from the body is to be present with the Lord"* *(2 Corinthians 5:8)*. At the moment of physical death, the immortal soul goes to be with Jesus in Paradise.

MAY 3   PARADISE?

Key Verse: *"Today shalt thou be with me in paradise" (Luke 23:43).*

Message: Jesus told the penitent thief on the cross: *"Today shalt thou be with me in paradise" (Luke 23:43).*

What is Paradise? Paradise is a Persian word meaning "garden" or "park." Thus, Paradise is a beautiful garden park like the Garden of Eden. Jesus said in Revelation 2:7 that overcomers would eat of the tree of life *"which is in the midst of the paradise of God."*

Where is Paradise? Today, it is in heaven. It is not in the first heaven where the birds fly. It is not in the second heaven where the planets are. Today, Satan is the prince of these two heavens. In Ephesians 2:2, Paul calls him *"the prince of the power of the air."* Paradise is in the third heaven, the throne room of God. How do we know that Paradise is in the third heaven? Paul said so. In 2 Corinthians 12:2, he says that he was *"caught up to the third heaven."* In verse 4, he says that *"...he was caught up into paradise."* So—the soul of all believers in Jesus (those saved in the church age and gone on before us) are today in Paradise in heaven with Jesus, waiting for us to join them.

MAY 4   THE SOUL IN HEAVEN

Key Verse: *"For we which have believed do enter into rest...."* *(Hebrews 4:3).*

Message: In heaven the soul of the believer has no covering. The covering went back to dust. The soul of the believer in heaven today will have no covering until he gets his final covering. Now you might ask, "What are those souls without a covering doing in heaven? What are my loved ones doing right now?" I believe they are resting in Jesus until they get their final covering.

The Bible does not say a lot about what is going on in heaven today, but let's examine what it does say.

In Hebrews we read about this rest. In chapter 4, verse 3, the writer wrote, *"For we which have believed do enter into rest...."* In verse 9, he wrote, *"There remaineth therefore a <u>rest</u> to the people of God."* The believer in heaven today is engaging in heavenly rest.

Now I am not saying that the believers in Jesus who are in heaven today are idle. I really don't know about that. I do know that their work on earth is complete. They will never again have to struggle with Satan. They are resting from all sorrow, all pain, all disappointment, all heartache. They are sitting at Jesus' feet, resting in Him. They still look like themselves because the soul is what they are, but their souls have no cover.

MAY 5   CAN THEY SEE ME?
Key Verse: *"The Lord looketh from heaven; he beholdeth all the sons of men." (Psalm 33:13).*

Message: Have you ever heard (for example) an athlete say, after a great performance in a game, "I know my dad in heaven was watching me today"? I immediately wonder what makes him think this could happen.

I know some Christians who think it can. The only verse they seem to use is Hebrews 12:1: *"Wherefore seeing we also are compassed about with so great a cloud of witnesses...."*

The footnote in my King James Study Bible says this: "These heroes of faith are <u>like</u> a cloud of witnesses....The Greek word for witnesses refers simply to those who testify or witness."

In his commentary on Hebrews, John Mac Arthur says, "I do not believe that the cloud of witnesses surrounding us is standing in the galleries of heaven watching as we perform....They are not looking at us: we are to look at them." I agree.

We said earlier that the saints in heaven today are resting from all sorrow, all pain, all disappointment, all heartache. I can assure you that if they were looking at us, they would be experiencing all of the above, not resting from them. I don't know about you, but I take comfort in knowing that my mother is not watching me.

By the way, I know someone who is watching us from heaven. Psalm 33:13 says, *"The Lord looketh from heaven; he beholdeth all the sons of men."* Proverbs 15:3 says: *"The eyes of the Lord are in every place, beholding the evil and the good."* Sobering thought, isn't it?

MAY 6 THE SOUL THROUGHOUT ETERNITY

Key Verse: *"...shall change our vile body..."(Philippians 3:21).*

Message: Throughout eternity the soul of the believer will be housed in a glorified covering. I have great news for you. Our bodies will be molded after Jesus' glorified body. We will look like ourselves, but our glorified bodies will be constructed like Jesus' glorified body.

In Philippians 3:21, Paul says that the Lord Jesus Christ *"...shall change our vile body, that it may be fashioned like unto his glorious body."* A perfect body at last!!! A perfect covering for our soul!!! That body will not experience corruption, disease, pain, nor death. How glorious!!! When will this be?

One day on God's timetable the last sermon will be preached; the last invitation will be given. Jesus will step out of heaven and give every believer in Christ his glorified body. How will this happen?

MAY 7 THE DEAD IN CHRIST FIRST

Key Verse: *"...and the dead in Christ shall rise first"* (1 Thessalonians 4:16).

Message: Very simply put, when Jesus steps out of heaven, some believers will have died physically. Their bodies will be in the grave; their souls will be with Him. In 1 Thessalonians 4:14, Paul says that those *"...which sleep in Jesus will God bring with him."* That means all those saved souls in Jesus without a covering, who have been resting in Jesus.

How will they get their glorified covering? In 1 Thessalonians 4:16, Paul says, *"For the Lord himself shall descend from heaven with a shout, with the voice of the archangel, and with the trump of God: and the dead in Christ shall rise first."*

The bodies in the grave will rise first. You might ask, "Didn't you tell us that those bodies return to dust?" Yes, I did; but Paul tells us some very good news. In 1 Corinthians 15:52, he says that *"...the dead shall be raised incorruptible...."* The corrupt covering, lying as dust in the grave will come out as a glorified covering—a perfect covering for your soul.

Here is what this means. Please get it. When Jesus comes with the souls of believers, He will reach down to the grave, or wherever the body is buried, and reconstruct the dust into a glorified covering for the soul.

At this point the souls of those who come with Jesus will get their eternal covering, their glorified bodies.

MAY 8   THE ALIVE IN CHRIST SECOND

Key Verse: *"Then we which are alive and remain shall be caught up together with them in the clouds, to meet the Lord in the air..."* *(1 Thessalonians 4:17).*

Message: After Jesus gives the glorified bodies to those who come with Him, He will turn His attention to those believers in Him who are alive. In 1 Thessalonians 4:17, Paul says, *"Then we which are alive and remain shall be caught up together with them in the clouds, to meet the Lord in the air: and so shall we ever be with the Lord."* But, folks, if Jesus were to appear right now, we could not meet Him as we are. Something would have to change. What would we have to shed? Our corrupt bodies!!!

As we have said, while we are alive, our soul is covered by a flawed body. That body will have to go. Paul tells us that it will. In 1 Corinthians 15:51-52, he says, *"We shall not all sleep (die), but we shall all be changed, in a moment, in the twinkling of an eye, at the last trump...."*

You may be alive when Jesus steps out of glory; but before you can blink your eyes, He will reconstruct your body. Your soul will shed its corrupt covering, and receive a glorified covering.

At this point every believer will have his forever body—a body that will not experience corruption, disease, pain, or death. How wonderful!

But something even more wonderful is that from this time on we shall *"ever be with the Lord."*

MAY 9   LITTLE CHILDREN

Key Verse: *"...I shall go to him, but he shall not return to me"(2 Samuel 12:23).*

Message: I am sure there is a question that many of you would like to ask: "What will happen to little children?" I believe the Bible teaches that all children who do not reach the age of accountability before they die or Jesus returns will all go to heaven and be with Jesus forever.

Back in 2 Samuel 12:15, we read, *"And the Lord struck the child that Uriah's wife bare unto David, and it was very sick."*

All the time the baby was sick, David would neither eat nor sleep. However, when the child died, David got up, took a bath, changed his clothes, and went to the house of God to worship.

When he came home, he had a meal. His servants were confused. They said to him, "We don't understand this change in you. You wouldn't eat when the boy was sick; but now that he is dead, you are eating."

Listen carefully to David's reply in 2 Samuel 12:23: *"...wherefore should I fast? Can I bring him back again? I shall go to him, but he shall not return to me."* David is saying, "When I die and go to heaven, I will be reunited with my son."

Also, let me remind you of Jesus' warning to anyone who would offend a little one: *"It were better for him that a millstone were hanged about his neck, and that he were drowned in the depth of the sea" (Matthew.18:6).*

I truly believe that little children will join the glorified church and *"...ever be with the Lord."* At this point all church-age believers will have glorified bodies and will forever be with Jesus.

MAY 10   UNFINISHED BUSINESS

Key Verse: *"...but that it should be holy and without blemish" (Ephesians 5:27).*

Message: At this point we will be with Jesus, but not quite ready to enter heaven. There will be some unfinished business to take care of. We will have a new body, but it will have to have some finishing touches. It will have to be refined.

In Ephesians 5:25-27, Paul says that *"Christ...loved the church and give himself for it....that he might present it to himself a glorious church, not having spot, or wrinkle, or any such thing; but that it should be holy and without blemish."*

In Revelation 21:2, John saw the church as *"a bride adorned for her husband."* However, when we meet the Lord in the air, we will not be ready for our wedding because we will still have some spots and wrinkles. We will have to have the spots and wrinkles dealt with because we cannot enter heaven with them.

They will be dealt with at the Judgment Seat of Christ, the Bema Seat (Greek).

MAY 11   THE JUDGMENT OF OUR WORKS

Key Verse: *"...every one of us shall give account of himself to God"* *(Romans 13:12).*

Message: In 2 Corinthians 5:10, Paul says, *"For we must all appear before the judgment seat of Christ."* Why? Paul tells us in Romans 14:12: *"...every one of us shall give account of himself to God."* We will all have to account to Jesus the Judge, but let me make one thing perfectly clear.

Our salvation will not be in jeopardy. Our sins will not be judged. They were judged in Jesus on the cross.

In John 5:24, Jesus says that people who accept Him as personal savior *"...hath everlasting life, and shall not come into condemnation (or judgment); but is passed from death unto life."*

Now our sins will not be judged; our works will be judged. We were sent into this world with a purpose. Our Lord will judge how well we fulfilled it. He will look at our works. Why? To determine our reward in heaven based on what we did down here in accord with His purpose for us!

In Matthew 16:27, Jesus said, *"For the Son of man shall come in the glory of his Father with his angels; and then he shall reward every man according to his <u>works</u>."* Paul says in the last part of

1 Corinthians 3:8: *"...and every man shall receive his own reward according to his own labor."*

Every person will one day stand before Jesus the Judge to answer for his service record. Believers in Jesus will do so at the Judgment Seat of Christ.

MAY 12   THE PROCEDURE

Key Verse: *"For other foundation can no man lay than that is laid, which is Jesus Christ" (1 Corinthians 3:11).*

Message: Now let's see what will happen at the Bema Seat or Judgment Seat of Christ. It all really depends upon what we do down here. You see, all through our Spiritual lives we are to build our work upon love for and obedience to the Lord Jesus Christ.

Paul says in 1 Corinthians 3:11: *"For other foundation can no man lay than that is laid, which is Jesus Christ."*

In other words, God has placed Jesus Christ as the only foundation. There is no other. Now, with Jesus as your foundation or motive, you are at liberty to build on this foundation; but always remember, God always gives you a choice. He gives you two sets of building materials. You must decide which you will use.

In 1 Corinthians 3:12, Paul lists these building materials: *"Now if any man build upon this foundation gold, silver, precious stones, wood, hay, stubble."* You may choose as your building materials either "gold, silver, and precious stones" or "wood, hay, and stubble."

MAY 13   THE RESULT OF YOUR CHOICES

Key Verse: *"And whatsoever ye do in word or deed, do all in the name of the Lord Jesus" (Colossians 3:17).*

Message: Every deed that you have ever done in the name of Jesus Christ will be brought out when you stand before Jesus the Judge. In 1 Corinthians 3:13, Paul says, *"And the quality of each person's work will be seen when the day of Christ (Judgment Seat) exposes it."*

Every deed that we have done in His name will have to pass through the fire of His judgment. Every deed will be either a "gold, silver, and precious stone" deed or a "wood, hay, and stubble" deed.

Now Jesus will not just examine your works; He will also examine your motives. The things you have done because you love Jesus and in obedience to Him will be called "gold, silver, and precious stone" deeds and will go with you to heaven.

The things you have done for self-glory or praise of man or honor or prestige or out of duty or guilt will be called "wood, hay, and stubble" deeds and will be burned up. They will not go with you to heaven. You will suffer loss, but not the loss of your salvation. That cannot be taken away, but you will suffer the loss of reward.

We would do well to heed Paul's advice in Colossians 3:17: *"And whatsoever ye do in word or deed, do <u>all</u> in the name of the Lord Jesus."*

Let me ask you a question: "Would your present service record stand the test of our Lord's fiery judgment?"

MAY 14   GOLD, SILVER, PRECIOUS STONE DEEDS EQUAL REWARDS IN HEAVEN

Key Verse: *"...and then he shall reward every man according to his works"* (Matthew 16:27).

Message: In 1 Corinthians 3:14, Paul said, *"If any man's work abide* (makes it through the fiery judgment) *he shall receive a reward."*

In Matthew 16:27, Jesus said, *"For the Son of man shall come in the glory of his Father...; and then he shall reward every man according to his works."*

Paul and Jesus both make it clear that there will be degrees of reward in heaven. We will be rewarded by what we do for Jesus because we love Him. However, let me hasten to add that every person will be happy with his position in heaven because he will know that a just God will have rewarded him fairly.

Let me assure you that the penitent thief on the cross will not have the rewards that Paul will have, but he will be happy in his rewarded position—and so will you.

Note: At this point we will be just about ready to enter the throne room of God. According to Revelation 4:4, we will all be *"clothed in white raiment; and* (we will have) *on our heads crowns of gold."*

We will all wear a white robe on our bodies and a golden crown on our heads. However, the reward service will not quite be over.

Jesus will hand out His greatest rewards to those with outstanding service records in special areas. These will be called "crowns." (I take it that these crowns will not look like crowns of other believers.) There are five of these crowns, and every one of us should be working to attain them. Let's look at them.

MAY 15   THE CROWN OF LIFE
Key Verse: *"...and I will give thee a crown of life" (Revelation 2:10).*

Message: Jesus promised this crown to the martyr church, the church at Smyrna. He told them not to fear suffering.

In Revelation 2:10, He promised, *"Be thou faithful unto death, and I will give thee a crown of life."* I believe this crown will be handed out to those who suffer for their faith as well as to those who suffer in the body but do not give up.

You see, the reward is based on "enduring" the suffering. In James 1:12, we read, *"Blessed is the man that endureth trials; for when he is tried* (at the Judgment seat of Christ) *he shall receive the crown of life, which the Lord hath promised to them that love him."*

This crown is reserved for those who love Him even though they are suffering. Please note the last phrase: *"to them that love him."*

You know, many older people have some physical problems; and I have observed that as they grow older, they become sweeter or meaner—better or bitter. *"Love of Jesus"* makes the difference.

For you see, if we do not really love Jesus with all our hearts, our suffering and our trials will cause us to become bitter and critical and filled with self-pity, and keep us from receiving the "crown of life."

Let me say this to you. If you are suffering at this moment and you wonder if Jesus cares, remember that He has something special for you—a special crown—reserved for you and all in Christ who suffer down here.

MAY 16   THE CROWN INCORRUPTIBLE

Key Verse: *"...let us run with patience the race that is set before us, looking unto Jesus the author and finisher of our faith...."* *(Hebrews 12:1-2).*

Message: In 1 Corinthians 9:25, Paul tells us that the Greek athlete trained and disciplined his body and ran a race for one reason: *"to obtain a corruptible crown"* (a laurel wreath that would not last).

Paul went on to say that the believer is to train and discipline his body and run life's race to obtain an *"incorruptible crown"* (one that would last forever). In verse 27, Paul says that he brings his body into subjection.

In Hebrews 12:1-2, the writer tells us to *"lay aside every weight, and the sin which doth so easily beset us, and let us run with patience the race that is set before us, looking unto Jesus the author and finisher of our faith...."* The one who receives this crown will be the one who sets his eyes on Jesus and runs the race of life all the way to the finish line.

Some people in the church say, "I've worked in the church for years. It's time for someone else to take over." These folks will not receive this crown. It is for those who <u>finish</u>. Remember! It is always too early to quit.

If you want this crown, you had better get out on the race track and keep your feet moving until the Lord calls you home.

The crown incorruptible is reserved for those who make their bodies a living sacrifice all the way through their lives. Vow with the Psalmist: *"I have decided to obey your laws until the day I die"* *(Psalm 119:112 GN).*

MAY 17   THE CROWN OF REJOICING

Key Verse: *"For what is our hope, or joy, or crown of rejoicing..."* *(1Thessalonians 2:19).*

Message: The crown of rejoicing is the soul winner's crown. In 1Thessalonians 2:19, Paul asked the Thessalonians: *"For what is our hope, or joy, or crown of rejoicing? Are not even ye in the presence of our Lord Jesus Christ at his coming?"*

When Paul stands before the Judgment Seat of Christ, he will receive the crown of rejoicing because he introduced the Thessalonians (and countless others) to Jesus.

The greatest work we are privileged to do for our Lord is to introduce others to Jesus. Under the leadership of the Holy Spirit, we are to let our witness count. We are to witness with our mouths; we are to witness with our lives; we are to witness with our money. Read on!

MAY 18   THE CROWN OF REJOICING AND $$$

Key Verse: *"Not because I desire a gift; but I desire fruit that may abound to your account" (Philippians 4:17).*

Message: We are to witness by bringing our tithes and offerings into the storehouse so that others might preach the good news. You probably haven't thought about giving as being part of soul winning, but it is.

Paul gave a good example of this is his letter to the Philippians. In 4:15 he said to them: *"Now ye Philippians know this also...no church communicated with me as concerning giving and receiving, but ye only."* No one was helping to support Paul on his missionary journeys but the Philippians.

Now I want you to listen carefully to Paul's next words to them. He commended them for sending support; then he said in verse 17: *"Not because I desire a gift; but I desire fruit that may abound to your account."*

Paul says that it wasn't the gift that thrilled him, even though it did allow Paul to continue to preach the Word and see people saved. What thrilled him was that the "givers" were sharing in the soul winning effort and as a result were laying up treasures in heaven.

You see, they were receiving fruit in their heavenly account. You can too. Jesus said in John 3:36 that when we witness we *"gather fruit into life eternal."*

Every time you witness—hand out a gospel tract—give so that others may go and tell—you are laying up fruit "against that day."

MAY 19 SHARING THE CROWN OF REJOICING

Key Verse: *"...both he that soweth and he that reapeth may rejoice together"* (John 4:36).

Message: Let's think for a moment. Suppose you witness to someone who doesn't get saved as a result of your witness but does get saved later as the result of some else's witness. Do you know what will happen at the Judgment Seat of Christ?

The answer is found in John 4:36: *"...both he that soweth and he that reapeth may <u>rejoice</u> together."* On that day you will see the one to whom you witnessed, and you will rejoice together—along with anyone else who had a part in pointing him to Jesus. There will be great joy on this occasion as you receive the crown of rejoicing.

Ponder this statement: The degree of our joy in heaven will be determined by the souls we have had a part in bringing to Jesus.

MAY 20 THE CROWN OF RIGHTEOUSNESS

Key Verse: *"...that love his appearing"* (2 Timothy 4:8).

Message: In 2 Timothy 4:8, Paul said, *"Henceforth there is laid up for me a crown of righteousness, which the Lord, the righteous judge, shall give me at that day; and not to me only, but unto all them also that love his appearing."*

You might ask, "Why is the crown of righteousness to be given to those *'that love his appearing'"*? Well, you see, if you look forward to Jesus' return, it will affect your whole life. It will cause you to live a righteous life. If you love Him, you will want to live like Him.

Now, most of us, if we are honest, cannot say that we are longing for His return because we're ashamed of the lives we are living. They are not righteous.

Folks, it is so important for us to live a life so right with Jesus that we might look with a heart full of love and anticipation for His return, so that we might receive the crown of righteousness.

MAY 21   THE CROWN OF GLORY

Key Verse: *"...ye shall receive a crown of glory that fadeth not away" (1 Peter 5:4).*

Message: This crown is a special reward for the God-called obedient pastor. In 1 Peter 5:4, Peter tells the pastor: *"Feed the flock of God... being examples...and when the chief Shepherd shall appear, ye shall receive a crown of glory that fadeth not away."* The pastor who feeds his sheep the Word of God and is an example before them will receive a crown of glory.

Did you know that you could share your pastor's crown? Matthew 10:41 (GN) shows how this is possible: *"Whoever welcomes (supports) God's messenger because he is God's messenger will share in his reward."* Be sure you understand this. The believer who supports his pastor simply because he is God's messenger will share his crown of glory.

Sometimes I do not feel that we truly understand who the pastor is. He is a man set apart by God just as Moses and Paul were. He is man set apart to feed the sheep. He is a man set apart to be an example to the sheep.

He is a man who has unique relationship to our Lord that you and I cannot understand. The pastor is my spiritual leader, and I yield to his authority. He gets his instructions for the church from our Lord. I will get mine from my pastor.

Let's all support our God-called pastor and share his crown of glory.

Transition: When we meet Jesus in the air, when we receive our glorified bodies, when our service record has been reviewed at the Judgment Seat of Christ, when our wood deeds have been burned up, when our gold deeds have been rewarded, when we are dressed in white robes and crowns—we will be ready to walk through the door of heaven to our new home.

Can you imagine what it will be like to see the door to heaven swing open and to step directly into the throne room of God—into the presence of our Lord and our God? I cannot fathom this wonderful meeting, but John gave us a glimpse of what we can expect.

MAY 22   THE THRONE OF GOD

Key Verse: *"...behold a throne set in heaven, and one sitting on the throne"(Revelation 4:2).*

Message: In Revelation 4:2, John saw what we shall see, and here it is, *"...behold a throne set in heaven, and one sitting on the throne."*

Revelation 4:3 describes the One sitting on the throne: *"And he that sat was to look upon like a jasper and a sardine stone: and there was a rainbow round about the throne, in sight like unto an emerald."* When John looked upon that throne, all he saw was a green rainbow and beautiful colors like precious stones.

John is not introduced to the One on the throne. He is not named here, but He is in other places in the Bible. Psalm 11:4 tells us that *"the Lord's throne is in heaven...."* Ezekiel saw *"the likeness of a throne...and upon the likeness of the throne was the likeness of a man above it"* (Ezekiel 1:26).

Although no one has ever seen God, this is His throne. God has never been photographed. In John 1:18, we read, *"No man hath seen God at any time...."* John did not see God. He could only describe the likeness of the One on the throne to precious stones and beautiful colors.

I can only imagine those beautiful gem colors and rainbow of green reflecting on that sea of glass, but I am going to see it some day. How beautiful heaven must be!

MAY 23   THE GLORIFIED JESUS

Key Verse: *"...one like unto the Son of man... " (Revelation 1:13).*

Message: John <u>did</u> see the glorified Christ and was able to describe Him. In Revelation 1:10-11, he tells us that when he was worshiping on Sunday morning on the Isle of Patmos, he *"...heard...a great voice behind him saying, I am the Alpha and Omega, the first and the last...."*

Here John is saying that as he stood there worshiping, the Holy Spirit came upon Him; and he heard a "great voice."

John is about to introduce Jesus as He is today in His glorified body. Let me say this. The average person pictures Jesus in His
human form and usually as the artists have painted Him. But folks,
Jesus does not look like that today. John describes for us the Christ
that we will see.

In essence John said, "I turned to see who had spoken to me.
I saw seven golden candlesticks, and I saw in the midst of them
'...*one like unto the Son of man...*'" (*Revelation 1:13*). (This was
Jesus' favorite designation for Himself.) John saw the Lord Jesus
Christ, and we will too.

MAY 24   WHAT WILL WE SEE?

Key Verse: *"His head and his hairs were white like wool, as white
as snow..." (Revelation 1:14).*

Message: We will see what John saw. He first saw Jesus' garment.
Revelation 1:13 goes on to say that He was *"clothed with a garment
down to the foot, and girt about the paps with a golden girdle."*

Jesus today is clothed in a priestly long robe with a gold band
around His chest. In Revelation 1:14-15, John describes Jesus'
appearance: *"His head and his hairs were white like wool, as white
as snow: and his eyes were as a flame of fire; and his feet like unto
fine brass, as if they burned in a furnace...."*

Well, we have just seen a picture of our Lord Jesus Christ who
is today at the right hand of the Father and the One into whose presence we will one day enter.

He has snowy white hair, a glowing white face, penetrating
eyes, and shining feet. He is dressed in a long robe with a gold band
around His chest.

On the day when the purified church enters the throne room of
God, we will be in the presence of the Father on the throne whom
we cannot see except in bright beautiful colors and in the presence
of Jesus Christ whom we can see seated at the right hand of the
Father.

The question now is, "What will we do in heaven?"

MAY 25   PREPARE TO PRAISE

Key Verse: *"...and upon the seats I saw four and twenty elders sitting..." (Revelation 4:4).*

Message: When we gather at the throne of God dressed in our white robes and golden crowns, we will sit down. What will we see?

In Revelation 4:4, John tells us that *"...round about the throne were four and twenty seats... (thrones)."* Read on in verse 4: *"...and upon the seats I saw four and twenty elders sitting, clothed in white raiment and they had on their heads crowns of gold."* Who are they? I believe they represent all believers in the Church Age.

Well, our representatives will be there; we will be there, and so will, according to Revelation 4:6, *"four beasts."* I cannot tell you much about these beasts, but they seem to be created beings who administer God's government. Who they are is not the important issue here. What they do is. They praise God!

MAY 26   PRAISE

Key Verse: *"... Holy, holy, holy, Lord God Almighty, which was, and is, and is to come"*
(Revelation 4:8).

Message: Revelation 4:8 says of these beasts: *"...they rest not day and night, saying, Holy, holy, holy, Lord God Almighty, which was, and is, and is to come."*

Now I believe that when the four beasts begin to chant, our twenty-four representatives will become the choir and lead all of us in a great praise service.

I want us to see what we will do. According to Revelation 4:9, *"When these beasts give glory and honor and thanks to him that sat (sits) on the throne,"* we will join them. Our representatives will rise from their thrones, and all of us will *"fall down before him that sat (sits) on the throne, and worship him that liveth forever and ever, and cast their (our) crowns before the throne, saying, Thou art worthy, O Lord, to receive glory and honor and power: For thou hast created all things, and for thy pleasure they are and were created"* (Revelation 4:10-11).

Just get the picture! At the sound of *"Holy, holy, holy"* coming from the four living creatures, we will fall before the Triune God to join in the praise. We will sing this great song of creation. Then as part of our worship, we will cast our crowns at the feet of Jesus. We will lay them there because He alone is worthy to receive crowns. We will lay our crowns at the feet of Him who saved us by His matchless grace.

MAY 27   MORE PRAISE

Key Verse: *"I saw a strong angel proclaiming with a loud voice..."* *(Revelation 5:2).*

Message: Let me tell you about another praise service in heaven. In Revelation 5:1, John said, *"And I saw in the right hand of him that sat on the throne a book written within and on the backside...."*

We will look at the right hand of God that will hold a scroll. Just what is that scroll? It is the title deed to the earth.

God gave it to the first Adam, but he let Satan wrestle it away from him. From that day until this throne scene in heaven, Satan has been allowed to have dominion over the earth. That will change.

In verse 2 of chapter 5, John said, *"I saw a strong angel proclaiming with a loud voice, Who is worthy to open the book...?"* In a very loud voice, the angel cried, "Who has the right to the title deed to the earth?"

S-I-L-E-N-C-E

The angel has a mighty loud voice. He will be heard in heaven, on earth, and in Hades.

However, *"No man in heaven, nor in earth, neither under the earth was able to open the book..."* *(Revelation 5:3).* No one in Adam's line spoke. Not one of us has a right to open the book and take charge of the earth, but someone will have to. The question is, "Who is going to be able to do it?"

MAY 28   WHO INDEED?

Key Verse: *"Thou art worthy to take the book...for thou wast slain and hast redeemed us to God by thy blood"* (Revelation 5:9).

Message: John wept because no man was found worthy, but one of the elders spoke up and said to him: *"Weep not: behold, the Lion of the tribe of Judah, the Root of David, hath prevailed to open the book..."* (Revelation 5:5).

The Lord Jesus is the *"Lion of the tribe of Judah"*; He is the *"Root of David."* He is the only one who has the right to reclaim the earth from Satan.

When the tears dried on John's cheeks, he looked up and saw what we will see. He said, *"And I beheld, and, lo, in the midst of the throne and of the four beasts, and in the midst of the elders stood a lamb as it had been slain"* (Revelation 5:6). Here we see Jesus the Lamb of God begin to move. *"And he came and took the book out of the right hand of him that sat upon the throne"* (Revelation 5:7).

When Jesus takes that title deed to the earth into His hand, we will break out in a new song: *"Thou art worthy to take the book... for thou wast slain and hast redeemed us to God by thy blood"* (Revelation 5:9).

Listen! When the Lamb of God stands up, turns to the One who holds the book in His right hand, and takes the book, every person who has been redeemed by the blood of the Lamb— millions and millions of people—will burst into a song that is a new song: the song of redemption. Because Jesus paid the price for our sins with His blood, He alone is worthy to rescue the earth now held by Satan.

We will sing the song of creation; we will sing the song of redemption, and a whole lot of other songs. Truly, we will praise and worship in heaven.

What else will we do? Get married!!!

MAY 29   PREPARING FOR A WEDDING

Key Verse: *"Let us be glad and rejoice, and give honor to him: For the marriage of the Lamb is come...."* (Revelation 19:7).

Message: We will prepare for a wedding, the wedding of Jesus Christ and the church. Jesus will be the bridegroom; the church will be the bride. This will cause rejoicing.

In Revelation 19:7, we hear a great shout of praise from the whole host of heaven: *"Let us be glad and rejoice, and give honor to him: For the marriage of the Lamb is come...."* This great host will proclaim, "It is time for the wedding!" Then they will add a very important chorus: *"...and his wife hath made herself ready..."* *(Revelation 19:7).*

You might ask, "Won't we be ready when we get to heaven? We will have on white robes." We <u>will</u> have on white robes, but they will be plain.

How many of you would ever envision a bride's gown as plain? We usually think of silk and satin and lace and pearls. Most brides do not have plain wedding gowns, and I hope that most brides in heaven won't either.

As I said, each of us will be arrayed in a gown of pure white linen, but something will be added to the gown.

MAY 30   AN EMBROIDERY JOB

Key Verse: *"...for the fine linen is the righteousness of saints"* *(Revelation 19:8).*

Message: No two wedding gowns will look alike. Why not? The answer is found in Revelation 19:8: *"...for the fine linen is the righteousness of saints."* What does *"righteousness of saints"* mean? The original Greek text shows that the word *"righteousness"* is literally "righteous deeds."

This means that before the wedding, we will decorate our white linen gown with the gold, silver, and precious-stone deeds we take with us to heaven.

Folks, today when you do something for the Lord because you love Him, you are accumulating jewels to sew onto your wedding gown. In other words, every one of us will wear an original.

Will your gown look more like the one worn by the penitent thief or the one worn by Paul? I do not want a plain gown. How about you? What we do down here in the name of Jesus will determine what our wedding gown will look like.

MAY 31   THE HONEYMOON

Key Verse: *"...clothed in fine linen, white and clean" (Revelation 19:14).*

Message: We will decorate our own gowns; we will be married. Then we will step out of heaven in our going-away gown. According to Revelation 19:14, we will once again be *"clothed in fine linen, white and clean"* and will accompany our Lord when He comes to reclaim the earth.

After He takes care of some unfinished business, we will have a thousand-year honeymoon with our Husband.

Then when He takes care of some more unfinished business, we will move with Him to our forever-after home, the New Jerusalem. Look for this in the next month.

Remember! The only passport to heaven is the shed blood of Jesus Christ. Be sure you have been washed in the blood of the Lamb—the only key to experiencing what is in this month's devotionals.

June

OUR ETERNAL HOME-THE NEW JERUSALEM

Last month we looked at our next home: heaven. This month we will look at our eternal home: the New Jerusalem.

In between we will live in a temporary home. We will live there for a thousand years. (To our Lord a thousand years is temporary.)

At the end of that thousand years, the Lord Jesus will take care of all unfinished business. He will wipe heaven and earth clean. Satan, his demon angels, the Antichrist, the false prophet, and the lost of all ages will be in their eternal home, the Lake of Fire. They will live forever in *"the fire that never shall be quenched" (Mark 9:45)*. They will live in this place where they will be *"tormented day and night forever and ever" (Revelation 20:10)*. How tragic! As I have said before, we should do everything we can to keep people from this fate.

After the lost move to their eternal home, the saved of all ages will move to theirs. The major focus of this month will be on the eternal home of those saved during the Church Age—the Age of Grace. That includes you and me.

JUNE 1   THE NEW JERUSALEM

Key Verse: John gave us this picture: *"And I John saw the holy city, new Jerusalem, coming down from God out of heaven prepared as a bride adorned for her husband" (Revelation 21:1).*

Message: Let's talk about the New Jerusalem. It will not originate on earth. It is not the earthly Jerusalem from which Jesus will reign during the one thousand years. It is not the earthly city of Jerusalem that we know today.

The New Jerusalem is the eternal home of the church. Jesus said, *"In my Father's house are many mansions....I go to prepare a place for you..." (John 14:2).* This home is being prepared for us in heaven. The New Jerusalem is its location. This city is a real city in which Jesus the Bridegroom will live with His perfected bride—the church—those saved in the church age—the day in which we live. The New Jerusalem is in heaven today, but one day it will change locations.

JUNE 2   A CITY A BRIDE

Key Verse: John saw *"the new Jerusalem...prepared as a bride adorned for her husband" (Revelation 21:2).*

Message: Before we go on, let's clear up something that might be a bit confusing. As we have said, the bride will descend from heaven, and at the same time her new home will descend with her.

The city and the bride are so closely related that they are spoken of as one. There is a literal city, and it is called the *"bride."* The terms *"Holy City"* and *"New Jerusalem"* are used to describe both the bride and her home.

JUNE 3   A GLIMPSE OF THE CITY

Key Verse: An angel said to John: *"Come hither; I will shew thee the bride, the Lamb's wife" (Revelation 21:9).*

Message: Just get the picture! Can you imagine the emotions that were running through John?

Here he was in exile on the Isle of Patmos, awaiting death, and he was about to get a glimpse of his eternal home. God was about to reward John's faithful service. He does the same for you and me. Isn't He wonderful?

Listen to John: *"And He carried me away in the spirit to a great and high mountain, and showed me that great city, and holy Jerusalem, descending out of heaven from God" (Revelation 21:10).* Just imagine what he saw!

JUNE 4   WHERE WILL IT LAND?

Key Verse: *"...descending out of heaven from God" (Revelation 21:10.*

Message: You will notice that we are told that the city will come down, but we are not told that it will touch earth.

Now, I cannot be dogmatic about the things I am about to say, but I want to share with you what God has laid on my heart.

As I have said so often, we are not earth people. In His high priestly prayer in John 17, Jesus made it clear that we are in the world but not of the world. Therefore, I do not believe that our eternal home will be on earth.

Also, note that John had to go to *"a great and high mountain in order to see it."* To me, this means that the city will stop in the air.

I do not know how far it will come down, but I do believe it will be suspended in the air above the earthly Jerusalem, the center of the earth.

JUNE 5   HOW BIG IS IT?

Key Verse: *"...the length and the breadth and the height of it are equal" (Revelation 21:16).*

Message: John goes on to give detailed dimensions; but since I have a problem with numbers, I'll just say that the dimensions given to John were these: The city is fifteen hundred miles long, fifteen hundred miles wide, and fifteen hundred miles high. This is a big city.

I read somewhere that if you can imagine a city stretching from Boston to Miami and from New York City to Denver, towering fifteen hundred miles into the air, you can visualize the dimensions of that place of many mansions which is being prepared for our eternal abode. (Incidentally I cannot picture a city with these dimensions sitting on earth.)

JUNE 6   THE OUTSIDE
Key Verse: *"… [it] had a wall great and high, and had twelve gates, and at the gates twelve angels, and names written thereon, which are the names of the twelve tribes of Israel…" (Revelation 21:12).*

Message: There are twelve gates to the city, three gates on each side. An angel will stand at each gate. Each gate will have the name of one of the twelve tribes of Israel on it. Every tribe of Israel will have its own entrance.

Perhaps you have a question at this point: "Why will the Jews come to the New Jerusalem?" One reason is to worship.

You see, there will be no earthly temple. In Revelation 21:3, right after John saw the Holy City coming down, he heard a voice from heaven proclaim: *"Behold the tabernacle (or tent) of God is with men, and he will dwell with them…and God himself will be with them."*

God the Father and God the Son will be present in the New Jerusalem, but they will be more than present. In Revelation 21:22, John said, *"And I saw no temple therein: for the Lord God Almighty and the Lamb are the temple of it."* They will be the temple. No building will be necessary.

Well, when the worship service is over, the Jews will return to earth. (They will be space travelers. No shuttles will be needed.)

JUNE 7   WHO ELSE WILL COME?
Key Verse: *"And the nations…" (Revelation 21:24).*

Message: The Jews will not be the only people who will come to the New Jerusalem to worship. The saved Gentile nations (other than church-age believers) will come also. In Revelation 21:24, we read, *"And the nations of them which are saved shall walk in the light of it, and the kings of earth do bring their glory and honor into it."* Now the Gentiles who inherit the earth will not live with us in the New Jerusalem. They will *"walk in the light of it."*

However, like the Jews, they will come there to worship and then go back home. I don't know which gates they will enter, since each gate has the name of a tribe of Israel on it. I can only speculate that they will enter the gate closest to where they live.

Now let's take a closer look at the city.

JUNE 8   HER GLORY
Key Verse: *"Having the glory of God..." (Revelation 21:11).*

Message: John said that the New Jerusalem would have the glory of God. What does this mean? In Revelation 21:23, John says, *"And the city had no need of the sun, neither of the moon, to shine in it; for the glory of God did lighten it...."*

The city will be filled with the Shekinah Glory of God. We get a picture of this in Exodus 40. Verse 33 tells us that Moses finished the tabernacle. Verse 34 says, *"Then a cloud covered the tent of the congregation, and the glory of God filled the tabernacle."* The cloud of His glory and His presence showed His approval of the completed tabernacle. He was now dwelling with His people.

His glory will fill the New Jerusalem, a fact that will show His approval of the completed great city. I don't know exactly what His glory is like, but I know it will permeate the whole place.

JUNE 9   HER LIGHT
Key Verse: *"...and the Lamb is the light thereof" (Revelation 21:23).*

Message: I can't actually describe the glory of God, but I can describe the light that will permeate the whole city. His name is Jesus Christ *"...the Lamb of God, which taketh away the sin of the world" (John 1:29).*

In Revelation 21:11, John said, *"And her light was like unto a stone most precious..."* Peter calls Jesus *"a living stone, rejected of men, but chosen of God, and precious" (1 Peter 2:4).* Jesus, the precious living stone, is the light of the New Jerusalem. Revelation 21:23 makes this clear: *"...and the Lamb is the light thereof."*

Jesus will be the source of all light for the New Jerusalem and for the whole earth.

What will His light be like? We see the answer in Revelation 22:11: *"And her light was like unto a stone most precious, even like a Jasper stone, clear as crystal."*

The light that will radiate from our Lord will be like a huge gem, a jasper stone. I am told that this stone could be an opal, a topaz, or a diamond. Since it will produce a lot of light and it will be *"clear as crystal,"* I believe it will be like a diamond. Jesus will light up the New Jerusalem and the world with a pure light—light as clear as a transparent diamond.

JUNE 10   THE WALL
Key Verse: *"And the wall of the city..."* (Revelation 21:14).

Message: You might wonder why there will be a wall around the city. I believe it is there to show how secure and protected we are in our new home. (I need to add that the wall has gates, showing that the city is accessible to those coming from earth to worship.)

How tall is the wall? Revelation 21:17 gives the answer. Once again let me say that since numbers aren't my thing, I will tell you that the measurements given in this verse translate to 216 feet.

Of what is it made? Revelation 21:18 says, *"And the building of the wall of it was of jasper...."*

Can you picture a 216-foot tall diamond wall? John added this to verse 18: *"...and the city was pure gold, like unto clear glass."*

What beauty! Can you picture pure light radiating from Jesus, a 216-foot tall diamond wall, and city of transparent gold? My! My! And our eyes won't need sunglasses!!!

JUNE 11   THE FOUNDATIONS
Key Verse: *"And the wall of the city had twelve foundations, and in them the names of the twelve apostles of the Lamb"* (Revelation 21:14).

Message: In his letter to the Ephesians, Paul said to them, *"You are built upon the foundation laid by the apostles and prophets, the cornerstone being Christ Jesus Himself"* (Ephesians 2:20 GN).

Truly, our Lord Jesus is the *"chief cornerstone"* of the church, but the church is built upon the foundation of the apostles.

In Acts 1:1-2, Paul told Theophilus that Jesus preached the gospel on earth until *"he was taken up; after that he through the Holy Ghost had given commandments unto the apostles whom he had chosen."*

When Jesus went back to heaven, He gave the Holy Spirit instructions on how to carry on the work, and He gave instructions to the Holy Spirit to pass on the information to the apostles.

Through the power of the Holy Spirit, these men started the first churches; they preached the first sermons; they wrote about the church. Thus it was fitting that their names be on the foundations of the New Jerusalem.

JUNE 12   THE DECORATIONS
Key Verse: *"...all manner of precious stones..." (Revelation 21:19).*

Message: In this verse we learn that something beautiful will decorate the foundations. They will be *"garnished with all manner of precious stones...."*

Each foundation will have in it a beautiful precious gem. I'll not name them, but I will say that they will be the most beautiful shades of blue, green, red, purple, and gold imaginable.

Think of the beauty! The wall is made of diamond; the city is made of pure gold, as clear as glass; the foundation stones are adorned by beautiful gems.

Truly, the New Jerusalem will be a city of light and a city of color.

JUNE 13   MORE ABOUT THE GATES
Key Verse: *"...one pearl..." (Revelation 21:21).*

Message: We have already talked about the twelve gates to the city. We said that each gate will have the name of one of the twelve tribes of Israel on it.

In Revelation 21:21, we see that *"every several gate was of one pearl...."*

Down here an oyster produces a pearl. How big is the biggest one you have ever seen? Not very big! But when our Lord produces one, He makes it big enough to cover a whole gate. Can you imagine a pearl large enough to cover an entire gate? Oh, the wonder of it all!!!

JUNE 14   NO MORES

Key Verse: *"...and there shall be no more..." (Revelation 21:4).*

Message: In Revelation 21:27, we read that the only ones who can enter the city are *"they which are written in the Lamb's book of life."* His book contains the names of those who are saved, those who have been redeemed by the blood of the Lamb.

For these folks, there are some great "no mores." We see these in Revelation 21:4: *"And God shall wipe away all tears from their eyes; and there shall be no more death, neither sorrow, nor crying, neither shall there be any more pain; for the former things are passed away."*

In this life there is no way we can escape death and sorrow and tears and pain, but in our eternal life we will experience none of these. They will all pass away. Just think! You won't even remember what tears are like!

JUNE 15   MORE NO MORES

Key Verse: *"There shall be no night there" (Revelation 22:5).*

Message: There will be some other "no mores." There will be no more sun and no more moon. They won't be needed. We have already said that they won't be needed because *"the Lamb is the light thereof" (Revelation 21:23).*

In our key verse we see that there will be no more night. Certain things we need down here, we will not need up there. Our bodies will not need sleep, so there will be no need of night.

There is another reason we won't need night. The Prince of Darkness loves to do his worst deeds at night, but he won't be around. He will have moved from this world to his eternal home—the Lake of Fire *"...where he shall be tormented day and night for ever and ever" (Revelation 20:10).*

JUNE 16   THE STREET

Key Verse: *"...and the street of the city was pure gold, as it were transparent glass" (Revelation 21:21).*

Message: We sing about the "streets" of gold, but this verse says "street." I believe it is a winding street that goes from the bottom to the top of this tall city, like a winding staircase or like a spiral on a notebook. It is a beautiful street of see-through golden glass. How beautiful!

In Revelation 22:2, we read that John saw the river (more on the river later) *"flowing down the middle of the city's street"* (not streets).

I picture this street to be like a divided highway with the river separating each side. Perhaps one side is for entering the New Jerusalem and one for leaving. I am speculating, but this idea makes sense to me.

JUNE 17   STOP AND REFLECT

Key Verse: *"...I go to prepare a place for you" (John 14:2).*

Message: And what a place He went to prepare! Our forever home, the New Jerusalem, will be so special. Can you visualize a wall of diamond, a city of pure translucent gold, gates of pearl, foundations of precious gems, and a street of transparent gold? This will be a beautiful city of color and light because *"the Lamb is the light thereof"* (Revelation 21:23).

Note: As I said, the New Jerusalem is a beautiful city of color and light. Now let's look at the other side of it. I am often asked, "Will we drink and eat in heaven?" (I guess this tells us what occupies our minds much of the time.)

JUNE 18   WATER

Key Verse: *"And He shewed me a pure river of water of life, clear as crystal, proceeding out of the throne of God and of the Lamb"* *(Revelation 22:1).*

Message: Today three-quarters of our globe is covered by water, but it will all dry up.

In Revelation 21:1, we see that when the first heaven and first earth pass away… *"there will be no more seas."* They will vanish. Today the seas serve as boundaries and barriers, but they will not be needed any more.

There will be only one place where water will be located in the New Jerusalem. It will originate at the throne of God and, according to Revelation 22:1(GN), it will flow *"down the middle of the city's street."* It will flow down the middle of that divided street.

Maybe your question at this point is, "Will we need water in eternity?" I believe we will because this river is called *"a pure river of water of life."* It seems to me that we will drink this water in order to live eternally.

JUNE 19   THE TREE OF LIFE

Key Verse: *"In the midst of the street of it, and on either side of the river, was there the tree of life, which bare twelve manner of fruits, and yielded her fruit every month…"* *(Revelation 22:2).*

Message: Now Ezekiel 47 is talking about the millennium, but it basically says what Revelation 22:2 says, so I believe we see in both passages a picture of eternity.

Ezekiel 47:7 says, *"…at the bank of the river were very many trees on the one side and on the other."* Ezekiel 47:12 says, *"and by the river upon the bank thereof, on this side and on that side, shall grow all trees for food, whose leaf shall not fade, neither shall the fruit thereof be consumed: it shall bring forth new fruit every month…and the fruit thereof shall be for meat."*

According to this verse, there will be many "trees of life." The tree of life, first found in the Garden of Eden, will one day grow in the New Jerusalem in abundance. These trees will grow between the street and the river.

Those trees will produce twelve kinds of fruit at a time, and there will be twelve crops a year. Water and fruit will be the drink and food in eternity. Learn to like your fruit, folks!

Well, will we need this fruit? I will repeat what I said about the water. I believe we will need the fruit because it will come from "the tree of <u>life</u>." It seems to me that we will eat this fruit in order to live eternally.

JUNE 20   THE LEAVES

Key Verses: *"...and the leaf thereof* (from the tree of life) *for healing" (Ezekiel 47:12).*
"...and the leaves of the tree were for the healing of the nations" (Revelation 22:2).

Message: These verses include all people who will live on earth. No further details are given to explain these statements, but it seems to me that the bodies of earth dwellers will need to eat of the leaves of the trees of life in order to keep their bodies perfect. I suppose that when they come to the New Jerusalem, they will worship and drink water and eat fruit and leaves.

This does not include us. The Bible does not say that the bride— the church—will need to eat the leaves for healing. Why not? What will keep our bodies perfect?

JUNE 21   COULD IT BE?

Message: I don't have a verse for what I am about to say. I realize that I am speculating, but could the Holy Spirit have something to do with our not having to eat the leaves for healing?

What will his role be in the New Jerusalem? Think for a moment. Today we are indwelled by the Holy Spirit, but we still have that old sin nature in us. It will be gone when we enter our eternal home.

Could it be that the Holy Spirit will completely fill us and thus keep us perfect? This is something to think about.

JUNE 22   KINGS AND PRIESTS

Key Verse: *"And (Jesus) hath made us kings and priests..."* *(Revelation 1:6).*

Message: In 1 Peter 2:5, the church is called *"a holy priesthood."* In verse 9, Peter calls the church *"a royal priesthood."* When the church becomes the bride, we will fulfill that role as Jesus intended.

We will also fulfill another role. We will reign with our Lord. In Revelation 22:5, we read that we *"shall reign forever and ever."* This is the heritage of the church of our Lord.

I'm not sure what He will have us do, but I believe we will be very busy reigning over the earth and helping in the worship services.

To lead in worship and reign over the earth are the highest privileges offered to man, but not to just any man. This honor is bestowed only on those people saved by the blood of the Lamb in the Church Age.

Pray that God will use you to increase this number.

JUNE 23   SERVANTS

Key Verse: *"...and his servants shall serve him"* *(Revelation 22:3).*

Message: When Jesus was on earth, the reverse was true. In Luke 22:27, He told His disciples: *"...I am among you as he that serveth."*

That is not exactly what the disciples wanted to hear. On one occasion Jesus and His disciples were walking toward Capernaum. When they got there, Jesus asked them, "What were you arguing about as we traveled?"

They didn't answer Him because they had been arguing among themselves about which one of them was the greatest. They didn't have to answer because Jesus knew exactly why they were arguing.

Mark 9:35 (GN) says, *"Jesus sat down, called the twelve disciples and said unto them, 'Whoever wants to be first must place himself last of all and be the servant of all.'"* Serving didn't appeal to these folks; and, unfortunately, it doesn't really appeal to us. We had rather be served.

But Jesus makes it clear that those He puts first are those who serve. He is our model. In Matthew 20:28, He said, *"...The Son of man came not to be served, but to serve...."*

The opposite will be true in our eternal home. We will serve Him. I'm not sure what He will have us to, but we will be thrilled to do His bidding because we will be so grateful to be the bride of the One who saved us by His matchless grace.

JUNE 24   SEE HIS FACE
Key Verse: *"And they shall see his face..." (Revelation 22:4).*

Message: Today this is not possible. An unglorified human being cannot see the face of God. In Exodus 33:20, God said to Moses: *"Thou canst not see my face for there shall no man see me and live."* In John 1:18, we read, *"No man hath seen God at any time...."* Today, God has never been photographed.

But that will change when we get to our eternal home. When John saw the throne of God, all he saw were beautiful gem-like colors and a rainbow of green. One day when we have our eternal glorified bodies, John and all the redeemed will behold the face of God. The greatest blessing we will have in our eternal home is that *"they (we) shall see his face."*

JUNE 25   A SPECIAL NAME
Key Verse: *"...his name shall be in their foreheads" (Revelation 22:4b).*

Message: We are familiar with the "mark of the beast." Revelation 13:16-17 says that the false prophet will make every person who wants to live *"receive a mark in their right hand, or in their fore-heads. And no man might buy or sell, save he that had the mark or name of the beast (Antichrist) or the number of his name (666)."*

This mark will show in a very visible place that the bearer belongs to the Antichrist and that he has to worship this villain.

Well, he, the false prophet, Satan, and the lost of all ages will be long gone to their eternal home, the Lake of Fire, when the name mentioned in Revelation 22:4 appears on our foreheads.

The name of our God will appear in a very visible place—on our foreheads—showing that we belong to Him and that we get to (not have to) worship Him in our new home the New Jerusalem, for all eternity. What a difference between "having to" and "getting to."

As you pray today, remind yourself that you have the privilege of "getting to" worship and serve a living God.

Note: We have just looked in detail at the eternal home of the bride of Christ. I think it only fitting that we look at the places where the rest of mankind will spend eternity.

JUNE 26   JEWS

Key Verse: *"And the Lord said to Abram....all the land which thou seest, to thee will I give it, and to thy seed forever" (Genesis 13:14, 15).*

Message: Palestine, the Promised Land, was given to Abram and his seed <u>forever</u>. In Genesis 15:18, the Lord said to Abram: *"Unto thy seed have I given this land, from the river Egypt unto the great river, the river Euphrates."*

No one knows the exact borders because it is not clear whether the *"river of Egypt"* in the south is the Nile or a stream that runs between Egypt and Canaan.

But one day the borders will be known. One day the Jews *"... shall look upon me whom they have pierced, and they shall mourn for him" (Zechariah 12:10).* They will accept Jesus as their Messiah.

When this happens, *"the Lord thy God will turn thy captivity... and will return thee from all the nations where the Lord thy God hath scattered thee" (Deuteronomy 30:3).*

Because of their disobedience, the Jews have been out of the land at least sixty percent of the time. But when they repent, God will bring them home to live forever in all of Palestine.

As you pray today, pray that America will always stand by Israel. In Isaiah 49:25, God said to Israel: *"I will contend with him that contendeth with thee."* In other words, God deals with nations as nations deal with Israel.

154

JUNE 27   ARABS
Key Verse: *"In that day shall Israel be the third with Egypt and with Assyria, even a blessing in the midst of the land"* (Isaiah 19:24).

Message: One day many of the Arabs will be saved and will live in Egypt and Assyria. There is no place called Assyria today, but I know that Iraq and Syria were part of ancient Assyria.

Looking at these folks today, we find it hard to believe that they will one day accept Jesus as Messiah and be saved. Who are the Arabs? Half brothers of the Jews! They are descendants of Ishmael, Abraham's son by the Egyptian handmaid Hagar.

Genesis 16:12 certainly describes Ishmael and his people: *"He will be a wild man, and every man's hand against him...."*

Yet, God made a promise to Hagar about Ishmael. In Genesis 16:9, He said to her: *"I will give you so many descendants that no one will be able to count them."* In 21:18, He said, *"I will make him a great nation."* This has come true. There are a lot more Arabs in the world today than Jews.

Now, at this point, Ishmael's people have one joint cry: *"...come, and let us cut them off from being a nation; that the name of Israel may be no more in remembrance"* (Psalm 83:4).

They will continue trying to drive Israel into the Mediterranean Sea until Jesus comes again.

Most of the Arab states will be judged and destroyed. Only Egypt and Assyria will remain and will be the great nation God promised Hagar.

But until then the Middle East will be in turmoil. Let us heed Psalm 122:6: *"Pray for the peace of Jerusalem; they shall prosper that love thee."*

JUNE 28   GENTILES
Key Verse: *"Come...inherit the kingdom prepared for you..."* (Matthew 25:34).

Message: This is a statement made by Jesus at the time He judges the nations. The nations in question are the ones who will have made it through the Great Tribulation and are alive when Jesus returns.

Matthew 25:32-33 says, *"And before him shall be gathered all nations, and he shall separate them one from another....And he shall set the sheep (saved) on his right hand, but the goats (lost) on the left."* Jesus will invite the sheep nations to *"come...inherit the kingdom prepared for you...."*

Then He will tell the basis for the invitation: *"For I was hungry, and ye gave me food: I was thirsty, and ye gave me drink: I was a stranger, and ye took me in: naked, and ye clothed me: I was sick, and ye visited me: I was in prison, and ye came unto me"* *(Matthew 25: 35-36).*

A puzzled group of people will ask, "Lord, when did we do these things?"

His answer will be, *"Inasmuch as ye have done it unto one of the least of these my brethren, ye have done it unto me"* *(Matthew 25:40).*

Who are His *"brethren"*? I believe they are the 144,000 Jewish evangelists who will be the preachers during the Great Tribulation. They will be constantly chased by the Antichrist but protected by God who will use these nations to hide them and take care of them. This group could also include any other believers hidden by and cared for by these nations.

The nations who are "sheep" nations will live in the world not occupied by the Jews and the Arabs.

JUNE 29   THE LOST
Key Verse: *"...depart from me..."* *(Matthew 25:41).*

Message: Jesus spoke these words to the "goat" nations, the ones who will not minister to Christ's "brethren" during the Great Tribulation. These folks will join the lost of all ages in their eternal home, the Lake of Fire.

In Matthew 25:41, we see that Jesus will say to them: *"Depart from me, ye cursed, into everlasting fire, prepared for the devil and his angels."*

As I said in the beginning of this month, all lost people will live forever in *"the fire that never shall be quenched"* *(Mark 9:45).* They will be in this place where they will be *"tormented day and night forever and ever" (Revelation 20:10).*

God prepared this place for the devil and his evil angels. He never intended for man to go there. But the choice must be up to the individual. If he rejects Christ, he will live forever separated from Him in the Lake of Fire.

As you pray today, ask the Lord to make a divine appointment for you with a lost person and use you to share the good news that will keep him out of this awful place.

JUNE 30   AN INVITATION
Key Verse: *"...come..." (Revelation 22:17).*

Message: Jesus has no desire for anyone to go to the Lake of Fire. 2 Peter 3:9 says that He is *"not willing that any should perish, but that all should come to repentance."*

The invitation to "come" will be given unto the last possible moment. Revelation 22, verse 17, gives four invitations to the unsaved to come to Christ in faith for eternal life: *"And the Spirit and the bride say, 'come,' and let him that heareth say, 'come.' And let him that is athirst come. And whosoever will, let him take the water of life freely."*

I like the way the Good News puts this invitation: *"The Spirit and the Bride (Holy Spirit and the church) say, 'Come!' Everyone who hears this must also say, 'Come!' Come, whoever is thirsty; accept the water of life as a gift, whoever wants it."*

When my pastor gives the invitation, I close my eyes and picture Jesus standing there with outstretched arms saying, "Whosoever will, come."

One day the last appeal will be made, the last invitation song will be sung. While there is yet time, get the message out: *"Behold, now is the accepted time; behold, now is the day of salvation" (2 Corinthians 6:2).*

Closing Note: We have looked at the eternal homes of all people. The church, the bride, will live with our Bridegroom in the New Jerusalem. Saved Jews will live in all of the Promised Land. Saved Arabs will live in Egypt and Assyria. Saved Gentiles, except the church, will live in the rest of the world. The lost of all ages will exist in the Lake of Fire.

Pray that everyone you know will one day live with you in the New Jerusalem and not in the Lake of Fire. Then put feet to your prayers.

July

GIVING

When you read the title, did you say, "She's going to write about money"? Well, I am, but not yet. We need to look at giving in other ways before we get to money. We must start with ourselves.

In Romans 12:1, Paul said *"…present your bodies a living sacrifice…."* The word *"present"* is a technical term for the offering of sacrifices to God. Paul is therefore telling us to offer ourselves to God—to hand ourselves over as slaves to Him—to give ourselves completely to Him. Follow along with me and take inventory of your life of giving.

I I GIVE MYSELF – All on the Altar

We are to be a living sacrifice. We are not to be lifeless people who get saved and then sit down and do nothing at all. I repeat: We are to be a living sacrifice. This is a day-by-day, hour-by-hour sacrifice that must never stop as long as we draw a breath.

JULY 1   IN PRAYER

Key Verse: *"...I give myself unto prayer"* (Psalm 109:4).

Message: In Psalm 55:17, David said, *"Evening and morning, and at noon, will I pray...."* Prayer was so important to him, and it must be to us also. As many of you know, I am a local church addict. One reason is that I have learned so much in the thirty plus years I have been a member of this church. I have learned so much about prayer. I have learned that nothing good happens in the life of a church without prayer.

This was made plain to me on the last three pastor-search committees on which I served. In the past when I was on a committee, someone opened in prayer and someone closed. But, when Jack Jackson was chairman of the pastor-search committee, that changed. The highlight of our meetings was the prayer time. We met in my living room every week, and every week every one of us prayed that God would lead us to His man for this church. We realized how helpless we were without God's revelation, so we cried out to Him. Bob Spring repeated this pattern when he was chairman of the next committee. What was true in these committees should be true in your life. To be a living sacrifice, you must give yourself to prayer.

In 1 Thessalonians 5:17, Paul said, *"Pray without ceasing."* He did not mean that we are to pray audibly at all times, but it does mean that we ought to remain in an attitude of prayer. When a person's name comes to your mind, stop and pray for that person.

JULY 2   IN SERVICE
Key Verse: *"(We all have) gifts differing according to the grace that is given to us..." (Romans 12:6).*

Message: Each of us is given a spiritual gift or gifts, and we are to give them back to the Lord. How? By using them in the body for the benefit of the whole church! Look again at the key verse: *"(We all have) gifts differing according to the grace that is given to us"*. Now look at Ephesians 4:7: *"But to every one of us is given grace according to the measure of the gift of Christ."* My study Bible has this note about this verse: "Jesus determines both what gift each believer is given and the amount (measure) of that gift, but one may have a greater measure of that gift than another and the grace to use it." I agree. In the next couple of days, let's look at illustrations. In Romans 12, Paul lists the spiritual gifts of prophecy, service, teaching, exhortation, giving, leadership, and mercy. Ask the Lord to show you your gift, and then use it to edify the church.

JULY 3   IN MINISTRY
Key Verse: *"In service, in serving..." (Romans 12:7a).*

Message: This is the gift of ministry or *helps*, as Paul calls it in 1 Corinthians 12:28. The gift of service is any sort of practical help that Christians can give one another in Jesus' name. People who have sat under my teaching have heard me say this many times: "If the Lord lays it on your heart to do something for someone, do it right then." I believe that if you do it right away, you will receive a great blessing. If you do it later, you will receive a blessing, but not as great. If you don't obey, you may not have this gift. However, you may. Have you ever said, "I wanted to prepare her a meal, etc., but I just didn't have time"? If so, you may be neglecting the gift that is in you. If you have the gift of ministry but are too busy to use it, you are too busy. Take a good look at your schedule.

Paul said to Timothy: *"Neglect not the gift that is in thee..." (1 Timothy 4:14).* He says the same to us. Be so in tune with the Lord that you will hear Him when He asks you to give yourself in ministry to someone else and obey immediately.

JULY 4 IN GIVING

Key Verse: *"...He that giveth, let him do it with liberality..."* *(Romans 12:8).*

Message: People who exercise this gift do not give for thanks or recognition. They give for the glory of God. They are at their happiest when they are giving. Paul said in 2 Corinthians 9:7: *"Every man according as he purposes in his heart, so let him give; not grudgingly, or of necessity for God loveth a cheerful giver."* Giving is a heart issue. I believe this is one of those gifts that varies from person to person. I am not talking about tithing. Everybody is to tithe. I am talking about giving. The person with the gift of giving gives above the tithe. The person with the greater measure of the gift gives way above the tithe, *with liberality.*

I know a young lady who has the greater measure. Recently she was standing in line at a local store waiting for her husband to finish witnessing to a clerk. The Lord impressed her to let several people go ahead of her and to pay their bills. Now, folks, only the person with the greater measure would have done that. If you give above the tithe, you have this gift, if your giving is to glorify God. If you give way above the tithe, you have a greater measure of this gift, if your purpose is to glorify the Lord. Giving must never be for the praise of man. It must be for the glory of God.

Paul said that our Lord loves a cheerful giver (a hilarious giver.) After one of our pastors, Brother Larry, returned from a visit to his children, he told the congregation that at offering time the minister of the church he visited said, "It's time to take the offering." When he finished speaking, everybody clapped. He had us do likewise. I loved it, and I believe the Lord did also. Why don't you be a cheerleader for the Lord when the offering plate comes your way?

JULY 5 IN PRAISE AND THANKSGIVING

Key Verse: *"I will praise the name of God with a song, and I will magnify him with thanksgiving" (Psalm 69:30).*

Message: How much of your quiet time do you devote to giving our Lord praise and thanksgiving? Why don't you try this: On July

5 begin your quiet time by meditating on the following verses. You might be amazed at how much richer your time alone with the Lord will be.

- *I will praise thee, O Lord my God, with all my heart, and I will glorify thy name forever more" (Psalm 86: 12).*
- *Praise ye the Lord. Give thanks unto the Lord; for he is good: for his mercy endureth forever" (Psalm 106:1).*
- *I will extol thee, my God, O King; and I will bless thy name for ever and ever. Every day will bless thee; and I will praise thy name for ever and ever" (Psalm 145:1-2).*

Now that you have meditated on these verses on July 5, try following the same pattern every day. Search out the praise and thanksgiving verses in Psalms and give them to the Lord in prayer. The Psalmist said, *"It is a good thing to give thanks unto the Lord, and to sing praises unto thy name, O Most High" (Psalm 92:1).* Praise Him and thank Him for who He is; bless His name every day.

II I GIVE BACK TO GOD—His Tithe

In this section I will be talking about only the tithe—the ten percent that belongs to God. The command is very clear to me: *"Bring ye all the tithes into the storehouse..." (Malachi 3:10).* However, it doesn't seem clear to a lot of believers. In fact, it seems to me that some people want to put a negative connotation on tithing. In the next few days, we will look at some comments I hear.

JULY 6   LAW, NOT GRACE
Key Verse: *"And he gave him tithes of all (Genesis 14:20).*

Message: Some people say that tithing is under law, not grace. Now in Genesis 14, we learn that the "he" is Abraham and the "him" is Melchizedek. Abraham paid tithes to Melchizedek long before the law was given to Moses. Therefore, it is not valid to say that tithing is under law, not grace. I like what Dr. J. Gerald Harris, our former pastor, said in his book, Pardoned to be Priests: "I declare that if a Christian would not do more under grace than a Jew would under

163

the law, he is a disgrace to grace." I quote again from Dr. Harris: "The story of Melchizedek teaches us that the principle of tithing is an eternal principle. It predates the Law, it continued throughout the dispensation of the Law, and it still continues in this day of grace."

The Lord owns everything we have in our possession. We are only stewards. All He requires is that we return ten percent to Him. My, what could be done to help more everyday people come to know and experience our Lord Jesus if every one of us returned the tithe to Him? I'll do my part. Talk this over with the Lord today.

JULY 7   THE OLD, NOT THE NEW
Key Verse: *"...Not to leave the other (tithing) undone" (Luke 11:42).*

Message: Some people say that tithing is the Old Testament plan for giving, not the New Testament. The New Testament does not stress it so much, but tithing is God's plan for the support of His work in every dispensation. Jesus mentioned tithing in Luke 11:42. Here, He chastises the Pharisees for tithing vegetables and withholding love, but He ends the verse by saying that they should have done both: *"...not to leave the other (tithing) undone."* To me this says that tithing is a "given" in the New Testament. The New Testament picks up here and emphasizes adding an offering, as we shall see later.

The Lord does not require much of us when it comes to giving— only ten percent. Now notice what God told the Israelites in Malachi 3:8: *"Ye have robbed me...."* When they asked how, He answered, *"...in tithes and offerings."* Don't be counted in that number.

JULY 8   CAN'T AFFORD
Key Verse: *"...Yet have I not seen the righteous forsaken, nor his seed begging bread" (Psalm 37:25).*

Message: Some people say, "I can't afford to tithe." Some say, "I want to, but I can't afford to." Why not step out on faith? In our key verse, David said, "I have been young, and now am old; yet have I not seen the righteous forsaken, nor his seed begging bread." Our Lord does not forsake the righteous, and the person who is righteous has a right relationship with the Lord. To have a right relationship with Him, you must be right in your pocketbook. Step out on faith. God takes care of His children.

Now, I am going to make a bold statement: "Every person is a tither!" Have you ever heard a tithing testimony in which the speaker said that when he began to tithe, the nine-tenths went as far as the ten? I hope I am not presumptuous in saying this, but I believe one reason is that he never did have the ten percent to spend the way he wanted to. Folks, you will not spend God's money. You may not give it to the church, but you will give it to a car repairman or a doctor or a carpenter or a plumber, etc. If you don't believe me, just check your unexpected expenses at the end of the year and see what the total is. You might be surprised! Step out on faith and return to God the portion that is His. You will be blessed.

I can remember a time when I didn't think I could afford to tithe. I am so glad that time is long past. I can testify that our Lord has kept His promise. I have brought His tithe into the storehouse, and He has opened the windows of heaven for me. I have never been forsaken and have never had to beg for bread. He will do the same for you. Why don't you be sure you are right with Him in your pocket book.

JULY 9   GROSS OR NET

Key Verse: *"Honor the Lord with thy possessions, with the first fruits of thine increase" (Proverbs 3:9).*

Message: Some people say, "I tithe my net income. After all, the net is all I get to take home." I have a problem with that kind of thinking. It may not be true, but it sounds as if some of these folks are trying to see how little they can tithe. But I have to add that I am sure many of them think they are doing the right thing. Let me point you to the Word. Our key verse says that we are to give the *first fruits*. Leviticus 27:30 says, *"and all the tithe of the land, whether of the seed of the land or of the fruit of the tree is the Lord's...."* Notice the words *"first"* and *"all."* I ran across these words often in reference to the tithe, whether it be in reference to the land or harvest or meat or oil or bread or corn or fruit, etc. I believe the

Bible supports tithing the gross. The words "all" and "first" equal "gross" income to me. The command in Deuteronomy 14:22 is this: *"Thou shalt truly tithe all the increase of thy seed."* Won't you join me in obeying that command?

JULY 10   SOME HERE, SOME THERE

Key Verse: *"Bring ye all the tithes into the storehouse..."* (Malachi 3:1.

Message: Some people say, "I tithe, but I give some to the church and some to a person in need or to a para-church group, etc." I believe it is great to give to others in addition to the church, but I see no Scripture that says it is all right to use part of the tithe to do so. In Exodus 23:19, we read, *"The first of the first fruits of the land thou shalt bring into the house of the Lord thy God."* I ran across a passage in Leviticus that settled this for me: *"All the tithe of the land. . .is the Lord's.....The tenth shall be holy unto the Lord. He shall not search whether it be good or bad, neither shall he change it"* (Leviticus 27:30, 32-33).

God's plan has always been for believers to bring the tithe to His house. He has never changed that plan, and neither can we. It is a joy to be a storehouse tither. Are you having fun?

JULY 11   A TESTIMONY

Key Verse: *"As newborn babes, desire the pure milk of the word, that ye may grow thereby"* (1 Peter 2:2).

Message: I chose to share my friend Cindy's testimony with you today for two reasons. First of all, I believe it shows she has followed our key verse, and it traces her personal growth. Second, it illustrates what we have covered in the last two days: "Gross or Net" and "Some Here, Some There," and reveals what the Lord has taught her in these areas. With her permission, I share her testimony.

When Cindy came to this church, she was single and called herself a tither. However, she tithed on the net, not the gross. When she heard Brother Richard preach that one should tithe on the gross, she changed immediately. Then one day she had this situation come up. Her nephew needed school clothes and his parents needed help in buying them. Cindy went to Brother Richard and asked whether it would be all right to give part of her tithe to the church and part to the boy's parents. He told her that she should give her tithe to the church and give an offering for the clothes.

She said to me, "I didn't listen. I couldn't afford to do both, so I sent a check for the school clothes. And do you know what happened? The check bounced!" She told me that she got the message. She remained a storehouse tither. Now that she and Dan are married, storehouse tithing is an "absolute" in their home. I love this testimony.

Truly, salvation is a one-time experience, and lordship is a life-time process. Isn't it a blessing that Cindy is in the process? Are you in the process? Settle this with the Lord today if you are not.

JULY 12   WHAT ABOUT A GIFT?

Key Verse: *"Honor the Lord with thy possessions, and with the first fruits of thine increase" (Proverbs 3:9).*

Message: I am using this verse again because of what I have learned from it. Two words stand out: *"possessions"* and *"increase."* The thought crossed my mind: Tithing is not based on my paycheck alone. It is based on my possessions and my increase. What does that mean? I began to think about money gifts, refunds, etc. I asked a former pastor how he handled this money. He told me that he tithes everything that comes into his hands. I immediately made that an "absolute" in my life. It surely is freeing not to have to decide if I do or if I don't. I love "absolutes."

When you make tithing an "absolute" and give of all you receive, the Lord will bless you. Try Him! He has told you to do so.

Note: I have now covered all the comments I have heard about tithing. I pray that God will use something you have read to make tithing clearer to you. Now I am going to move to "giving."

III. I GIVE TO GOD—an Offering

Please hear Jesus' words to Nicodemus: *"For God so loved the world that he gave his only begotten Son. . ." (John 3:16).* Now hear Paul's words to the Ephesians: *"And walk in love, as Christ also hath loved us, and hath given himself for us and offering and a sacrifice to God. . ." (Ephesians 5:2).* Our Father <u>gave</u> Jesus to us; Jesus <u>gave</u> Himself for us. In each case the motive for the gift was *"love."* Love must also be the motive for all our giving. In the following days we will look at giving, based on love.

JULY 13   A HEART ISSUE

Key Verse: *"Every man according as he purposeth in his heart, so let him give..." (2 Corinthians 9:7).*

Message: Giving is never an issue of the mind. It must be an issue of the heart. Any service for Jesus that will be rewarded must come from the heart. Remember Daniel? He "purposed" in his heart that he would not eat the king's food or drink his wine. He also "purposed" in his heart to continue his daily prayer schedule, even though he had been told that to do so meant death. In our giving we must have this same kind of "purposeful heart." In 2 Corinthians 9:7, Paul went on to add: *"not grudgingly."* Folks, if it pains you to give, you might as well not give. It will be an offering not received by our Lord. He commands that we be *"cheerful givers."*

Proverbs 22:9 says, *"He that hath a generous eye shall be blessed."* Ask the Lord to turn your eyes where there is a need and let your heart lead you to give.

JULY 14   A SPECIAL BANK ACCOUNT

Key Verse: *"...I desire fruit that may abound to your account" (Philippians 4:17).*

Message: In his letter to the Philippians, Paul said to them in essence, "When I left Macedonia in the early days of my ministry, you were the only ones who helped me. When I needed help in Thessalonica, you provided for me on more than one occasion." Then he added, *"not because I seek a gift; but I desire fruit that may abound to your* *account.*" Paul was grateful to the Philippians, not because he had to have their money, but because they were adding to their bank account in heaven. God doesn't have to have our money, but we need to give it cheerfully out of a heart of love to add to our reward account in heaven.

In Matthew 6:20, Jesus said to *"lay up for yourselves treasures in heaven."* These treasures are for faithful service. May your giving be a treasure for you in heaven!

JULY 15   A PROMISE
Key verse: *"But my God shall supply..." (Philippians 4:19).*

Message: Paul had just received more gifts from the Philippians. In effect he said, "Because of you I have everything I need." Then he told them how God viewed their giving. It went up to Him as a sweet-smelling aroma, *". . .a sacrifice acceptable, well-pleasing to God" (Philippians 4:18).* Paul knew that their giving had been a sacrifice that pleased the Lord, so he made them this wonderful promise: *"But my God shall supply all your need according to his riches in glory by Christ Jesus" (Philippians 4:19).* Because the Lord was aware of their sacrifice, He would meet their need "gloriously" by Christ Jesus. Giving the last dollar in your wallet in Jesus' name is one of the greatest feelings there is. He will replenish your wallet.

The widow of Zarepath used her last meal and oil she was planning to use for the last meal for her and her son to make a little cake for Elijah. Because she stepped out on faith, God saw that she had food every day until the famine was over. We know that this kind of faith pleases the Lord. Remember Hebrews 11:6: *"But without faith it is impossible to please him."* Do you need to examine your faith? Now is a good time.

JULY 16   GIVE AND RECEIVE
Key Verse: *"Give and it shall be given unto you. . ." (Luke 6:38).*

Message: This is one of my favorite verses, and I am going to take several days to cover it. It is wonderful to know that we have this promise: *"Give and it shall be given unto you...."* There is no way you can out-give God. He gave it all when He gave us Jesus, but He didn't stop there. As we give, He gives all the more. But I must stop here to say that our motive must not be selfish. In 2 Corinthians 9:10 (LB), Paul says, *"For God, who gives seed to the farmer to plant, and later on, good crops to harvest and eat, will give you more and more seed to plant and will make it grow so that you can give away more and more fruit from your harvest."* Here is the principle: You give to get to give to get more to give more to get even more to give even more. Folks, God's plan never stops with the "getting."

Paul gave us a saying of Jesus that is not recorded in the Gospels. It is this: *"...It is more blessed to give than to receive"* (Acts 20:35). Tell the Lord that you will do as He leads with what you receive.

JULY 17   GOOD MEASURE

Key Verse: *"Give and it shall be given unto you; good measure, pressed down, and shaken together, and running over..." (Luke 6:38).*

Message: When I look at this part of Luke 6:38, I always think of what my long-time friend and prayer partner, Doris Evans told me about her parents. They raised a lot of vegetables and gave many of them away. But sometimes someone would come by and want to buy a bushel of peas, butter beans, etc. Doris' mom would load that basket, shake it down, put more in, until it was running over. The person would say, "Mrs. Gunn, you are putting too much in that basket." She would just smile and quote Luke 6:38 to him. The buyer would usually end up with more like a bushel and a half than a bushel. This is a picture of what God does for us when we are cheerful givers.

I thank the Lord Jesus for godly friends like Doris whom He has put in my life and for her godly heritage. I also thank Him that His bushel always turns into a bushel and a half when we give because we love Him. Do you have a godly friend for whom you need to pray? Why don't you do so right now?

JULY 18   SHALL MAN GIVE

Key Verse: *"Give, and it shall be given unto you; good measure, pressed down and shaken together, and running over, <u>shall men give into your bosom</u>. . ." (Luke 6:38).*

Message: When I have heard this verse preached, I have never heard anyone address this part of the verse. I looked at my commentaries to see if any of them contained comments on this part: *". . . shall men give into your bosom" (or lap).* Not one did. I don't know why not because I believe it is a very important point. Now, I truly believe Paul's words: *"But my God shall supply all your needs..." (Philippians 4:19).* I know that God is our source of supply, but He uses man as an instrument. I believe Jesus says that if you give, He will use a person of His choice to meet your needs—maybe an employer, relative, a friend, a brother in Christ, an ex-spouse, etc. The choice will be God's. When you decide who is going to meet your needs, it doesn't always work out that way.

I often say to a single-again lady: "Don't become consumed with how much money your ex should give you. This will only lead to your becoming bitter. I believe your ex should pay; but if he doesn't honor his obligation, trust God to meet your need." I truly believe that the first step out of financial difficulty is to give God something to work with. He only promises to bless what we give, not what we keep. You give and God will use some person to meet your needs.

Please know that God is our source of supply and have faith that He will decide how to meet our needs. Our part is to give; His part is to supply. If we are obedient, He will honor our obedience. He said to His people through Isaiah the prophet: *"If ye be willing and obedient, ye shall eat of the good of the land" (Isaiah 1:19).*

JULY 19   THE MEASURE

Key Verse: *"Give and it shall be given unto you; good measure, pressed down, and shaken together, and running over, shall men give into your bosom. <u>For with the same measure that you use shall be measured to you again</u>"* (Luke 6:38).

Message: Here at the end of verse 38, Jesus is saying, "Give and you will receive, and the measure you use for others is the one that God will use for you." This is really the law of sowing and reaping. Paul said, *"For whatsoever a man soweth, that shall he also reap"* (*Galatians 6:7*). I heard the following story somewhere. A young man who had been a Christian for only two months asked his pastor how much he should give to the Lord's work. The pastor answered by asking these questions. "How much do you want God to prosper your life? How much do you covet God's blessings upon your family?" The pastor continued, "You see, whatever you give to God is going to increase, so you decide how much you want to give." Good advice!

In the key verse we learn that whatever measure we use to give—large or small—will be used to measure what is given back to us. May we "sow bountifully."

JULY 20   SOW AND REAP

Key Verse: *"But this I say, he which soweth sparingly shall reap also sparingly; and he which soweth bountifully shall reap bountifully"* (2 Corinthians 9:6).

Message: This verse took on new meaning to me several years ago. It was time for us to build the family life center. Our pastor at the time, Brother Gerald, said that he felt that we should pay cash for the building, and he challenged us to give everything that came into our hands during a designated forty-day period. I did not have to ponder about whether I would participate (that is, after I got over the initial shock).

To me, this was a call to obedience; I would participate. But the question became, "How?" I had never faced such a big challenge. Forty days! Three paychecks! Two house payments! My first thought was that in preparation, I had better start saving my money. But my second thought was that I should keep giving. I did. It seemed that every time I felt I had given enough, that still small voice would whisper, "Give some more!" The result? That forty days to victory was one of the high peaks of my spiritual journey, and I did not suffer financially.

Truly, the Lord has shown me the blessings of sowing bountifully. He always amazes me with the harvest. I can testify that there is no way to out-give Him. I challenge you to try.

JULY 21 THE GREATER MEASURE

Key Verse: *"...He that giveth, let him do it with liberality" (Romans 12:8).*

Message: I used this verse earlier, but I believe there is something else very important for us to see. King David was one of those people who exemplified the greater measure of the gift of giving. He so wanted to build the house of the Lord, but God wouldn't let him because he had shed "too much blood." Did David sit down and quit? No! He used his gift of giving. In 1 Chronicles 29:2, he said *"I have made every effort to prepare materials for the temple—gold, silver, bronze, iron, timber...."* Then he used the greater measure of his gift of giving. In 1 Chronicles 29:3 (GN), David said, *"...Over and above all this that I have provided, I have given silver and gold from my personal property because of my love for God's temple."*

David gave "with liberality" to build God's house because he loved the Lord. Can we do less? When God chose David's son Solomon to build the temple, how did David react? He showed us another example of generous giving. 1 Chronicles 28:11 (GN) tells us that *"David gave all the plans for all the Temple buildings..."* to Solomon. May we learn by David's example!

JULY 22   DAVID'S CHALLENGE

Key Verse: *"...Now who else is willing to give a generous offering to the Lord" (1Chronicles 29:5 GN).*

Message: David gave above and beyond; then he challenged the people to do likewise. The result? *"Then the heads of the clans, the officials of the tribes, the commanders of the army, and the administrators of the royal property volunteered to give...."* They gave, and what a happy group of people! Listen to verse 9 (GN): *"The people had given willingly to the Lord, and they were happy that so much had been given. King David also was extremely happy."* But we know that they were not the only ones who were happy because our Lord..."*loveth a cheerful giver"* (2 Corinthians 9:7). In obedience to our Lord, the church to which I belong is in the middle of a building program. Our pastor has echoed David's challenge: *"...who is willing to give a generous offering to the Lord?"* The people in David's day gave. How about you in our day? Will you participate willingly so that more people will be able to know and experience our Lord?

JULY 23   INITIALS IN MY BIBLE

Key Verse: *"...He that giveth, let him do it with liberality (Romans 12:8).*

Message: I'm not quite ready to leave this verse. You will remember that Paul said that some people have a gift and some have a greater amount of that gift. I have a friend who has the greatest amount of the gift of ·giving than any other person I know. I was flipping through Proverbs the other day and saw the initials "R.C." that I had written by the following verses:

- *"The generous soul shall be made prosperous: and he that watereth shall be watered also himself"* (Proverbs 11:25).
- *"He that hath pity upon the poor lendeth unto the Lord, and that which he hath given will he pay him again"* (Proverbs 19:17).
- *"The righteous giveth and spareth not"* (Proverbs 21:26).
- *"He that hath a generous eye shall be blessed for he giveth his bread to the poor"* (Proverbs 22:9).

These verses fit my friend. The ways he thinks up to give are unbelievable. If he could, he would give all the money needed to build the new church. It is a blessing for me to see "R.C." by these verses. Those initials stand for Dr. Roger Collins. May God raise up more like him! Could you be one of them?

I have also written "R.C." by Psalm 37:21 and 26: "...*the righteous showeth mercy and giveth....He is ever merciful and lendeth; and his seed is blessed."* I have also written "Adam" by verse 26. He is Roger's son. How many of you realize that your cheerful giving will bless your children?

JULY 24   PROSPERITY

Key Verse: *"The Lord hath pleasure in the prosperity of his servant"* *(Psalm 36:27).*

Message: When giving becomes your lifestyle, the Lord will sometimes prosper you, because you cannot out-give God. Let me say a couple of things about this:
1. It is all right for you to prosper because it pleases God. That is what the key verse says. I truly believe that our Lord wants you to prosper in this life as well as in the next.
2. It is all right for you to prosper when you keep prosperity in the proper perspective. Psalm 62:10 says, *"...If riches increase, set not your heart upon them."*

But let me hasten to add that there are more important things on which to set your heart. In Colossians 3:2, Paul says, *"Set your affection on things above, not on things on the earth."* In Matthew 6:33, Jesus said, *"But seek ye first the kingdom of God, and his righteousness; and all these things shall be added unto you."*

You know, most people cannot handle wealth. I am one of them, so my prayer is Proverbs 30:8: *"...give me neither poverty nor riches; feed me with food you prescribe for me."* Do you need to pray this prayer?

III I PLANT SEEDS OF FAITH

Two verses have played a part in my learning about planting seeds of faith. One is Galatians 6:7: *"Whatsoever a man soweth, that shall he also reap."* The other is Matthew 17:20: *"Verily I say unto you, if ye have the faith as a grain of mustard seed...."* I will now take you on my seed-faith journey.

JULY 25   THE BEGINNING

Key Verse: *"Whatsoever a man soweth, that shall he also reap"* *(Galatians 6:7). "...A grain of mustard seed...is the least of all seeds; but when it is grown...it becomes a tree..." (Matthew 13:32).*

Message: The Lord laid these verses on my mind when a lady in the class I was teaching at the time had a real need. The thought kept going through my mind, "You have to sow seed if you expect to reap; and if you plant a tiny seed, in faith, you will watch it become a tree. One little seed planted in the earth can bring forth much fruit." My next thought was, "What about one little coin or one little bill planted in the offering plate?"

I went to my class and said, "Ladies, when the offering plate comes by you this morning, I want you to plant a seed of faith for our sister. You may plant a quarter or a dollar or whatever. As you put it into the plate, tell the Lord that you are planting the seed-faith money for our sister and ask Him to bless it to that purpose." Then I said to them, "All next week I am going to ask the Lord to bless that seed so that you will be able to participate in this love gift." Folks, the Lord blessed! One week later these ladies came with their harvest and their testimonies. Both were great. The Lord gave these ladies well over $600 to give to our sister. I will never look at an offering plate the same way again.

God's Word says, *"Upon the first day of the week let every one of you lay by him in store, as God hath prospered him..."* *(1 Corinthians 16:2).* As the offering plate comes by, will you plant God's tithe and your gift into the plate as an act of worship?

JULY 26   EFFECT ON ME

Key Verse: *"Give unto the Lord the glory due his name; bring an offering and come into his courts" (Psalm 96:8).*

Message: One day when I was reading this verse, the Lord convicted my heart: *"bring an offering and come into his (house)."* I had always put my tithe and offering in the plate on Sunday morning, but I didn't stop to think what I was doing. I just wanted to get the plate on by me so that I could hear the special music. But when this verse touched my heart, I realized that the offering plate was not passed by accident. I began to realize that it was passed as part of the worship experience.

    Then something else happened. My Sunday School class planted seeds of faith for our sister. When I saw what God had done, my heart was full and overflowing. And you know, God got my attention with Psalm 96:8 and with the planting for our sister. As a result I promised Him that I would never let an offering plate go by without participating in that part of the worship service—that I would never let an offering plate go by me, Sunday morning, Sunday evening, Wednesday evening without planting some seed-faith money. And I haven't! I want to tell you that my corporate worship has risen to a new level since I endeavored in my heart to worship through offering-plate giving.

    I have planted a seed of faith for many things and for many people. Each time I just say, "Lord, I am planting this seed for ____ __. Please increase it in any way that you see fit." I am thankful for all the victories I have seen in this area.

JULY 27   OTHER EFFECTS

Key Verse: *"Trust in the Lord with all thine heart; and lean not unto thine own understanding. In all thy ways acknowledge him, and he shall direct thy paths (Proverbs 3:5-6).*

Message: I believe that if we meet the first part of these verses, He will direct our path. Let me tell you how I once saw this played out. After my pastor Brother Gerald left our church, the pastor-search committee was formed. We met at my house on Monday evenings.

One evening when we were sitting there, we were concerned because we didn't seem to have a clear direction to pursue. We had about exhausted our list of prospects. Then there was another concern. One of the committee members told us that the church was in financial difficulty and asked if any of us had any ideas of how to get the offering up. I replied, "Well, I can tell you what my Sunday School class just did." He asked, "Would you be willing to present this plan to the church?"

We did one Sunday evening. At the end of the service when the plates were passed, they came back full and running over with coins and bills. There was a great planting of seed that night. Let me tell you what I believe was an immediate result. We made the presentation on a Sunday evening, as I said. On Monday evening at our meeting, we were drawn to Brother Richard's resume'. Jack Jackson, our chairman, began to talk with Brother Richard, and the rest is history. He became our pastor. Another result happened a little over a month later. There was a great harvest. The Lord multiplied that seed into a $117,000 harvest. What a blessing to see God work!

I am thankful that when our church had a need, God's people planted their seed of faith and He gave the increase. I pray that every one of us will be an offering-plate planter.

JULY 28   TWELVE YEARS LATER

Key Verse: *"Now after the death of Moses. . .the Lord spoke unto Joshua,. . .saying,. . .Go over this Jordan, thou, and all this people, unto the land which I do give to them, even to the children of Israel"(Joshua 1:1-2).*

Message: Twelve years after my former class had planted seed faith for our sister and for our church, we began a new study in my current Sunday School class of younger women—many of whom were young wives and mothers. I began the lesson by saying that as the book of Joshua begins, the people were situated on the eastern shore of the Jordan River, ready to enter the promised land. God had given them the land, but they had to possess it.

As I studied this, the Lord began to impress upon my heart that we too had been given land to be used for a new church location, but that we would have to possess it. We would have to take a faith venture. I asked the ladies to do just that. I explained the principal of planting seed faith. Then I gave all the ladies a quarter. I asked them to place the quarter into the offering plate that morning and to plant whatever they could for the next month. I asked them to pray this prayer as they planted: "Lord, I believe you have given us land for our future use. I plant this seed in faith, asking you to take it and multiply it and make it possible for me to have a part in claiming the land."

Then I told them that God would choose how He would multiply their seed of faith, that he might choose to send unexpected money, impress them to use entertainment money, let them have some of their grocery money left over, impress them to get a part-time job, etc. I told them specifically not to ask their husbands for any money. I left the ladies that morning with these words. "I believe the Lord wants to make the first payment on the land through us. Let's be faithful to plant our seeds of faith."

They were, and the Lord was. On harvest day the Lord gave through these special ladies over six thousand dollars. We presented this same appeal to the whole church family. I asked every person to plant seed. I said to the children and the youth, "Do not ask your parents for money." I said to the women, "Do not ask your husbands for money. Make this a personal journey of faith." They did, and God blessed. On harvest day, the Lord gave through these dear people $167,000. What a day!!!

We know that our Lord is rich. Haggai 2:8 comes to my mind: *"The silver is mine, and the gold is mine, saith the Lord!"* He has the wealth of the whole world in His hand, and I knew that He would give us from His bountiful supply the money to pay for the new land and the new facility if we would just take a faith venture with Him. We are on the land and in the building. Praise His holy name.

JULY 29   A TESTIMONY
Key Verse: *"...and test me now herewith, saith the Lord of Hosts, if I will not pour you out a blessing..." (Malachi 3:10).*

Message: This verse fits the testimony I am going to share with you. I asked my friend, Becky if she would allow me to share her seed-faith testimony. She agreed and gave me her journal in which she had written it. She was in my class when we planted seed for the land. I will now quote from her journal:

"Today, March 21, 2000, I celebrate my miracle from planting seed faith. I want to give God all the glory for being my great provider. Our family has been challenged through our finances lately. Bill's job has been harder in the financial area. A few weeks ago Miss Nan taught our class a special lesson on Joshua and how to claim the land. She challenged us to begin planting a seed-faith offering and to seek God in giving a special offering toward our new land (for our church). Bill and I have planted a seed-faith offering each Sunday morning and evening. Last night I asked the Lord to wake me up for my quiet time. He did. Little did I know, this same morning Miss Nan was praying and asking God to give Bill and me a miracle to show that the Lord is our provider.... Later that day I began to go through our bills while I was on the phone with my friend, Rene. I opened a bill—thinking it was a late notice—but instead, it was a totally unexpected check for $835. I screamed in Rene's ear, 'I just got my seed-faith harvest money!'... One of my first thoughts was, 'How much do I give?' I believe if I had not been in the middle of this planting season, my focus would have been, 'What can I pay off or buy?' I praise the Lord. To Him be glory!"

Here is Becky's prayer from her journal: "Lord, I pray my heart will be now: 'what can I give, not what I can buy.' I praise you Jesus. You are my rock and my redeemer. Jesus is Lord!"

Note: God has been faithful to Bill and Becky. He has allowed them to be partners in a special company. God honors faithfulness.

JULY 30   FROM A MOTHER AND A DAUGHTER
Key Verse*: "...God loveth a joyful giver" (2 Corinthians 9:7).*

Message: Here is a testimony from Dana, another lady—a mother—who was in my class. I think her testimony shows that God has a sense of humor. Dana loves chicken salad from the Beagle Bagel. All month (when we were planting seed), she craved that chicken salad, but she felt the Lord telling her to eat at home and put that money in her little bank for harvest day. Well, she went to a planning meeting for Vacation Bible School. Guess what was on the menu? Chicken salad from the Beagle Bagel!

She was obedient, and God blessed. Now I want to share another testimony from Emily, Dana's daughter. I just love it when children participate in what the church is doing. Emily was nine at the time. She received $50 from her grandmother for Valentine's Day. She told her mother that she didn't usually get money from her grandmother for Valentine's Day, so this must be her harvest money. She gave it all. That blessed my heart.

Dana teaches Emily and Graham, her son, what our Lord has taught her, and they have received seed-faith blessings. I don't know anyone else who has depended on our Lord more than Dana. Here are a couple of verses that describe her: *"...in his word do I hope" (Psalm 30:5). "...thy word hath given me life" (Psalm 119:50).* Do these verses describe you? I pray that they do. If not, claim them today.

JULY 31   CHILDREN

Key Verse: *"Lo, children are a heritage of the Lord..." (Psalm 127:3).*

Message: Once people have learned seed-faith planting, many of them don't just practice it during a campaign. Let me tell you how this is demonstrated in the births of two precious children. The first is Jack. One evening Crull and Ashley were at my house. The subject of their having a baby came up. We discussed the financial and other adjustments that a baby brings. Then Ashley said, that for the first time, she felt the Lord was telling her that it was time to have a baby. She and the Lord were right. She was soon pregnant. I told her that I would begin planting a seed of faith for them. She said that she would also.

This is the prayer I prayed before the offering plate came my way the first day and many others. "Lord, Ashley felt that you were impressing on her heart that the time had come for her to have a baby. She was obedient, and little Jack is on the way. Lord, when you placed him in her womb, you had a plan for his life, and that includes how he is to be cared for when he arrives. I plant this seed of faith asking you to make your plan known when the time is right. Until then, we will practice Philippians 4:6-7."

Note: Jack has been here for over six years and is being well cared for. He is truly *"a heritage of the Lord."*

The second child is Hannah. Marsha and Don wanted another child. The years passed, and a baby did not appear. They decided to try adopting. Marsha began to plant a seed of faith. She thought she was planting the mustard seed so that God would multiply it and bring a child into their home. Well, He did, but not in the way she expected. Marsha and Don got the paper work and began the process to adopt; but they put the paper work aside because they found out, to their utter amazement, that Marsha was with child. Soon a precious baby girl with curly red hair graced their home. They named her Hannah. Marsha calls her her mustard-seed child. Praise the Lord! *"He maketh the barren woman to be a joyful mother of children" (Psalm 113:9).* By this verse in my Bible I have written: Marsha, Kayla, and baby Hannah.

I am thankful for the way our Lord brought Hannah into the world. She is a precious child and truly "a heritage of the Lord." I am sure that, just as Hannah in the Bible, who had her child later in life, gave him to the Lord, Marsha and Don have done likewise. They planted a seed at the point of their need. May you learn to do likewise!

Conclusion: Jesus said, *"I am come that they might have life, and that they might have it more abundantly" (John 10:10).* Jesus came to earth so that we might have life and have it in its fullest measure. But this I believe. You might be right in many areas of your walk with the Lord, but you will only know true abundant living when you practice true abundant giving. I close with these words from a song, "Little Is Much When God Is In It," written by my friend Doris Evans.

> "Oh may we know the joy of giving!
> From want the widow gave her mite.
> So small to all except the Master.
> It was the best gift in His sight."

August

GLEANINGS FROM PRAYERS IN THE BIBLE

I do not want you to get the wrong idea about what I am about to share. I <u>do</u> want you to know that I pray the armor prayer before I get out of bed every morning, and I <u>do</u> want you to know that I pray in my quiet time every morning. *"But unto thee have I cried, O Lord; and in the <u>morning</u> shall my prayer prevent thee (come before thee)" (Psalm 88:13).* These two morning prayer times are "absolutes."

However, I am going to admit to you that praying is not always easy for me. I sometimes doze off when I am putting on the armor, but God always wakes me up at the point that I left off. I will also admit to you that it is easy for me to read God's Word in my quiet time, but not so easy to stay on track with my praying. I sometimes get distracted when someone else is in the house with me or when my mind wanders all over the place. At times I do not know how to pray. Others have admitted to me that there are occasions when they find it hard to pray—times when they are hurting so badly because of some tragic personal experience or even when they are feeling so great because of some wonderful personal experience.

I am sure that most of you will agree that we need help with our prayer lives and that the best place to get that help is the Bible. I began to look at prayers in the Word of God and have received encouragement. I believe you can also. Therefore, this month will focus on what I have gleaned from prayers in the Bible.

AUGUST 1   PRAYER OF A THIEF

Key Verse: *"And he said unto Jesus, Lord, remember me when thou comest into thy kingdom" (Luke 23:41).*

Message: Two thieves hung on crosses, one on the left and one on the right of Jesus. One hurled insults at Him; the other answered those railings with, "Our punishment is right; we are getting what we deserve, but He has done nothing wrong."

Then the thief turned and cast himself on Jesus' mercy and spoke to Him in prayer: *"Remember me when thou comest into thy kingdom."* He wanted to be remembered when Jesus set up His earthly kingdom in the future. But Jesus said to him, "You will not have to wait that long. *'Today thou shalt be with me in paradise'"* *(Luke 23:43).*

In his book, <u>Saving a Fallen World</u>, Michael Bentley quotes Bishop Ryle who sums up this event with these words: "The dying thief was never baptized, belonged to no visible church, and never received the Lord's Supper. But he repented and believed, and therefore he was saved."

This man was saved at the last minute. He was the only one in the Bible who was saved on his death bed, but he was one. That can bring hope, but it is dangerous to presume that there will be a last-minute opportunity. In 2 Corinthians 6:2, Paul said, *"Behold, now is the accepted time; behold, now is the day of salvation."*

If you have not prayed the sinner's prayer, now is a good time to do so. The following prayer taken from the pamphlet, "God's Greatest Gift," suggests how you might call upon Jesus to save you:

"Dear Jesus, I open the door of my heart to You right now. Please come into my life, forgive me of all my sins and save my soul. Dear Jesus, to the best of my ability, I will live for You and serve You. I promise to make my decision public and to follow you in believer's baptism. Thank you, Dear Jesus, for hearing my prayer and saving my soul. In Jesus' name, Amen."

If you prayed this prayer, you are saved. Now follow Paul's words in Colossians 2:6: *"As ye have therefore received Christ, so walk in him."* Pray that He will guide your steps.

AUGUST 2   PRAYER FOR BLESSING

Key Verse: *"...I will not let thee go, except thou bless me"* (Genesis 32:26).

Message: Let's see what led up to this prayer. Jacob was a scheming, deceiving worldly man, who, on one occasion, *"was left alone..."* (Genesis 32:24). But he was not alone for long. Verse 24 continues *"...and there wrestled a man with him until the breaking of the day."* This *man* was the pre-incarnate Christ. You will notice that the Word does not say that Jacob wrestled with Christ. Rather, it says that Christ wrestled with him. Why? To get Jacob to come to the end of himself and be dependent on God!

The task was not easy. The wrestling match took all night. Jacob would not yield. Verse 25 says, *"And when he saw that he prevailed not against him, he touched the hollow (socket) of Jacob's thigh (hip)...."* With his hip out of joint, Jacob could no longer wrestle. He was helpless. He came to the end of himself.

When Christ Jesus started to leave, Jacob prayed this prayer: *"I will not let thee go, except thou bless me."* He couldn't wrestle any more. He could only cling. And when he did, God answered his prayer and changed his name from Jacob which means "deceiver" to Israel which means "Prince with God."

This change did not happen until Jacob realized his helplessness. The same is true of us. It is only when we realize our helplessness that we are brought to God and really seek His blessing.

There will be times when God will wrestle with you. When He has to put your hip out of joint to bring you to the end of yourself, hold on to the hem of our Lord's garment and pray, *"I will not let thee go, except thou bless me."* He will bless you in His time. Pray for strength to hold on until He does.

AUGUST 3   PRAYER FOR GUIDANCE

Key Verse: *"...shall I go..." (2 Samuel 2:1)?*

Message: 2 Samuel begins with these words: *"And it came to pass after this* (after David had lamented over the deaths of Saul and Jonathan) *that David inquired of the Lord, saying, 'Shall I go up into any of the cities of Judah?' And the Lord said unto him, 'Go up,' And David said, 'Whither shall I go up?' And He said, 'Unto Hebron.' So David went...."*

David felt that it was time to move, but he did something very important before he took the first step:

- He asked the Lord if he were to move.
- He asked the Lord where he should go.

When he got the answer from God, he went. As directed, he went to Hebron where he received the blessing of being anointed king of Judah.

There is a great lesson here. The only time you are to make a move is when God leads—whether it is to another city or state, to a bigger house, to a better job, to a greener pasture, etc. If you make a move for any of these reasons without seeking God, you might be making a mistake.

I know you don't want to make a mistake, so what do you do? First of all, you pray with David, "Shall I go? Where shall I go?" You may not have the answer at this point. What else can you do? I believe the answer is found in Proverbs 3:6: *"In all thy ways acknowledge him, and he shall direct thy paths."*

If you lead the Spirit-filled life wherever you are—at home, at work, at school, at play—our Lord will direct your path. Pray that you will live close to the Lord wherever you happen to be, especially in the hardest place, your home.

AUGUST 4   PAUL'S ADVICE ON PRAYER

Key Verse: *"I exhort therefore, that, first of all, supplications, prayers, intercessions, and giving of thanks, be made for all men"* *(1 Timothy 2:1).*

Message: In this verse Paul tells us some important things about praying. He makes it clear that we are to pray *"for all men"*—for the lost who need to be saved and for the saved who need to be growing.

What does Paul say should be included in our prayers?

1) *Supplications*—specific requests
2) *Prayers*—adoration and worship
3) *Intercessions*—prayers for others
4) *Giving of thanks*—praise and thanksgiving

(These need to be included in all your prayers.)

Now in verse 2, Paul gets specific about those in the "all men" group for whom we are to pray. Let's hear him: *"For kings, and for all men that are in authority...."* Paul gave a message to Titus for the church: *"Remind them to be subject to rulers, to authorities..."* *(Titus 3:1).*

Paul goes on to tell the reason we are to pray for those in authority: *"in order that we may lead a tranquil life in all godliness and dignity"* *(1Timothy 2:2b NAS).* If we are to live a "tranquil life," we must be subject to our Lord and to our leaders.

I'll be honest with you. Until this verse got my attention, I didn't have "rulers" as a priority on my prayer list. I didn't always remember to pray for them. I will also admit that I still am not consistent. Let's all do better. What would our country be like today if all believers prayed for all leaders every day? Tell the Lord that you will be one.

AUGUST 5   JEHOSHAPHAT FOR PROTECTION

Key Verse: *"O our God...We have no might against this great company that cometh against us; neither know we what to do, but our eyes are upon thee" (2 Chronicles 20:12).*

Message: Jehoshaphat was a good king of Judah who brought the *"people back unto the Lord God of their fathers" (2 Chronicles 19:4).*

One day he was told: *"A great multitude is coming against you" (20:2).* Verse 3 says that *"Jehoshaphat feared,"* but he did the right thing. Verse 3 says that he *"set himself to seek the Lord...."* Then he sent out a call for all the people of Judah to come to Jerusalem. They came. Verse 13 says, *"And all Judah stood before the Lord, with their little ones, their wives, and their children."* Jehoshaphat stood before the people and began to pray for protection.

What a wonderful sight! There was a great need, and all the people stood with their leader and prayed. Oh that this were a picture of the Lord's church! Jehoshaphat began his prayer with *"O Lord God of our fathers..." (20:6).* Then he began to recall God's help in the past and to call on His help for the present.

Next came these words in verse 12: *"O our God...We are powerless against this great multitude that is coming against us. We do not know what to do, but our eyes are upon thee."*

Jehoshaphat certainly prayed the right prayer. When you don't know what to do, look up.

This is great advice for an individual and for a church. I recall serving on the pastor search committee. We met in my living room on Monday evenings. When we started, we didn't "know what to do." We didn't know where to start looking for a pastor, but we did know where to put our eyes. Prayer time was special. We didn't just open and close with prayer. Every person on the committee prayed every time we met, and God answered our prayers. He led us to His choice to pastor this church.

And God answered Jehoshaphat's prayer also. All the people were full of joy *"for the Lord had made them to rejoice over their enemies" (20:27).* There is just something special about a praying church. Ask the Lord if He would have you become part of your church's prayer ministry.

AUGUST 6   JOB'S PRIORITIES
Key Verse: *"...Thus did Job continually (regularly)" (Job 1:5).*

Message: What did he do regularly? Let's see. Job 1:1 says, *"There was a man in the land of Uz, whose name was Job...."* He was a very special man. He loved the Lord with all his heart. The last part of verse 1 says that he *"feared God and shunned evil."* He was also a very wealthy man. He had lots of sheep and camels and oxen and female donkeys and a large number of servants. Verse 3 says that he *"was the richest man in the East."*

But his "houses and lands" were not the top priority in his life. His God and his family were. He had seven sons and three daughters. Every week a noon meal was held at each son's house (7 sons), and the daughters were invited. Job was so concerned about his children that he did something special. Verse 5 (GN) says that *"The morning after each feast, Job would get up early and offer sacrifices for each of his children...."*

Men, what are your mornings like? Do you wake up with business on your mind? Do you hurry out of the house to catch a plane or attend a meeting? Is your job your top priority? Or do you do as Job did? I hope so.

However, I am afraid that rising up early and praying for your family is not an "absolute" with many of you. What a difference your home would be if you had that quiet time every day! I urge you to do so and to pray the protective hedge around your children and pray for them to have discernment as they face the temptations of the day.

Men, also teach your children God's Word. Don't leave all the training to your wives. Psalm 78:4 says that you are to *"show to the generation to come the praises of the Lord, and his strength, and his wonderful works that he hath done."* Paul says, *"And ye fathers... bring them* (your children) *up in the nurture and admonition of the Lord" (Ephesians 6:3).* This command will be a lot easier to do if you pray for them every morning. Make it an "absolute" to do so.

AUGUST 7   A SHORT PRAYER

Key Verse: *"...Jehoshaphat cried out, and the Lord helped him..."*
(2 Chronicles 18:31).

Message: King Ahab of the northern kingdom of Israel and King Jehoshaphat of the southern kingdom of Judah were sitting in their royal robes in Ahab's palace. Ahab called about four hundred (false) prophets and asked the question, "Should I go and attack Ramoth, or not?" They all said, "Go! You will win."

However, one true prophet called Micaiah said, *"The Lord has made these prophets of yours lie to you. But he himself has decreed that you will meet with disaster"* (18:22 GN).

Of course, Ahab didn't listen, and he persuaded Jehoshaphat to join him. They got ready to go attack Ramoth. Now notice what sly, conniving Ahab said to Jehoshaphat: *"As we go into battle, I will disguise myself, but you wear your royal garments. So the king of Israel went into battle in disguise"* (18:28).

Well, the king of Syria had told his military commanders not to attack anyone but Ahab. When they saw Jehoshaphat dressed in his kingly robes, they started to attack him, thinking he was Ahab. Notice what happened when the Syrians circled around Jehoshaphat: *"Jehoshaphat cried out, and the Lord helped him; and God moved them to depart from him..."* (18:31). Jehoshaphat prayed. It was a mighty short prayer. *He "cried out."* I don't know what he cried out, but it was enough to get God's attention.

My point is that a prayer doesn't have to be long to be effective. You know that I believe that the morning is the best time for your quiet time. However, I realize that, because of your schedules, some of you cannot have yours until later.

But I do urge you to spend a little time with God before you face your family and your day. A moment alone with our Lord before you face the devil's world will make your day easier. You might not have time to do more than cry out, but cry out!

Make an early-morning visit with our Lord another "absolute" in your life and pray that He will do for you what He did for Jehoshaphat: *"And the Lord helped him and God moved them (his enemies) to depart from him."* By the way, Ahab was wounded and later died. He should have listened to God. Folks, it always pays to do so.

AUGUST 8   PRAY SILENTLY?

Key Verse: *"...and he cast himself down upon the earth, and put his face between his knees" (1 Kings 18:42).*

Message: Elijah told King Ahab that there was going to be a drought in the land and there was. The time came for it to end. 1 Kings 18:1 says that *"After many days the word of the Lord came to Elijah... saying, go, show thyself unto Ahab, and I will send rain upon the earth."* Elijah went and said to Ahab: *"Get thee up, eat and drink; for there is a sound of abundance of rain" (18:41).*

Now notice what Elijah did. James 5:18 says that he prayed. But look what 1 Kings 18:42 says: *"And Elijah went up to the top of Carmel; and he cast himself down upon the earth, and put his face between his knees."* Was he praying? No prayer is recorded, but James says so. I believe he was praying silently.

What about praying silently? Ever so often I am asked this question: "Can the devil read my mind?" I explain that he cannot because he is a created being, an angel, albeit a fallen one. Only the Creator can read your mind. When Jesus healed a paralyzed man, the scribes standing by thought to themselves: *"This man blasphemeth" (Matthew 9:3).* Verse 4 begins, *"And Jesus, knowing their thoughts...."*

Now the question I get when I say that the devil cannot read our minds, is this: "Should we pray silently so that he cannot hear what we pray and attack us?"

My answer is that it is all right to pray silently. Sometimes it is the right way. However, it is equally all right—probably more so—to pray out loud. I am not willing to let the evil one influence my praying. Incidentally, I think about him and talk about him as little as I can. He loves to hear his name. It doesn't easily roll off my tongue. Be very careful about calling anything unpleasant that happens to you a "Satanic attack." Could it be God???

Folks, whether you pray silently or out loud, just be sure to pray today and every day.

AUGUST 9   HEZEKIAH FOR DELIVERANCE

Key Verse: *"Lord, bow down thine ear and hear..." (2 Kings 19:16).*

Message: Sennacherib, king of Assyria, sent a letter to Hezekiah, king of Judah. In essence the message was, "Your God has told you that you will not fall into my hands. Don't be fooled. I've taken every country I've faced. What makes you think you are any different?"

When King Hezekiah got that letter, he did the right thing. He took it to the*" house of the Lord and spread it before the Lord" (19:14).* Then he began to pray: *"O Lord God of Israel...thou art the God, even thou alone, of all the kingdoms of the earth; thou hast made heaven and earth. Lord, bow down thine ear and hear; open thine eyes and see, and hear the words of Sennacherib..." (19: 15-16).* He went on to acknowledge that what the king had said about destroying nations in his path was true.

Then he lifted up the main part of his prayer: *"Now therefore, O Lord our God, I beseech thee, save thou us out of his hand that all the kingdoms of the earth may know that thou art the Lord God, even thou only" (19:19).* The answer came: *"That which thou hast prayed to me against Sennacherib King of Assyria I have heard" (19:20).* And God answered. Jerusalem was saved, but Sennacherib was assassinated.

I believe that Hezekiah's prayer for deliverance has a message for us. He didn't pray that Jerusalem be spared because of its importance or because the temple was there or because his kingship was at risk. No, he prayed for victory so that everyone would know that God, and God alone, had delivered them.

Have there been times that you have prayed for deliverance? Did you make promises such as, "Lord, if you will get me out of this situation, I'll be a better spouse or I'll be a more responsible person or I'll go to church or I'll serve you"? Our prayers for deliverance are usually "I" prayers.

Why not pray like Hezekiah, "Lord, deliver me so that people will know that you are God *'even thou only.'"* As you pray today, acknowledge that you know that all deliverance comes from Him.

AUGUST 10   HEZEKIAH FOR HEALTH
Key Verse: *"...I have heard thy prayer..." (2 Kings 20:5).*

Message: 2 Kings 20 begins, *"In those days was Hezekiah sick unto death."* God sent Isaiah to him with this message: *"...Set thine house in order, for thou shalt die and not live" (20:1).*

Hezekiah began to weep and pray and remind God of how he had *"done that which is good in thy sight" (20:3).* God sent Isaiah back with this message: *"...I have heard thy prayer..." (20:5).* Then He said, "I will heal you and let you live fifteen more years." That sounds like a good thing, doesn't it? Well, let's see. God's perfect will was that it was time for Hezekiah to die; God's permissive will was that he could live fifteen more years. Good idea?

Well, let's see what happened during those fifteen years. The first thing that happened was that he got a visit from some ambassadors of Babylon with a letter and a present from the king. Pumped up with pride, Hezekiah showed them all the gold and silver and armor and *"all that was found in his treasures: there was nothing in his house, nor in his dominion that Hezekiah showed them not" (20:13).*

This action prompted another visit from Isaiah who said in essence, "You just did a no-no. The day is coming when everything you showed those ambassadors will be carried off to Babylon. Nothing will be left." The point is that the information learned by the Babylonian ambassadors would contribute to Jerusalem's eventual capture. Again I ask, "Were fifteen more years a good idea?" I believe not!

Folks, God's perfect will is always best for you. Your will sometimes results in God's permissive will. You may beg Him for something you know is not God's will, and He may let you have it, but you will not have complete happiness living in God's permissive will. He may do with you as He did with the children of Israel when they tempted Him in the desert: *"And he gave them their request; but sent leanness in to their soul" (Psalm 106:15).*

Let me give you an example. In 2 Corinthians 6:14, Paul said, *"Be ye not unequally yoked together with unbelievers...."* You know this is the perfect will of God. You may ask God to partner with an unbeliever in marriage, in business, in friendship, etc. He may allow you to do so as part of His permissive will, but He will send you *"leanness of soul."*

Pray that you will seek and follow God's perfect will for your life.

AUGUST 11   PRAY EARNESTLY

Key Verse: *"Continue in prayer..."* (Colossians 4:1).

Message: Beginning in verse 18 of Colossians 3, Paul gives advice on domestic life. In verse 18, he said, *"Wives, submit yourselves unto your own husbands...."* In verse 19, he said, *"Husbands love your wives...."* In verse 20, he said, *"Children, obey your parents...."* In verse 21, he said, *"Fathers, provoke not your children to anger...."*

If you look at these commands, I am sure you will agree that not one of them comes easy. That is the reason I believe Paul said to these folks: *"Continue in prayer..." (4:1).* This actually means "persevere in prayer." If you are going to fulfill the commands that apply to you, you are going to need to do some serious praying.

I have found that the more important something is to you, the more time you spend in prayer. This was true in the Bible. When Peter was in prison, a local prayer meeting was held for him. Acts 12:5 says that *"Prayer was made without ceasing of the church unto God for him."* Luke 6:12 says that before Jesus chose the twelve, *"He went out into a mountain to pray, and continued all night in prayer to God."*

Persevere in prayer! Pray without ceasing! Pray all night! Let me ask you this. How important is it to you to be a godly family member? Important enough to persevere in prayer? How much time do you spend praying that you would be a godly person in the role assigned to you? How earnestly do you pray? Your success at home just might depend on the importance you place on praying that you be all God intends you to be as a husband or wife or father or mother or child.

Men, pray that you will be a "Psalm 112" man. Ladies, pray that you might be a "Proverbs 31" lady.

AUGUST 12   PRAY FOR ENEMIES

Key Verse: *"Without any reason they laid a trap for me..."* *(Psalm 35:7 GN)*.

Message: In Psalm 35, David asked God for help with his enemies, and he had a lot of them. In verse 4, he said that there were some men who wanted to kill him. In verse 11, he said that they accused him of crimes about which he knew nothing. In verse 12, he said that they paid him back evil for good. So how did David respond?

Listen to what he said: *"But when they were sick, I dressed in mourning; I deprived myself of food; I prayed with my head bowed low, as I would pray for a friend or a brother (Psalm 35:13-14 GN).* Jesus Himself said, *"...pray for them which despitefully use you and persecute you"* (Matthew 5:44). I am sure you will agree that praying for those who falsely accuse you and persecute you is hard to do.

I mentioned what I was writing for August 12 to my friend Doris Evans. She said to me, "My dad always prayed for those who 'despitefully use us and persecute us.'" She said that she didn't understand why he did this until she matured more in her faith, and I believe I have grasped what Doris has come to know. I began to think about her dad, Mr. Gunn; He was a godly man. Most people would pray this prayer to get relief from the persecution through which they were going. I don't believe Mr. Gunn did. I believe he followed all of Matthew 5:44: *"But I say unto you, love your enemies, bless them that curse you, do good to them that hate you, and pray for them which despitefully use you, and persecute you."*

I believe Doris' dad lived verse 44 and that he did so for one reason: in order to win these folks over to Jesus. Oh, that we had more men like Mr. Gunn!

Pray that you will do what our Lord said and act as David and Mr. Gunn did.

AUGUST 13   PRAYER OF A PROPHET

Key Verse: *"Yet I will rejoice in the Lord; I will joy in the God of my salvation" (Habakkuk 3:18).*

Message: God gave Judah chance after chance to turn back to Him from idol worship, but they would not. As a result, their fate was to go into Babylonian captivity. God chose Babylon to punish Judah. Habakkuk was deeply disturbed by the violence of these pagan Babylonian people, so he went to God with his concerns.

Now let me make one thing clear. Habakkuk loved God. He began his prayer; *"Lord, from the beginning you are God. You are my God, holy and eternal. Lord my God and protector, you have chosen the Babylonians and made them strong so that they can punish us" (1:12 GN).* After professing that God was his God and protector, Habakkuk questioned God: *"How can you stand these treacherous, evil men?.... Why are you silent while they destroy people who are more righteous than they are" (1:13 GN)?*

Habakkuk just couldn't understand why bad things happen to good people. He went to the right place for his answer, to Holy God, who said to him in essence, "Evil people will not survive; the righteous will live." However Habakkuk had to hear what we do not want to hear: *"...What I show you will come true. It may seem slow in coming, but wait for it; it will certainly take place" (2:3 GN).*

I am sure there are times when you feel like questioning God. If you are going to do so, make sure you, like Habakkuk, love God, know that He is always good, and that He makes no mistakes. You may not get your answer immediately, but hang on to the hem of His garment until the answer comes and be prepared to accept God's answer, whatever it may be.

Then take 3:17-18 as your very own testimony: *"Although the fig tree shall not blossom, neither shall fruit be in the vines; the labor of the olive shall fail, and the fields shall yield no food; the flock shall be cut off from the fold, and there shall be no herd in the stalls, yet I will rejoice in the Lord; I will joy in the God of my salvation."*

Pray with Isaiah: *"I will greatly rejoice in the Lord; my soul shall be joyful in my God..." (Isaiah 61:10).*

AUGUST 14 SECRET SINS

Key Verse: *"Direct my steps in thy word, and let not any iniquity have dominion over me"* *(Psalm 119:133).*

Message: David knew the importance of knowing and obeying the Scriptures. In Psalm 19:11, he said, *"By them is thy servant warned; and in keeping them there is great reward."*

He knew, from the Scripture, the importance of praying that sin not have dominion over him, particularly secret sin. In verse 12, he prayed, *"Cleanse thou me from secret faults."* His prayer was that he be kept from hidden sins. In this Psalm, David is asking the Lord to keep him from saying or doing anything that would cause him to try to hide a sin.

Then in verse 14, he prays about the thoughts in his head and the words from his mouth. This man after God's own heart prays that he may be acceptable to the Lord and his thoughts might be pleasing to God; *"Let the words of my mouth, and the meditation of my heart, be acceptable in thy sight, O Lord, my strength and my redeemer."*

Can you pray the prayer of Psalm 119 with David? I hope so. I pray that you do not have any secret sins. Actually, you don't. I know One who sees them. In Psalm 90:8 (GN) we read, *"You place our sins before you, our secret sins, where you can see them."* If you do have a sin that is secret from everyone but God, listen carefully to Proverbs 28:13: *"He that covereth his sins shall not prosper: But whoso confesseth and forsaketh them shall have mercy."*

With this is mind, I hope that you can pray with David: *"I acknowledged my sin unto thee, and mine iniquity have I not hid. I said, I will confess my transgressions unto the Lord; and thou forgavest the iniquity of my sin"* (Psalm 32:5).

If you are walking around with secret sin in your life, confess it and forsake it. There is mercy with the Lord.

AUGUST 15   THOUGHTS

Key Verse: *"How precious are thy thoughts..." (Psalm 139:17).*

Message: What kind of thought life do you have? I am sure that things creep into your mind that you would not dare utter to anyone, but there is One who knows your thoughts. In Psalm 94:11, we read, *"The Lord knoweth the thoughts of man...."* In Psalm 139:2, David prayed, *"O Lord, ...thou understandest my thought afar off."* He knows all your thoughts. He even knows when your thoughts are rebellious toward Him.

What kinds of thoughts does our Lord have toward you? David tells us in Psalm 139:17-18: *"How precious are thy thoughts unto me, O God! How great is the sum of them! If I could count them, they are more in number than the sand."* In Psalm 40:5, David prayed that if he were to declare and speak of our Lord's thoughts toward us, *"they are more than can be numbered."*

Have you ever stopped to think that our Lord thinks about us all the time and that He only thinks "precious" thoughts? Many times ours are not precious at all. In fact, ours are often thoughts of greed and lust and anger and revenge and a lot of other things we would not voice.

Now, in lieu of the fact that our Lord knows all our thoughts and that He thinks only good things about us, shouldn't we work on our thought life?

I have a verse for you to learn. When you start to have unhealthy thoughts, force yourself to quote Paul's words to the Philippians: *"...Whatsoever things are true, whatsoever things are honest, whatsoever things are just, whatsoever things are lovely, whatsoever things are of good report; if there be any virtue, and if there be any praise, <u>think on these things</u>" (Philippians 4:8).*

As you learn to redirect your thoughts, you will be ready to pray with David: *"Search me, O God, and know my heart; try me, and know my thoughts" (Psalm 139:23).*

AUGUST 16   CORNELIUS

Key Verse: *"...Thy prayers and thine alms are come up..." (Acts 10:4).*

Message: Cornelius was a religious man who responded to all the light that he had. Acts 10:2 says that he was *"a devout man, and one that feared God with all his house, which gave much alms to the people, and prayed to God always."* Cornelius was a remarkable person. He revered God; he was the spiritual leader of his household; he gave to the needy; he prayed very often. According to verse 30, he also fasted.

Because Cornelius lived up to the light he had, God saw that he got introduced to the Light of the World. An angel paid Cornelius a visit and said to him. *"Thy prayers and thine alms are come up for a memorial before God."* The result was that Peter was sent to him.

Peter asked, "Why have you sent for me?" His answer was, "The angel told me to send for you." But before Cornelius gave his reply, he repeated the message of the angel: *"Thy prayer is heard, and thine alms are remembered in the sight of God" (Acts 10:31).*

Now, what struck me were the two things that got God's ear: Cornelius' prayers and his giving. Does this give you an idea about how God feels about giving? It obviously pleases Him. How do you feel about giving? I hope it pleases you. Let me share with you some good advice: *"Every man according as he purposeth in his heart, so let him give, not grudgingly, or of necessity; for God loveth a cheerful giver" (2 Corinthians 9:7).*

Giving depends on the condition of the heart. Pray that your heart is so right with the Lord that you give joyfully and to the right place: *"Bring ye all the tithes into the storehouse..." (Malachi 3:10).* Don't ever get into this conversation with our Lord: *"...Ye have robbed me. But ye say, wherein have we robbed thee? In tithes and offerings" (Malachi 3:8).*

Let me leave you today with this promise: *"He that hath a bountiful (generous) eye shall be blessed..." (Proverbs 22:9).*

AUGUST 17   WHEN THE CHURCH PRAYS

Key Verse: *"...Prayer was made without ceasing..." (Acts 12:5).*

Message: At a time when there was great famine in the land, King Herod began to harass certain followers of Jesus. Acts 12:2 says, *"He killed James, the brother of John with the sword."* James was the first disciple to be martyred; Herod intended for Peter to be the second. However, he decided to wait until after Passover to do away with Peter, so he had Peter put in prison and had four soldiers to guard him at all times.

Acts 12:5 says, *"Peter therefore was kept in prison: but prayer was made without ceasing of the church unto God for him."* Now, sometimes we get after the people at the prayer meeting for their lack of faith when Peter stood at the door, and rightly so; but we need to commend them for praying *"without ceasing."*

I believe that what happened to Peter was a result of their prayers. They didn't realize it at the time, but God began to answer their prayers while Peter was asleep in his jail cell. How? Well, when Herod *"would have brought him forth, the same night Peter was sleeping between two soldiers, bound with two chains; and the guards before the door kept the prison" (12:6).*

There was no human way of escape, but I believe that because the church was praying *"without ceasing,"* God made a way of escape. How? A bright light awakened Peter from a deep sleep. An angel touched him and said, "Get up, get dressed, and follow me." Peter did so. He thought he was having a vision, but he wasn't. They passed the first two guard posts. They reached the main gate. It flew open! The angel departed and Peter walked through, a free man. He said, *"Now I know for certain that the Lord hath sent his angel, and hath delivered me out of the hand of Herod..." (12:11).*

The prayers of the church folks were answered. They didn't know it at the time and couldn't believe it had happened, even when Peter first joined them. But when they realized that Peter was in their midst, there was great rejoicing. The point I want to make is that when the church prays *"without ceasing"* God answers. I believe that whatever the church needs, God will provide if <u>all</u> the church prays *"without ceasing."*

How can this be done? It can be done when every member becomes a part of the Watchman Prayer Ministry (or whatever it is called in your church) that is scheduled 24/7. Do you participate? If not, now is a good time to sign up. Make this a matter of prayer.

AUGUST 18   LEAD ME
Key Verse: *"O send out thy light and thy truth..."* *(Psalm 43:3).*

Message: The writer of this Psalm was having a very difficult time. In verse 1, he prayed, *"O deliver me from the deceitful and unjust man."* In verse 3, he prayed, *"O send out thy light and thy truth: let them lead me...."* His desire was to be led by the light from above as revealed by the Word. In Psalm 119:105, the Psalmist prayed, *"Thy word is a lamp unto my feet, and a light unto my path."* In Psalm 23:3, David says that the Lord *"leadeth me in the paths of righteousness."*

The rest of Psalm 43:3 tells where the Psalmist wants that path to lead him: *"O send out thy light and thy truth: let them lead me; let them bring me unto thy holy hill, and to thy tabernacle."* His desire was to be led to God's house. What would he do when he got there? *"Then I will go to your altar, O God; you are the source of my happiness. I will play my harp and sing praise to you, O God my God"* *(Psalm 43:4 GN).*

Now, if you are having a difficult time, do as the Psalmist did. In essence he prayed, "Lead me to your house, O God, where I will kneel at your altar. I will serve you by playing my harp and singing praises to you."

If you are having a difficult time, follow the path of righteousness to the house of God. Make your way to the prayer altar. Then use your spiritual gift in service and in praise. There is no better place to be when you <u>have</u> a serious need than in God's house. There is no better place to be when you <u>don't have</u> a serious need. There is just something about being with other believers and with Jesus who has promised to be where "two or three are gathered in his name." Attend! Serve! Make both "absolutes" in your life. Pray to this end.

AUGUST 19   DELIVERANCE

Key Verse: *"...You have brought us to a place of safety" (Psalm 66:12 GN).*

Message: In verses 10 and 11 of Psalm 66, the Psalmist prays to God and lays before Him the trials the children of Israel had gone through. He prayed, *"You have put us to the test, God; as silver is purified by fire, so you have tested us. You let us fall into a trap and placed heavy burdens on our backs."*

Can you identify with these people? Have you been tested—been through the fire, fallen into a trap, had heavy burdens on your back? The Psalmist made it through. In verse 12, he prayed, *"But now you have brought us to a place of safety."* I pray that you have made it through and have this testimony. I also pray that you have the next testimony that the Psalmist prayed, *"I will go into thy house with burnt offerings..." (66:13).*

When the Psalmist got victory, he went to God's house; and he brought an offering. When you got victory, what did you do? You might have gone to God's house, but did you bring an offering? Folks, I believe these two go hand-in-hand. You should be so grateful for what our Lord has done for you that you show your gratitude by going to His house and by being a "hilarious" giver.

And by the way, the Psalmist added, *"I will give you what I said I would when I was in trouble" (66:14 GN).* Be sure that you do likewise!

Ask the Lord to help you be right in your pocketbook. Don't go to God's house empty-handed.

AUGUST 20   THE HOLY SPIRIT AND PRAYER

Key Verse: *"...But the Spirit itself maketh intercession for us..." (Romans 8:26).*

Message: In Romans 8:26, Paul says, *"...We know not what we should pray for as we ought...."* Sometimes we just have to tell God, "I just don't know how to pray about this situation." You might not, but the right prayer still goes up to God. How does it get there? The Holy Spirit takes it. When you confess your weakness, the Holy

Spirit takes over. Verse 26 begins. *"The Spirit helpeth our infirmities (our weaknesses)."* It ends with *"...but the Spirit itself maketh intercession for us with groanings which cannot be uttered."* We cannot hear what he is praying, but he is praying the right way for you. How do I know this?

Verse 27 begins, *"And he that searcheth the hearts...."* Who is this? Let's let the Scripture tell us. 1 Chronicles 28:9 says, *"...for the Lord searcheth all hearts...."* It is God who searches our hearts, and He knows the *"mind of the Spirit."* When you don't know how to pray, the Holy Spirit *"maketh intercession for us according to the will of God" (8:27).*

The Holy Spirit knows the will of God, and that is the prayer he takes from your "I-don't-know-how-to-pray" prayer to the throne of grace.

When you don't know how to pray, ask the Holy Spirit to take your prayer to the Lord the way it should be prayed, and you keep on praying until your prayer lines up with what the Holy Spirit prays and our Father receives.

AUGUST 21   WHEN TO PRAY

Key Verse: *"And He spake a parable unto them to this end, that men ought always to pray, and not to faint (lose heart)" Luke 18:1).*

Message: The point of the key verse is that when we are tempted to say, "What's the use?" we ought to be resolved in our hearts to keep praying. Paul said in 1Thessalonians 5:17: *"Pray without ceasing."*

Obviously, we cannot stay in the prayer closet all the time. So what does Paul mean? He means that we are to stay in an attitude of prayer. To me that means that when a person comes to my mind, I should pray for him. To me this also means that if I wake up thinking of someone, I am to pray for him. In other words, we should always be ready to pray.

But we must also have regularly scheduled times to pray. When King Darius was tricked into signing a decree that all who bowed before any god or man beside the king for thirty days should be cast in the lions' den, did that stop Daniel from praying? No!

When he heard about the decree, he went home, opened his windows toward Jerusalem, and *"kneeled upon his knees three times a day, and prayed, and gave thanks before his God as he had been doing before this" (Daniel 6:10).* In Psalm 55:17, David said, *"Evening, and morning, and at noon, will I pray...."* When I think of praying "three times a day" or "evening and morning and noon," I think of meal-time prayers, which I hope are a pattern at your house.

But I also believe that at least once a day we should spend some serious time in prayer. As you know, I believe the morning is the best time; but you have to make the choice. Just make this time alone with the Lord an "absolute." Ask the Lord to remind you of your daily date with Him.

AUGUST 22   THE MOUTH
Key Verse: *"Set a watch, O Lord, before my mouth; keep the door of my lips" (Psalm 141:3).*

Message: This verse is a prayer we should pray more often but probably pray less often. Why is it so important for us to pray that our mouths be bridled? James 3:8 gives the answer: *"But the tongue can no man tame; it is an unruly evil, full of deadly poison."* In short, you cannot control your tongue. How often has something slipped out of your mouth that you wished you could take back? Rather often, I am sure!

Well, since you cannot control your tongue, you must pray that the Lord will set a watch over your mouth and ask the Holy Spirit to guide your tongue. Do you know that there are benefits to you if you do just this? There are. Listen to some of them:
- Proverbs 12:18: *"...the tongue of the wise promotes health."*
- Proverbs 13:3: *"He that guardeth his mouth preserves his life...."*
- Proverbs 15:2: *"The tongue of the wise uses knowledge rightly...."*

One of the best ways I know to be healthy and wise is to let the Holy Spirit control the words that come out of your mouth.

I suggest that you move this prayer of David to the top ten on your prayer list: *"Set a watch, O Lord, before my mouth; keep the door of my lips" (Psalm 141:3).* By the way, do you need a proverb for today? Listen to this one: *"If you want to stay out of trouble, be careful what you say" (Proverbs 21:23 GN).*

AUGUST 23   GOD'S GRACE
Key Verse: *"...I besought the Lord thrice..." (2 Corinthians 12:8).*

Message: Paul was given the rare privilege of being lifted to Paradise where he saw sights too wonderful to describe. In 2 Corinthians 12:7, he told the Corinthians that to keep him from boasting about his experience *"to me was given a thorn in the flesh, the messenger of Satan to buffet me, lest I should be exalted above measure."* We cannot know for sure what that thorn was; but whatever the case, it was a tool of the devil. It was painful to Paul, so what did he do? He prayed.

He said, *"For this thing I pleaded with the Lord three times that it might depart from me" (12:8).* Three times he prayed, "Lord please take this thorn away." But we know that was not God's will. In verse 9, God said to Paul: *"My grace (my unmerited favor) is sufficient for thee: for my strength is made perfect in weakness."* In essence God said, "Paul, my grace is all you need, for my power is strongest when you are weakest."

That answer stopped Paul from praying for the thorn to be removed. Instead, he said, "If that is the case, I am content with my weakness and whatever other difficulties I face for Christ's sake *'for when I am weak, then I am strong'" (12:10).* The lesson the Lord has here is this: The weaker a person is, the more clearly God's grace shines forth!

Have you a thorn that you asked God to remove, but He didn't do so? How did you react when it didn't go away? Did you become bitter? Did you give up? Did you complain? Did you get depressed? I hope not. I pray that you reacted as Paul did. He did not allow the thorn in his flesh to interfere with his ministry. He relied on God's grace to help him accomplish what he was sent to earth to do.

Pray that you will do likewise. Rely on that "marvelous grace of our loving Lord."

AUGUST 24   PRAYER FOR CLEANSING

Key Verse: *"...Create in me a clean heart, O God, and renew a right spirit within me" (Psalm 51:10).*

Message: Psalm 51 was written sometime after David's sin with Bathsheba. Surely, David was not perfect; but he was more sorrowful for his sins than any other person I can think of in the Bible. He pleaded with God for forgiveness.

He began the Psalm with this prayer: *"Have mercy upon me, O God, according unto the multitude of thy tender mercies, blot out my transgressions. Wash me thoroughly from mine iniquity, and cleanse me from my sin. For I acknowledge my transgressions..." (Psalm 51:1-3a).* Here David, a broken-hearted man, confessed his sin.

Then he prayed for inner renewal. In verse 7, he prayed, *"Purge me with hyssop, and I shall be clean; wash me and I shall be whiter than snow."* Then in verse 10, he prayed, *"...Create in me a clean heart, O God, and renew a right spirit within me."*

After David acknowledged his sins and prayed for inner renewal, he told God what he would do when he was restored: *"Then will I teach transgressors thy ways; and sinners shall be converted unto thee (51:13).* In verse 14, he prayed, *"Deliver me... O God... and my tongue shall sing aloud of thy righteousness."* In essence he promised God that if he were delivered, he would offer praise and would perform service.

Was David's prayer answered? Oh, yes, it was! He went on to serve God in a mighty way. He is a good example of the principle that those who fail God may be restored to service.

If you have sinned and feel that God cannot use you again, think of David. If you acknowledge your sin and ask to be cleansed from it, God will forgive you and restore you to service. Truly, God is the God of the second chance. If you need one, ask Him for it.

AUGUST 25   CONSISTENT PRAYER

Key Verse: *"... (He) maketh his petition three times a day" (Daniel 6:13).*

Message: The key men in King Darius' government hated Daniel because the king favored him and was about to set him over all the realm.

These men vowed to get rid of Daniel, but they couldn't find any fault with him. They determined that the only way they could do away with him was to find something *"against him concerning the law of his God" (6:5).* They tricked the king into putting out a decree to the effect that all who bowed to anyone other than the king for thirty days would be put into the lion's den. Then they rushed to Daniel's house, hid in the bushes, and spied. Sure enough, they caught Daniel praying.

Off they ran to the king and said, *"That Daniel...regardeth not thee, O king, nor the decree that thou hast signed, but maketh his petition three times a day" (6:13).* The king loved Daniel and did not want him to be thrown into the lion's den, but he could not free Daniel because the law of the Medes and the Persians could not be changed.

Thus, verse 16 says, *"Then the king commanded and they brought Daniel, and cast him into the den of lions."* Daniel did not utter one word. He didn't make excuses, give reasons why he didn't deserve to go there, or ask to be spared. He just went. Why didn't he protest? *"...because he believed in his God" (6:23).* The outcome was in God's hands. As we know, he came out unhurt.

The point I got from this is that consistent prayer causes you to believe in your God—that He makes no mistakes. I am not talking about occasional praying or even most-of-the-time praying. I am talking about being alone with God in prayer every day, no matter what. Every day! In the good times and the bad! It is in your prayer closet that you grow in your relationship with our Lord. It is in your prayer closet that you learn to "believe in your God" and know that He works out everything for your good and His glory. Is daily prayer an "absolute" in your life? If not, make it one and see what God will do.

AUGUST 26　　MORE ON CONSTANT PRAYER

Key Verse: *"...our God whom we serve is able to deliver us..."* *(Daniel 3:17).*

Message: I decided to continue with this theme of consistent prayer because I do not believe that Shadrach, Meshach, and Abednego could have taken the stand they did had consistent prayer not been an "absolute" in their lives. Here is the situation.

King Nebuchadnezzar built a huge golden image of himself and invited all the important people in his kingdom to come to a dedication service. When they got there, they soon learned that the king had a different reason for assembling them. They heard this command: *"When the music plays, 'fall down and worship the golden image that Nebuchadnezzar the king has set up'" (3:5).* Then came the consequences of disobedience: "If you do not bow, you will be thrown into a fiery furnace." Immediately, everyone fell on his face, except the three Hebrew children.

To them the king said, "I'll give you one more chance; but if you do not bow, you will be cast into the fiery furnace." To the king these three said something I do not believe anyone could have said had he not had a consistent prayer life. Listen to them:

"If it be so, our God whom we serve is able to deliver us from the burning fiery furnace, and he will deliver us out of thine hand, O king. But if not, be it known unto thee, O king, that we will not serve thy gods, nor worship the golden image which thou has set up" (Daniel 3:17-18).

They proclaimed that God was able to deliver them; but if he chose not to, they still would not bow. They didn't bend; they didn't bow; and as a result, they didn't burn. The evil one had no victory over them.

Folks, a consistent prayer life will be your help when you face a major challenge from the world. It is here that you will find the strength to take the first step—not to bend—that will keep you from experiencing the next two. Our God is "able" to deliver you. Be consistent in your prayer life, and He will in His own way and in His own time deliver you.

AUGUST 27   SPEAK BOLDLY

Key Verse: *"...that with all boldness they may speak thy word"* (Acts 4:29).

Message: Peter and John were brought before the religious leaders because they were boldly preaching Jesus, whom the leaders hated. They couldn't do away with the two disciples for fear of the people, so they *"commanded them not to speak at all nor teach in the name of Jesus" (Acts 4:18)* and let them go. After replying, *"For we cannot but speak the things which we have seen and heard" (4:20),* Peter and John went to join their company and told them what the chief priests had said.

When the people heard the report, *"they lifted up their voice to God with one accord, and said, Lord, thou art God..." (4:24).* In verse 29 they prayed, *"And now, Lord, behold their threatenings: and grant unto thy servants, that with all boldness they may speak thy word."* Truly, they did speak the Word of God with boldness.

I really believe we need to pray this prayer because of the command found in 1 Peter 3:15: *"Sanctify the Lord thy God in your hearts: and be ready always to give an answer to every man that asketh you a reason of the hope that is in you...."*

Peter says that we are to be ready at all times to share Jesus with anyone who asks us why we are Christians. Can you do that? I suggest you put your answer down on paper. Even then, it is sometimes hard for many of us to share. Since this is true, I suggest that you prepare your testimony and pray daily that *"with all boldness"* you may share Jesus. Pray for holy boldness!

AUGUST 28   THE WORD

Key Verse: *"...thy word is truth" (John 17:17).*

Message: John 17 is called the high priestly prayer of our Lord Jesus. In it He prayed for Himself, then for His disciples, and then for all who would believe as a result of their testimony. This number includes all, who throughout the centuries, until the end of time, shall believe on Him. You and I are in this group.

I believe that something He prayed for His apostles is very important for us also. In John 17:8, He prayed, *"For I have given them the <u>words</u> which thou gavest me."* In verse 14, He prayed, *"I have given them thy <u>word</u>."* In verse 17, he prayed, *"Sanctify"* (set apart for the Father's service) *them through thy truth: thy <u>word</u> is truth.*

What do these verses say about God's Word? They say that God gave the Word to Jesus, and Jesus gave it to His followers. Verse 17 says that the *"Word is truth."* Folks, the Bible is the inerrant, infallible Word of God. It truly contains no errors. Every word of it is true. Paul says in 2 Timothy 3:16: *"All scripture is given by inspiration of God, and is profitable for doctrine, for reproof, for correction, for instruction in righteousness."*

Here, Paul is saying that God has given us His perfect Word, and in that Word is everything we need in order to live the Christian life. How well do you know God's Word? Study it daily; meditate on it; memorize it.

Teach your children to memorize it. One of the joys of my life is to have a child come up to me and say, "I have a verse for you." Teach your children to hide God's Word in their hearts and pray that the Word might come to their minds when they are tempted to sin. Psalm 119:9 (GN) says this: *"How can a young man keep his life pure? By obeying your commands."* One can only obey what he knows. Be sure that everyone in your house can pray: *"Thy word is a lamp unto my feet, and a light unto my path"* (Psalm 119:105).

AUGUST 29   THAT THE WORLD MAY KNOW

Key Verse: *"Neither pray I for these alone* (His disciples), *but for them also which shall believe on me through their word"* (John 17:20).

Message: In His high priestly prayer, Jesus prayed for us after He had prayed for Himself and His disciples. What did He pray for us? In verses 21 through 23, He prayed for us to have spiritual unity. What was His reason for praying for us to have spiritual unity with our brothers?

He tells us in verse 21: *"...that the world may believe that thou hast sent me."* He repeats this in verse 23. In Matthew 28:19-20, Jesus gave us the Great Commission: *"Go ye therefore, and teach all nations, baptizing them in the name of the Father and of the Son, and of the Holy Ghost; teaching them to observe all things whatsoever I have commanded you: and lo, I am with you alway, even unto the end of the world."*

Here is the lesson I see here. We are commanded to go to the world with the message of Jesus Christ, but the world will only believe us if we are all one in the Spirit—that we tell the same story. What is that story? Here it is.

Jesus left His throne in glory, covered His deity with humanity, walked among men, taught and healed, suffered false accusations, died on a cross for our sins, rose from the dead, and returned to His rightful place in heaven. Today He is at the right hand of the Father, calling out a people to His name and interceding for us. One day He will come for us *"that where I am, there ye may be also" (John 14:2).* We are to be in one accord *"that the world may believe that thou hast sent me."*

AUGUST 30   THAT WHERE I AM

Key Verse: *"Father, I will that they also, whom thou has given me, shall be with me where I am" (John 17:24).*

Message: We have been talking about Jesus' high priestly prayer. One thing He prayed for us concerns our future. What does it hold in store for us? We get the answer in 17:24: *"Father, I will that they also, whom thou hast given me, shall be with me where I am...."* Please get this. Jesus wants us to be where He is. He is in heaven. Heaven would be incomplete for us without Jesus. We can be sure of this.

But the opposite is also equally true. Heaven is incomplete for Jesus without us. He promised in John 14:2-3: *"In my Father's house are many mansions; if it were not so, I would have told you. I go to prepare a place for you. And if I go and prepare a place for you, I will come again and receive you unto myself; that where I am, there ye may be also."* Here in John 17:24, He restates this:

"Father, I will that they also, whom thou hast given me, shall be with me where I am."

Can you grasp that heaven is incomplete for Jesus without us? If so, you can understand Psalm 116:15: *"Precious in the sight of the Lord is the death of his saints."* Our Lord is looking forward to our coming home. Why? What reason does He give? *"...that they may behold my glory, which thou hast given me..." (17:24).*

Jesus wants us to see Him in all of His glory. He wants us to see Him as He really is in all of His whiteness and brightness. Folks, beholding Him in all of His glory is awaiting us. Lord, hasten the day!

AUGUST 31   MY PRAYER
Key Verse: *"...I give myself unto prayer" (Psalm 109:4).*

Message: Why is it so important for us to give ourselves to prayer? In a recent Watchman Prayer guide, Brother John quoted from a book by Dr. Gregory R. Frizzell entitled, How to Develop A Powerful Prayer Life. I believe this quotation from his book answers the question:

"Prayer is the heart and soul of every successful relation-ship with God. In fact, prayer is absolutely crucial to every area of a believer's life. To illustrate the point, consider the following questions. How did you receive Christ as your Lord and Savior? How do you abide in Christ and allow Him to live His life through you? How do you grow as a Christian? How do you overcome temptation and weakness? How do you resist Satan and wage effective spiritual warfare? How do you confess your sins? How are you filled with the Holy Spirit? How do you obtain guidance and wisdom from God? How do you experience the power to serve God effectively? The answer to every single question is prayer.

"In view of the awesome importance of prayer, I confi-dently make the following statement. 'No one's relation-ship with Christ will ever rise above the level of his or her praying.' Put simply, if your prayer life is inconsistent and weak, so will be your relationship with God! But take heart, dear friend, you can develop a dynamic prayer life. And when you learn to walk in powerful daily prayer, God will transform your entire life."

Let me repeat one thing Dr. Frizzell said, "No one's relationship with Christ will ever rise above the level of his or her praying." I agree, so pray, Christian, pray! Make this an "absolute" in your life. *"...I give myself unto prayer."*

September

EYES, EARS, HEART, MOUTH

Recently I sat in the parking lot after prayer meeting and talked with one of my spiritual children. She was concerned about how to help her family live the Christian life in today's world. I sensed in her the frustration I see in many people who come to me for counseling. (I am not a trained counselor, but I listen to a lot of people.) Many of them are frustrated. Some are frustrated because of the influence of the world on their lives. Some are doing things they would not have thought possible a few years ago. Some have children who are bombarded on every side by the lure of the world. Some are frustrated because of a spouse who is a Christian but has one foot in the world.

At this point, I am not really sure where I am going with this month. I can tell you that it is for Christians. It is for you if you have been saved by the blood of Jesus. But the book is not just for Christians, but for Christians who are becoming more like the world and might not even be aware of it.

So how do we stop this trend? I believe the answer lies in God's Word. In my Spirit, our Lord impressed on my heart to focus on the eyes, the ears, the heart, and the mouth. In this month I will do just that. As you take a trip through the month, examine yourself and see if you have let the world creep more and more into your walk and allow our Lord to get you back on the path of righteousness.

SEPTEMBER 1   EYES

Key Verse: *"I will set no wicked thing before mine eyes..." (Psalm 101:3).*

Message: When David became king, he made a commitment to holy living. One of his resolves was that he would *"set no wicked thing before mine (his) eyes...."* He did just fine until he was in the wrong place at the wrong time. He should have been in battle with his men, but instead he put himself in the place of temptation. His eyes caused his resolve to break down in practice. 2 Samuel 11:2 says that David was walking on his roof *"and from the roof he saw a woman...."* He saw; he lusted; he sinned with her. You know the rest of the story.

I pray that you have resolved to "set no wicked thing before your eyes." If you go where sin reigns, you could have appealing alcohol or drugs or gambling or even a Bathsheba pass before your eyes. The best way to keep your resolve from breaking down in practice is to stay away from tempting places.

David has some very good advice in 101:6: *"Mine eyes shall be upon the faithful of the land, that they may dwell with me...."* Here, David is vowing to keep company with those who were faithful to God. Ask the Lord to lead you to such friends.

SEPTEMBER 2   EYES

Key Verse: *I will set no wicked thing before mine eyes..." (Psalm 101:3).*

Message: In yesterday's message, I used this verse to warn against going to places where sin reigns—where your resolve can break down in practice.

Today I want to talk about the home. Is your home a place in which no wicked thing is set before the eyes of the family? I could give you other examples, but I will focus on only one: movies— movies that you watch on television or movies that you bring into your house.

I am amazed that active believers think nothing of watching a movie that flaunts sexual women in front of their eyes. They don't seem to think that their eyes are seeing anything harmful. Wrong! Men, if you are of this mindset, think about your children. At this time they are not seeing you as the spiritual leader in the home. Also, men, if you are of this mindset, think about your wife. You are demeaning her by gazing on a seductive other woman.

Also, men, if you are of this mindset, think about Jesus. If He came to your home, would you invite Him to sit down and watch one of these movies with you? I think not!

If your resolve is to *"set no wicked thing before your eyes,"* you must change the direction of your eyes. In Philippians 4:8, Paul said, *"whatsoever things are pure...think on these things."* Ask the Lord to direct your eyes in this direction.

SEPTEMBER 3   EYES

Key Verse: *"I will set no wicked thing before mine eyes..."* (Psalm 101:3).

Message: In the last two messages, I used this verse to warn against going to the devil's turf and watching sex on the screen in the home. Today I want to talk about your eyes in the worldly workplace. How much of the world is before your eyes every day?

In 1 John 2:15, John admonishes believers not to love the world nor the things that are in the world. Then in verse 16, he lists some things that are of the world. One of them is this: *"...The lust of the eyes is...of the world."* Here, John is talking about the evil desires that pop up in our hearts. It can happen to anyone who puts himself in the wrong environment.

Let me give you an example. You work with a member of the opposite sex. Your eyes are perfectly innocent in your work relationship. But one day that person begins to share that the spouse doesn't appreciate or understand him/her, etc. Gradually, your eyes see each other in a different light—a not-so-innocent light. Then, after a while, an affair can happen.

Listen carefully! The <u>first</u> time a member of the opposite sex starts talking to you about personal things, stop him/her right then and say, "You need to talk about this with a member of your sex or a counselor." Then you flee! Paul told Timothy to *"flee youthful lusts" (2 Timothy 2:22)*. This is good advice for any age. Men, don't counsel women; women, don't counsel men. Doing so might begin in innocence but end in an affair. People I talk with who have had affairs most always say to me, "I never intended for it to happen." It won't if you run for your life at the first sign that an ungodly relationship could develop. Don't go alone to lunch with a member of the opposite sex. Don't ride alone with him/her in a car. Avoid that water cooler. These are good places for Satan to get a toe in the door.

Guard your eyes, folks. Let me leave you with this proverb: *"Adultery is a trap—it catches those with whom the Lord is angry" (Proverbs 22:14 GN)*. Ask the Lord to keep you out of that group.

SEPTEMBER 4   EYES
Key Verse: *"I will set no wicked thing before mine eyes..." (Psalm 101:3)*.

Message: I can't seem to get away from this verse. It just seems to apply to many things that I deal with in counseling. The subject I am going to discuss is one I never dreamed that I would have to address. It is pornography. I don't have any first-hand knowledge of this evil, because I don't counsel men. But I do talk to wives whose husbands have trouble in this area.

The obvious place that many men go to is the internet, but I have observed something that seems to have even more attraction for them: the actual pictures, as seen in magazines. What I have heard from these women is that their husbands try to hide these magazines in the house. After I had heard this several times, I remembered something from my youth. One of my girlfriends told me that she had found an adult magazine in her dad's sock drawer. It was gone the next time she looked, but finding that magazine affected her, and it did me too. He was the Sunday School director.

I can't even begin to tell you the places where these husbands hide their filth. Men, let me tell you that you are not hiding your pornography from God: *"The Lord is in his holy temple...his eyes behold...the children of men" (Psalm 11:4)*. And you probably are not hiding it from your children. If my friend could find her dad's adult magazine, your children can find yours.

Men, if you are addicted or are on your way there, get help! I have seen first hand what addiction to pornography can do to wives. Why don't you pray Psalm 119:37 today: *"Turn away mine eyes from looking at worthless things...."*

SEPTEMBER 5   EYES

Key Verse: *"I will set no wicked thing before mine eyes..."* *(Psalm 101:3).*

Message: Before I leave this verse, I want to go back to the home. I pray that you, like David, have resolved to set nothing evil before your eyes in your home. You know, you might have something evil there that you haven't really thought of as evil.

I'll give you an example. When I moved here almost thirty years ago, my pastor, Brother Len and his wife, Pansy came by to visit. It wasn't long until they felt quite at home at my place. One day Brother Len picked up a paper weight that someone had given me. It had my horoscope sign on it. I hadn't given any thought to it until he asked me, "What are you doing with this in your house?" Well, I got rid of it in a hurry. As I began to grow in my walk and to read God's Word on the subject, I saw the danger. Today, I try not to let my eyes focus on that page of the newspaper.

Let me give you another example. A few years ago, an elderly lady who lived with me greeted me when I got home from school with these words: "Two nice ladies came by to visit with me today and left me this book." I didn't have to read the title to know who had been by and left the book with her. I calmly explained to her that we didn't open the door to people who won't accept the gospel of Jesus Christ as the Bible teaches it. When I went to bed that night, I was restless. That book popped into my vision. I had to get out of bed and put it outside the door until the next morning when I could put it into the trash. I am very sensitive about having evil things in my house.

Here is another example. My friend Terri had a very fine painting of Buddha on her wall as part of her oriental decorations. When she began to grow in her faith, that picture began to bother her. It just kept bothering her more and more. Finally, she took it outside and burned it. She well understood the commandment: *"Thou shalt have no other gods before me" (Exodus 20:3).*

Folks, here is another resolve of David that I hope you have claimed: *"I will walk within my house with a perfect (blameless) heart" (Psalm 101:2).* This walk will be a lot easier if you do not have evil things set before your eyes. Take inventory of your home. Ask the Lord to point out to you anything that is evil; and when He does, destroy it.

SEPTEMBER 6   EYES
Key Verse: *"Search the scriptures..." (John 5:39).*

Message: I can think of no better place for your eyes to go than to the Word of God. This truth was made plain to me recently. I have a special pen that I keep in my "quiet time" Bible. It is a good pen that does not leak through the pages.

Well, I took it out of my Bible to use it for something else. When I finished, I couldn't find the top. I looked all over the place—on the floor, on my blue couch, and even under the cushions. I gave up looking and settled for another pen, one not so good. Then I opened my Bible to start my quiet time, and there was the top, right before my eyes.

This illustration is an example of what so many of us do. When we have a trial, we are much like a pen with a misplaced top. We look for help in many places—from counselors, from ministers, from friends, from relatives, from self-help books—often to no avail. Maybe you do what I did last. After looking many places, I found the top in my Bible. The last place I looked should have been the first. Here is my advice for you. When the top is off your pen, look first at the Word before you look anywhere else. John said, *"Search the scriptures...."* In 2 Timothy 3:16, Paul said, *"All scripture is given by inspiration of God, and is profitable for doctrine, for reproof, for correction, for instruction in righteousness."* In Romans 15:4 (GN), he said, *"Everything written in the scriptures was written to teach us."*

When the top is off your pen, pray with the Psalmist: *"Give me understanding according to Thy Word."* Then, *"Search the scriptures...."*

SEPTEMBER 7   EYES

Key Verse: *"...Women (should) adorn themselves in modest apparel..." (1 Timothy 2:9).*

Message: I believe there is a need for us to look at the first part of Paul's words in 1 Timothy 2:9, because this command is so violated in today's world. Nearly every Sunday I hear some people say things to me about dress that their eyes have beheld: "Can you believe that her mother let her wear such a short skirt?"—or—"Can you believe she is wearing such a tight shirt?"—or—"Can you believe how low her neckline is?" You get the idea.

I have heard mothers justify what their daughters wear. They say such things as, "There's nothing else out there to buy."—or—"My daughter insists on dressing like the other girls, and I let her."—or—"I don't like what she is wearing, but she wants to dress like the other girls so that she will fit in."

Parents, you are not to be rearing your daughters to fit in; you are to be rearing them to be individually different. The problem is that we spend more effort on the outward appearance rather than on what really counts. Peter says that what really counts is what is inside the person. Parents, you need to be teaching your girls to wear the *"ornament of a gentle and quiet spirit, which is in the sight of God of great price" (1 Peter 3:4)*. If you help your daughter to develop these inner qualities, you will probably spend less time arguing with your daughter about what she should wear.

Girls, here is a word for you. Men are visual. They will respect you more if certain parts of your body are less visible. Be careful how you dress. Ask the Lord for the strength to be more concerned about your inner self than your outward self. (By the way, I do believe you are to look your best, but to do so in a way that would be pleasing to our Lord's eyes.)

SEPTEMBER 8   EAR

Key Verse: *"...a name which is above every name" (Philippians 2:9).*

Message: In Philippians 2, Paul instructed us to have the mind of Christ. Then he proceeded to elaborate. In verse 9, he said, *"...God* *hath highly exalted him, and given him a name which is above every name."* In Ephesians 1:21, Paul says that Jesus is in heaven *"far above all principality, and power, and might, and dominion, and every name that is named...."* Since Jesus' name is above every name in heaven and on earth, it should be above every name in your home.

I am a firm believer that the name of Jesus should flow into the ears of everyone in your home, especially your children's. There are many good stories that are out there for children, but I would suggest that you choose some that name the name of Jesus. Play praise songs that exalt Jesus. Read stories about Jesus from the Bible. As soon as your children can read, let them read about Jesus from the Word. Help them to memorize verses about Jesus. A good one is Luke 2:52: *"And Jesus increased in wisdom and stature, and in favor with God and man."* Explain to your children that they are to have consistent and well-rounded growth just as Jesus did. Parents, this is a good prayer for you to pray for your children.

Have the name of Jesus heard in your home. As you do so, you will have a calmer home and calmer children. It also helps to have Jesus' name visible in your home. I use the wall next to my stairway as a gallery for pictures and plaques that people have given me. One plaque says, "Jesus is Lord." These wonderful words catch my eye when I climb the stairs. I believe that one way to keep Jesus alive and above every name in your home is to keep His name flowing into the ears of every family member. As you pray today, ask the Lord to remind you to do so.

SEPTEMBER 9   EAR

Key Verse: *"At what time ye hear the sound of...all kinds of music"* *(Daniel 3:5).*

Message: King Nebuchadnezzar built an image of gold—90 feet high and 9 feet wide—to represent the kingdom he had built. Then he sent an invitation to all the important people in his kingdom *"to come to the dedication of the image..." (3:2).* Well, this ceremony was not a dedication service. As those people stood there looking at that impressive image, their attention was drawn to a herald who stood up and proclaimed in a loud voice. *"At what time ye hear* *the sound of...all kinds of music, fall down and worship the golden image that Nebuchadnezzar the king hath set up" (3:5).— "all kinds of music!"* Folks, this was the kind of music that would induce people to worship a false god.

Parents, would I be safe in assuming that if you have teenage children in your home, you disagree about the music they choose to let enter their ears? Unfortunately, a lot of modern music exalts false gods and ultimately Satan himself. So what do you do? Don't argue. Set rules. I suggest that you consider doing what a good friend of mine did. He said to his teenagers, "If you can understand the words and the contents are acceptable to your mom and me, you may listen to that music." Folks, listen to the songs your teenagers choose and check out the artists. Don't make a big production out of this, but be sure your rules are obeyed.

You might say, "Is it worth doing all this? My child will listen to what he wants to when he gets out of the house." Yes, it is worth it!! Let me make this suggestion. If you are having trouble with your teenager, play praise music in your home when your child is at home and play praise music in his room when he is not at home. Choose music that contains the name of Jesus. Ask the Lord to help you and your children get on the same page concerning appropriate music.

SEPTEMBER 10   EAR
Key Verse: *"I hear the sound..." (Exodus 32:17).*

Message: While Moses was on the mountain getting the Ten Commandments, the people got tired of waiting for his return, so they persuaded Aaron to build the golden calf. Gathered around that idol, the people ate; they sang; they drank; they offered burnt offerings. In fact, they turned their "worship" service into a sexual orgy. It was time for Moses and Joshua to come down from the mountain. As they descended, they heard sounds coming from the camp. Joshua said, *"There is a noise of war in the camp" (32:17).* Moses replied, "No, what you hear is *'the noise of them that sing'" (32:18).*

Joshua didn't get it, but Moses did. He heard the sound of this unfamiliar music in the camp of Israel and knew before he arrived at the camp that the people were not singing "as unto the Lord" but as unto a golden idol. Now, I asked myself, "Why was Joshua not able to recognize this idolatrous music and Moses was?"

Could this be the reason? Let me explain. In Exodus 24:13-18, we see that both Moses and Joshua went up to the mountain, but that only Moses was called into the cloud to commune with God for *"forty days and forty nights" (24:18)*. Where was Joshua? I don't know, but I know where he wasn't. He wasn't in the cloud where Moses communed with God. Apparently, he was sitting all alone on the mountain.

Now, here is my point. Moses recognized the idolatrous singing that made him furious because he had spent much time in the presence of the Lord. Folks, the more time you spend with the Lord, the more you will abhor idolatrous music. Start your children listening to Jesus songs early in their lives. Change your "rocking" lullaby from "Hush Little Baby" to "Sweet Little Jesus Boy."

The more time spent with the Lord, the more the ear will be turned off to pagan music and on to praise music. Ask the Lord to help your children discern what music is pleasing to our Lord. By the way, it is all right for your teenager's music to be loud. Read Psalm 150. Verse 5 says, *"Praise Him upon the loud cymbals."* Music in heaven is going to be loud. Get ready for it, folks!

SEPTEMBER 11   HEART
Key Verse: *"But Daniel purposed in his heart..." (Daniel 1:8).*

Message: Success in living the Christian life in this world depends on the condition of the heart. In Psalm 108:1, David prayed, *"O God, my heart is fixed...."* He is telling God that his heart is steadfast. He had determined in his heart to obey God.

Another young man named Daniel determined to do the same thing. He was one of the young men taken into Babylonian captivity. The pagan king was determined to make him into a strong Chaldean by offering him the finest food and wine from his own table. But Daniel's diet did not include the king's food and wine. I daresay that many of the young Jewish men indulged at the king's table. Why didn't Daniel? Because he had *"purposed in his heart that he would not defile himself"* with the king's food and wine! The king's wine!

It was right there in front of Daniel. It would have been so easy for him to drink it. Those all around him were. But he didn't!

Like Daniel, young people today are surrounded by alcohol. They see their friends drink, sometimes even their church friends. They see adults drink, sometimes even their parents. They see alcohol glamorized in movies, on television, etc. So how do young people resist becoming part of the drinking crowd? They do as Daniel did. They must purpose in their hearts not to drink the king's wine. Proverbs 23:20 says, *"Don't be among winebibbers...."* He is saying, "Don't go where people are drinking." That is good advice. Ask the Lord to give you friends who have a "purposed heart."

SEPTEMBER 12   HEART
Key Verse: "But Daniel purposed in his heart..." (Daniel 1:8).

Message: Yesterday, I wrote about Daniel. The thing that made him so special is that he *"purposed in his heart that he would not defile himself..." (1:8).* Daniel was a wonderful role model for young men. I have often said, "If your name is Daniel, you have a lot to live up to." The Lord laid on my heart to lift up every Daniel in prayer every day. I always pray that they will purpose in their heats to be true to the Lord, no matter what their circumstances and no matter where they are.

I want to share this story with you. For several years Thad Daniels has been on my list of "Daniels." (I include first and last names.) Recently, his parents, Ray and Rhonda, who have great parenting skills, told me this story.

Thad wanted to take FAITH (a course that teaches one how to share his faith). Ray and Rhonda discussed this and decided that Thad might need to wait a while because every night would then be full with football, church, etc. When they gave Thad the news, he looked downcast and then said, "I've been put here for a purpose, and it doesn't include football. I'll give up whatever I have to in order to take FAITH." Needless to say, Ray and Rhonda let him enroll. Thad made this decision because he understands "purpose."

Praying for these folks named Daniel has been my privilege. Adults, ask the Lord to lay some teenagers on your heart and pray the Daniel prayer for them every day. Who knows how the Lord will answer your prayers!

SEPTEMBER 13 MOUTH

Key Verse: *"Out of the same mouth proceedeth blessing and cursing..." (James 3:10).*

Message: James goes on to say, *"My brethren, these things ought not so to be."* He is saying that there should be no place in your life for cursing. James went on to illustrate this point by saying, *"A fig tree, my brothers, cannot bear olives; a grapevine cannot bear figs..." (3:12).* His point is that blessing and cursing are not to come from a saved mouth.

I am sorry to have to tell you this, but blessing and cursing do come out of the mouths of some Christians. Some bless the Lord on Sunday and let curse words slip out when they hit their fingers with a hammer or when they get angry with someone during the week. Some, especially young people, bless the Lord at church and exchange text messages with friends that are filled with cursing during the week. Folks, this ought not to be.

Will you ever mess up? Possibly? Probably? If you do, you need to do as Peter did after he cursed Jesus and declared that he never knew Him. When he came to his senses, he was so sorry that he had messed up. He went out and wept bitterly. I pray that you will do likewise.

A former pastor's wife told me that this is what she has said to her children concerning their language: "You may say any word you hear your dad and me say." Would this rule work in your home? Wouldn't you like for it to apply" If so, you might resolve with David *"...I will take heed to my ways, that I sin not with my tongue: I will restrain my mouth with a bridle..." (Psalm 39:1).* Ask the Lord to help you do just that.

SEPTEMBER 14   MOUTH

Key Verse: *"A soft answer..." (Proverbs 15:1).*

Message: Proverbs is full of good parenting advice. Listen to what 15:1 (GN) says, *"A soft answer turneth away wrath (A gentle answer quiets anger)."* Also listen to Proverbs 25:15 (GN): *"A soft tongue breaketh the bone (breaketh down the strongest resistance)."*

Does a *"soft answer"* or a *"soft tongue"* describe your mouth when you are dealing with a child determined to have his own way? If so, you are in the minority. Recently I read this in the local newspaper: "According to a 2003 study published in the Journal of Marriage and Family, 88 percent of nearly 1,000 parents interviewed reported shouting, yelling or screaming at their children." You probably are in this group.

You have probably said, "I know that I shouldn't yell at my children, but I just can't help it." I may not be able to tell you how to stop raising your voice all the time. I realize that we all mess up occasionally. But I can tell you what will help. Before you face your child each morning, ask the Holy Spirit to produce patience and self-control through you as you deal with him/her. If you make this an "absolute," you will be amazed at how the friction will be cut down.

By the way, when I taught school, I did not raise my voice. I was not willing to let the student see that he had the upper hand. I found that staring at him did more good than yelling. You might try this with your children.

Remember! Patience and self-control are parts of the gift from Jesus to you that can only be produced by the Holy Spirit within you. Ask him to produce them through you as you deal with an angry child or with anyone else who is angry with you.

SEPTEMBER 15   MOUTH

Key Verse: *"But let your word be, yea, yea; nay, nay: For whatever is more than these cometh of the evil one" (Matthew 5:37).*

Message: Today we will continue on yesterday's theme of what causes raised voices in the home. I believe this behavior often happens when parents are indecisive—when "no" wears down to "yes."

Does this ever happen in your home? Your child wants to do something. You say "no." He begs; you say "no"; he begs some more; you say in a raised voice, "All right! Go ahead." Here is what happens so often. If you say "no" and mean it, the child gets angry. If you change your "no" to "yes," you get angry at yourself. No one really wins in this type of situation.

What can be done? Here is what I tell parents. "The Bible says that your 'no' is to be 'no' and your 'yes' is to be 'yes'." This is a simple command but so hard to follow.

I go on to say, "Make sure of your final answer before you respond to the child. If the answer is 'no,' say something like this. 'I am telling you that my answer is 'no.' I will not change my mind.'"

The child will probably begin to plead with you. Here is an important point. Do not get into a discussion with your child that usually would end in raised voices. In fact, do not say one word after you have said "no" (unless it is to send the child to his room, etc.) Try staring at the child. When he understands that your "no" means "no," there will be fewer raised voices.

By the way, I had never paid much attention to the last part of the key verse: *"Whatever is more than these (Yea, Yea; nay, nay) cometh from the evil one."* From where else would words that lead to yelling come? Certainly not from the Lord!

Let me leave you with this thought from Proverbs 10:19: *"The more you talk, the more likely you are to sin. If you are* <u>wise</u>, *you will keep quiet."* Ask the Lord to give you a <u>wise</u> mouth.

SEPTEMBER 16   MOUTH

Key Verse: *"A word fitly spoken (spoken at the right time) is like apples of gold in pictures (settings) of silver" (Proverbs 25:11).*

Message: Another Proverb says this: *"...A word spoken in due season, how good is it" (Proverbs 15:23).* Here is another: *"Pleasant words are as a honeycomb, sweet to the soul, and health to the bones" (Proverbs 16:24).*

Are encouraging words spoken in your home? Let's take an example. Your child is having a hard time in math. He works hard. He gets his final grade. He rushes home to say, "Dad, I got a B in the course," only to hear, "You could have done better." This is the way to discourage, not encourage. Wouldn't it have made for a better father-son relationship if the dad had said, "Son, I know you worked hard for that B. I'm proud of you." Do you see yourself anywhere in this example?

Let me ask you another question. Are pleasant words the norm in your home? It seems to me that words like these are more the norm in many homes: "Don't bother me. Can't you see that I'm busy?"— "Shut up! I don't want to hear another word out of your mouth."— "Can't you ever do anything right?"—"That was a stupid thing to do." I'm sure you can add more to this list. There's an old adage that says, "Sticks and stones may break my bones, but words can never harm me." Wrong! Words do harm. Folks, why not concentrate on exchanging those unhealthy words for *"pleasant words."*

I have said over and over that kindness is a lost art in the home. Consider making this your family verse: *"Be ye kind one to another, tenderhearted, forgiving one another, even as God for Christ's sake hath forgiven you" (Ephesians 4:32).*

Parents, let your children learn by your example. Make it a habit to say encouraging words and pleasant words to each other in front of them. This will not be easy, so ask the Lord to bring kind words to your lips.

SEPTEMBER 17   MOUTH

Key Verse: *"Not forsaking the assembling of ourselves together..."* *(Hebrews 10:25).*

Message: I hate to have to tell you this, but occasionally I have a mother say to me: "My child asks me, 'Why do I have to go to church? Daddy doesn't. Why can't I stay home with him?'" These are sad words to me.

Several years ago a lady in my class asked for my advice. She said that her six-year-old son didn't want to come to church. He wanted to stay home with his dad who didn't attend church. She asked me, "What should I do? Should I let him stay with his dad?" My answer was swift in coming: "Under no circumstance (unless he is ill) do you allow this to happen. You cannot control your husband, but you can control your son. Teach him that he 'gets' to go and make sure he understands that going to church every Sunday is an absolute for you and him." She did so, and I believe God honored her faithfulness. Today her husband and her son are both active in church.

Folks, I go back to the promise to parents found in Psalm 92:13-14: *"Those that be planted in the house of the Lord shall flourish in the courts of our God. They shall still bring forth fruit in old age...."*

The best way to assure that your child will still be faithfully serving the Lord in old age is to "plant" him in the house of God when he is young. Ask the Lord to give you strength to stand firm when your child wants to resist.

SEPTEMBER 18   MOUTH
Key Verse: *"Better to live..." (Proverbs 21:9,19).*

Message: I am going to give you a couple of Proverbs that will probably make you chuckle, but they really are not funny. Here they are: *"Better to live on a roof than share the house with a nagging wife" (21:9). "Better to live out in the desert than with a nagging, complaining wife" (21:19).*

Are you a nagging wife? I'm sure you don't want to be but probably are. I could go in many directions with this theme, but I want to continue with the husband who does not go to church. Ladies, do you ever play the Holy Spirit with your husband on Sunday morning? Do these words ever come out of your mouth? "Aren't you going to church today?"—or—"Staying home is not setting a good example for our children."—or—"Please go to church with me today."

When you get home from church, do these words ever come out of your mouth? "You don't know what you missed today."—or—"So-and-so asked where you were."—or—"The sermon was one you needed to hear." Words like these do more harm than good. Your husband already knows that you want him to go to church with you without your saying so—so what should you do? Here is what I suggest. Get up on Sunday morning in a cheerful mood. Get you and your children dressed for church. Don't say anything to your husband about going. (If he is going, he will get dressed.) Kiss him good-bye and say, "We'll see you in a little while." When you come home, don't volunteer a word about the church service. Come in cheerfully and put the best meal on the table that you can prepare. Then have a good afternoon.

Peter has some good advice for you. He says that if you have a husband who does not obey the Word, he might be *"won by the conduct of the wife" (1 Peter 3:1)*. He goes on to say in verse 4 that you are to take on *"the ornament of a gentle and quiet spirit, which is in the sight of God of great price."* Great advice!

This saying of Benjamin Franklin just came to my mind: "A spoonful of honey will catch more flies than a gallon of vinegar." Honey and nagging are not synonyms. Choose honey! You never know how God will work in the life of your husband if you do. Ask God to keep nagging words from leaving your mouth.

SEPTEMBER 19   MOUTH

Key Verse: *"...He spoke without stopping to think" (Psalm 106:33 GN).*

Message: Anger is a terrible emotion. When it hits you, it makes you say things you shouldn't and often gets you into trouble. It did Moses. Let's see how. *"At the springs of Meribah the people made the Lord angry, and Moses was in trouble on their account. They made him so bitter that he spoke without thinking." (Psalm 106:32-33)*. Anger makes a person do this.

In Colossians 3:8, Paul gives a list of things that the new creation in Christ Jesus should put off. The first word on the list is *"anger."* Is it hard for you to put it off? Do you stop to think before you speak when a driver cuts in front of you or a waiter messes up your order or a child spills his milk or a spouse spends too much money or someone accuses you of something you didn't do, or do you speak before you think?

Let me give you a Proverb to paste on your mirror: *"If you are sensible, you will control your temper. When someone wrongs you, it is a great virtue to ignore it" (Proverbs 19:11 GN).* I know this is hard to do; therefore, ask the Lord to teach you anger management.

Let me add this. I often have women say to me. "When my husband has said something to me that hurts, he does little things to make it up to me, but he doesn't say that he is sorry." Men, it would do your wife good to hear you say, "I'm sorry," and it would do you good also. Try it!

SEPTEMBER 20   MOUTH

Key Verse: *"For I am the Lord, I change not..." (Malachi 3:6).*

Message: In our church right now, we are going through a lot of changes. It is so easy for these words to come out of your mouth: "I don't like change." These are words that you will never hear in heaven. Since that is the case, these words should not leave your mouth down here. Maybe we wouldn't have so much trouble with the word "change" if we were to concentrate on things that do not change:

1. **The Word of God does not change**. Psalm 119:89 says, *"For ever, O Lord, thy word is settled in heaven."*
2. **The will of God does not change.** 1 Peter 3:9 says that our Lord is *"not willing that any should perish, but that all should come to repentance."* Once we are saved, it is His will for us to fulfill the purpose for which He sent us down here. In 1 Corinthians 7:7, Paul said, *"...every man hath his proper gift of God...."* In Ephesians 4:12, Paul said that we are to use this gift *"...for the edifying of the body of Christ."*
3. **The mission of God never changes**. Before He returned to heaven, Jesus gave us His Great commission: *"Go ye therefore, and teach all nations, baptizing them in the name of the Father and of the Son, and of the Holy Ghost; teaching them to observe all things whatsoever I have commanded you..." (Matthew 28:19-20).*
4. **Our God does not change.** Our key verse makes this plain: *"For I am the Lord, I change not..." (Malachi 3:6).* Hebrews

13:8 says of Him: *"Jesus Christ the same yesterday, and today, and forever."*

I am sure that when the leaders came up with the mission statement of our church: "Inviting everyday people to experience Christ in every way," they had these four truths in mind. The Word, the will, the mission of God, and God Himself never change. The changes our staff are making are not to make us comfortable, but to make it possible for those outside our walls to come in. So, won't you drop "I don't like change" from your vocabulary and add, "I'm for change if it helps us to carry out our mission." Ask the Lord to change your focus from the "Big I" to the "Great I Am."

I must tell you that this outline is not original with me. I got it from a Christian brother whose name you will know if you know me.

SEPTEMBER 21   MOUTH

Key Verse: *"...every tongue shall confess that Jesus Christ is Lord..."* *(Philippians 2:11).*

Message: One day every tongue <u>will</u> confess that Jesus Christ is Lord. For many this confession will come too late, but they will acknowledge from the Lake of Fire that Jesus is Lord. Unfortunately that confession will not save them from eternal hell. For believers, we have the privilege of proclaiming that He is Lord now and for all eternity. There's just something about that name. David said, *"Our help is in the name of the Lord" (Psalm 124:8).* Proverbs 18:10 says, *"The name of the Lord is a strong tower; the righteous runneth into it and is safe."*

Let me give you a practical suggestion concerning the name of the Lord. Many times I have had mothers say to me, "My child is afraid (for example) of the dark." I say to them, "Teach your children to say, 'Jesus is Lord.'"

I have had many stories from mothers. One told me that she stopped outside her young son's door and heard him saying, "Jesus is Lord" over and over until he fell asleep. One mother told me that she overheard her eight-year-old telling his little brother who was afraid, "You have to say 'Jesus is Lord.'" She went on to say how precious it was to hear that two-year-old trying to say, "Jesus is Lord." One mother has three sons. Over the door of each room she has a sign that says, "Jesus is Lord." I have one also on the wall by my stairway.

I could give you other examples, but you get the idea that there is power in the name of the Lord. Satan hates the name of Jesus. He trembles when he hears it. The best way to make him flee is not to speak to him but to proclaim, "Jesus is Lord." Adults, when you are afraid or when you think danger is lurking near you or when you think the evil one is trying to mess up your mind, say loud and clear, "Jesus is Lord." I do so quite often, actually, several times a day.

I urge you to do likewise and tell the Lord how thankful you are that God hath *"...given him a name which is above every name" (Philippians 2:9).*

SEPTEMBER 22   MOUTH
Key Verse: *"Bring ye all the tithes into the storehouse..." (Malachi 3:10).*

Message: I have had many people ask various questions about tithing and giving, but I have chosen to address this one, "My husband gives his tithe through the church, but he doesn't approve of some of the things the church is doing right now, so he is designating where it should be used. Is it all right for him to do this?"

The best answer comes from God's Word. Malachi 3:10 says, *"Bring ye all the tithes into the storehouse...."* Psalm 96:8 says, *"Give unto the Lord the glory due his name; bring an offering and come into his house."* These verses say that we are to bring our tithes and offerings to God's house. They do not say that we are to decide how they are to be distributed. I firmly believe that we are to give and then trust our leaders to use the money as God directs.

As you can see, I do not believe it is Scriptural to designate what you give through the church. The early church didn't. They all brought their money and laid it at the feet of the apostles. If we did likewise, we would have more resources to use to accomplish our mission of inviting everyday people to experience Christ in every way.

Let me leave you today with a prayer request that our pastor of administration, Geno Lucas, made in a recent Watchman Prayer Ministry booklet.

"Please pray for Biblical stewardship for every member of Colonial Heights Baptist Church. God gives us one area in which we may test Him, the area of stewardship. Pray that every member of Colonial Heights will give at least ten percent to the church budget so we can continue to reach the Metro Area for Christ." I will be part of the answer to this prayer. How about you?

SEPTEMBER 23   MOUTH
Key Verse: *"...greet....avoid..." (Romans 16:3, 17).*

Message: In his lesson to the Roman, Paul told the believers to greet certain members, names with which we are familiar: Phoebe, Priscilla, and Aquila. These people were obviously leaders in the church.

Then he listed others who were to be greeted: Epaenetus, Andronicus, Junia, Amplias, Urbane, Stachys, Apellas, and several others. Are you familiar with any of these folks? Probably not! Who were these folks? I believe they were the ones who went quietly about the business of serving the Lord in the local church. You know, I know these folks, although they have different names. I thank God that I serve in a local church with these folks.

Paul had a different word about some other folks. He said to the faithful: *"Now I beseech you, brethren, note them which cause divisions...and avoid them" (16:17).* These are the ones who "murmur." (I dislike that word!) In Philippians 2:14, Paul said, *"Do all things without murmurings and grumbling."*

Paul says to avoid these folks or "turn away" from them. This means that the faithful were not to try to change the murmurers or argue with them—just to avoid them. Then in verse 18, he tells why: *"For they that are such (murmurers) serve not our Lord Jesus Christ..."* Well, whom are they serving? Their own interests! They may be working in the church; but if they say something that hurts the unity of the local church, they are not serving our Lord. If you are listening to anyone who puts his own interests above the welfare of the local church, stop him. A good way to stop him is to turn the conversation by telling him how wonderful the church is and how it has ministered to you and your family. That will usually stop the murmurer. If not, avoid the person.

In the local church you will be a leader, a follower, or a murmurer. Ask the Lord to deliver you from the last category.

SEPTEMBER 24   MOUTH

Key Verse: *"...bring an offering and come into his house" (Psalm 96:8).*

Message: *"Bring an offering!"* Parents, what do you say to your children about the offering they bring to God's house? Do you ever say, on the way out of the door, "Don't forget your offering for Sunday School"? Let's spend some time talking about that offering.

Usually, you lay out clothes, etc., on Saturday for Sunday. Do you get the offering envelopes ready? I urge you to do so. Gather the family around the kitchen table. Give each person his envelope. Then teach this principle to your children. In Numbers 18:24, God told the ministers that the people were giving their offering *"as an offering to the Lord."* Tell your children that they are to give their offering to the Lord Jesus. Then get the lesson on their level. Explain that the church will use some of the money to send missionaries to tell other children about Jesus and even to buy food and shoes for them, etc.

If you give an allowance, now is the time to give it. If you give a dollar, don't give a bill; give change. Show your child that one dime belongs to God and that it must be put into the envelope to give back to Him. Stress that we never spend God's money. Then explain what an offering is and give him the option of adding to the dime. Parents, let your children see you prepare your envelopes and tell them why you give what you do.

Why is it so important to teach young children the right way to give? Because what they learn in those formative years will most likely stay with them and be part of their adult lives! Parents, are you an example for your children in the area of giving? If not, ask the

Lord to help you to be so. If so, ask Him to help you be consistent. Make Saturday night around the table an "absolute" in your house.

SEPTEMBER 25   MOUTH

Key Verse: *"...freely ye have received, freely give" (Matthew 10:8).*

Message: In his little book, *The Treasure Principle,* Randy Alcorn tells of a young man who got saved at age 21. He was so thrilled with his "free" salvation that he wanted to sell his house and "freely" give the money to the Lord's work. But when he shared his plan with older believers in his Bible study group, they talked him out of it. How tragic! What would you have said to him?

What would you say if your child came to you and said, "I want to give all of my allowance to Jesus so that other children can have shoes and toys"? Would you try to talk him out of doing so? Would you throw a negative into the picture by saying something like, "Now, if you give it all, you won't have any spending money this week"? Don't!

When a child wants to give, let him do so. My friend Jane and young son Jared were at my house the day before they moved to Florida. Jane was saying how expensive houses were in Florida. Evidently, Jared had heard his parents talking about the cost of houses because he said to me, "I know how 'spensive' houses are in Florida. I'm giving my dollars (from his allowance) to my daddy to help pay for us a new house."

When your child has a giving heart, be thankful. Let him give when he feels led to do so and praise him for having a generous spirit. Parents, ask the Lord to give you and your children the will to *"freely give."*

SEPTEMBER 26   MOUTH

Key Verse: *"Behold I set before you this day a blessing... A blessing if ye obey the commandments of the Lord your God..." (Deuteronomy 11:26-27).*

Message: Here, God promises a blessing to all those who obey His commandments. In Exodus 24:7, the children of Israel said, *"...all* *that the Lord hath said will we do, and be obedient."* Obedience brings blessings. I have already written a month on this subject, but I want to make another point. I want you to understand how you can receive the greatest blessings.

Let's take this command: *"Bring ye all the tithes into the store-house..." (Malachi 3:10).* You say, "I will do this. I will make it an absolute in my life. I will follow Proverbs 3:9: *'Honor the Lord... with the first fruits of all thine increase.'"*

If you make this an absolute and obey no matter what your circumstances, you will receive the blessing of God. He says in Malachi 3:10 that if you obey, He *"will pour you out a blessing, that there shall not be room enough to receive it."* The blessing is promised for absolute obedience, not partial obedience. What is partial obedience? It is giving God's tithe for some other cause. The cause may be worthy, but you must not use the ten percent to fund it.

Try the same formula with Hebrews 10:25: We are *"not to forsake the assembling of ourselves together."* If going to God's house every Sunday is an absolute in your home and you go (unless providentially hindered), you will receive a blessing of God. He says in Proverbs 28:20: *"A faithful man shall abound with blessings...."* God honors and blesses the faithful. On the other hand, if you go to church when you feel like it, you do not fit the definition of "faithful." Thus, you are not promised a blessing. Our Lord is after total obedience.

Have you other "absolutes" in your life? How about your quiet time? If this is an absolute, have it every day, no matter what, no matter how short or long. Just have it! You will be blessed. If you have made something an "absolute," you have made a vow to the Lord. We read in Deuteronomy 23:21: *"When you make a vow to the Lord your God, do not put off doing what you promised; the Lord will hold you to your vow...."*

My point in this lesson is not to tell you that you won't receive blessings. My point is to tell you that you receive the greatest blessings when you have "absolutes" in your life and stick to them. Ask the Lord to direct your "absolute" path.

SEPTEMBER 27   MOUTH
Key Verse: *"...Hosanna to the Son of David..." (Matthew 21:15).*

Message: Listen to the words that came out of the religious leaders' mouths when they heard the youth proclaim: *"Hosanna to the Son of David. They were sore displeased" (21:15).* The scribes and Pharisees were adamant in their denial that Jesus was their Messiah. As a result they could not believe that Jesus was allowing these young people to praise Him as such.

So what did Jesus do? I am sure that He made them even more furious because He quoted from the Old Testament Scriptures that they purported to follow. He asked them, "Haven't you ever read this Scripture?" Then he actually quoted Psalm 8:2: *"You have trained children to offer perfect praise" (Matthew 21:16).*

Parents, I hope that you have trained your children to *"offer perfect praise."* I would imagine that you chose the songs when the children were young. Then they became teenagers and their praise music changed. Students choose their own style of praise music to bring into the house of our Lord.

Adults, have these words ever come out of your mouth, "I don't like to listen to this music"? You might not like students' style of praise, but you need to support these young folks.

Come to church when they are in charge of the praise service. Keep smiling when they sing the same chorus more than once. Don't stand there with your arms crossed. Clap your hands and rejoice with them. Just thank the Lord that they are in the Lord's house praising His name. Ask the Lord to lead others to join their ranks.

SEPTEMBER 28   MOUTH
Key Verse: *"And such were some of you..." (1 Corinthians 6:11).*

Message: I am sometimes asked the question, "Can homosexuals get out of that lifestyle?" This is the only question I will attempt to answer in this message; and I will admit that much of what I am saying is based on my opinion, but my opinion based on God's Word.

I do not believe that a person who openly flaunts this lifestyle in the face of our Lord can change. Paul talks about him in Romans 1.

In verse 24, Paul says that *"God gave them* (those who refused to believe and change even though they had light) *up to uncleanness...* *to dishonor their own bodies between themselves."* In verse 24, Paul says that God *"gave them over to vile affections."* He went on to say in essence, "Women with women and men with men." The key here is, *"God gave them over."* If He has given someone over to homosexuality, I don't see his being able to change.

Now I do believe that some of these folks can change. Who are they? In my opinion they are the ones who have not been given over. I feel that the reason they have not been given over is that they are not happy in this lifestyle and would like to be delivered. My reason for believing they can be delivered is based on 1 Corinthians 6. In verse 9, Paul lists some lost people who *"shall not inherit the kingdom of God."* One on the list is *"Homosexuals."*

Here is my reason for believing they can change. Paul is talking to Corinthian believers. In verse 11, he said, *"And such were some of you, but ye are washed...."* I take it that some of these believers had been homosexuals but were now saved and washed clean. I believe the same is true of some people today and can be true for others who want to be set free—who are willing to seek the face of God and biblical counseling.

Let me add this. In Romans 1, Paul talked about the ones given over to homosexuality. Then he began Chapter 2 this way: *"Do you, my friend, pass judgment on others? You have no excuse at all, whoever you are..."* *(2:1 GN).*

It seems to me that we are quicker to judge homosexuals than any other group of people. Here Paul warns us not to do so. We must never forget that God hates the sin but loves the sinner. We must do likewise. Instead of criticizing, pray that the Lord has not given these folks over and that they will be delivered by His matchless grace. And remember this: You don't know which ones God has given over, so pray for all in this lifestyle.

SEPTEMBER 29   MOUTH

Key Verse: *"...not to please ourselves" (Romans 15:1).*

Message: Here are some concerns I have heard from ladies who come to sit on my blue couch: "My son wants to know why it is wrong for him to drink. His argument is that his dad does."—"My son wants to know why it is wrong for him to have a beer. His argument is that his friend's dad, who is a church leader, keeps it in the refrigerator."—"My husband got angry with me because I wouldn't go with him to a certain movie. His argument was that So-and-So saw it, and he's a deacon."—"Is it wrong for me to go to the casinos? I enjoy the food; and, besides, I have seen my Sunday School teacher there." I could go on, but you get the point.

Dad, church leader, deacon, Sunday School teacher—Paul has a word for you. In 1 Corinthians 8, he was making the case that our liberty makes it all right to eat meat or not to eat meat. Maybe you think the things I have mentioned fall into that category (I hope not!). But if you do, Paul has a further word for you: *"But take heed lest by any means this liberty of yours becomes a stumbling block to them that are weak" (8:9).*

Folks, if you have to justify your actions (If you have to justify them, you probably should not do them), ask yourself if what you are doing could possibly be a stumbling block to a weaker brother. Paul begins Romans 15 with these words: *"We then that are strong ought to bear the infirmities (weaknesses) of the weak, and not to please ourselves."* When you do something that causes a brother to stumble, you please yourself. When you refrain from doing something that could cause a brother to stumble, you please the Lord. Pray that you would use your liberty to strengthen, not weaken, a brother in Christ.

SEPTEMBER 30   MOUTH

Key Verse: *"All things work together for good to them that love the Lord..." (Romans 8:28).*

Message: I can tell you that this verse has been true in my life. I can give you a personal testimony, but not about Katrina or Rita. I can give you a personal testimony about the Easter flood of 1979. Everything I had went floating down the river. It was a shock at first; but since I have no attachment to inanimate objects, I was not devastated. Those belongings were just "stuff."

Now let me tell you how this experience worked out for my good. This might sound trivial, but I had lost weight and needed new clothes. I got a whole new wardrobe. Also, I had always lived in an apartment; but after the flood, I was able to buy a patio home that houses my blue couch. But most important of all, the Lord confirmed that I am to teach His Word. Here is how this confirmation came.

When the flood hit, I was in Dallas. I received the call to come home. Before I left for Texas, I had placed my Bible and Sunday School material on top of my magazine rack, which was shaped like a cradle.

Our pastor at the time, Brother Len, went down Ridgewood Road in a boat to my apartment. He came back to say that five feet of water was standing in the apartment. Then he said, "You are not going to believe this, but that cradle was rocking, and your Bible and your Sunday School material were as dry as could be."

That experience had two major results. It taught me to focus on things not of this world, and it confirmed that I am to spend the rest of my life teaching His Word. I have done so for over thirty years and will keep going. I truly believe that it is always too early to quit. In the last few years, our Lord has given me a new assignment—writing these devotionals. I pray that they have helped you in your journey down the path of righteousness.

I can think of no better way to end this month than to pray the key verse for you—that you will truly believe that *"all things work together for good to them that love the Lord..." (Romans 8:28).*

October

WORDS THAT INFLUENCE ONE'S WALK

P salm 23:3 says that our Lord "…*leadeth me in the paths of righteousness….*" He will point us in the right direction, but He will not make us travel down that road. We must, as an act of our will, follow as He leads.

As I began to ponder what the Lord would have me write in this month, the Holy Spirit began to put on my heart some words in the Bible that affect my walk down *"the path of righteousness"* — words such as love, command, require, anger, do, obey, hear, and several others. I call these words, "words that influence one's walk." As you read these messages, check yourself on how you relate to these words. Your answers will show you how closely you are following our Lord down *"the path of righteousness."*

OCTOBER 1   COMMANDMENT

Key Verses: *"...Love the Lord....Love thy neighbor..." (Matthew 22: 37, 39).*

Message: One day a Pharisee, a doctor of theology, in an effort to trick Jesus, asked, *"Master, which is the Great <u>Commandment</u> in the law" (22:36)?* Without hesitation, *"Jesus said unto him, Thou shalt love the Lord thy God with all thy heart, and with all thy soul, and with all thy mind. This is the first and great <u>commandment</u>" (22:37-38).*

I am sure that you have said to someone special in your life, "I love you with all my heart." Well, you will have to go one better than that if you are going to follow our Lord down that narrow road of righteousness. You are going to have to love Him with all your heart, soul, and mind—with every ounce of your being.

How serious was our Lord that we get this message? Serious enough to have it repeated in Mark 12:30 and Luke 10:27!

Do you take this commandment as seriously as Jesus does? If so, you must commit your all—your entire being—to Him. Pray that you will be faithful to do just that.

OCTOBER 2   COMMANDMENT

Key Verses: *"...Love the Lord....Love thy neighbor..." (Matthew 22: 37, 39).*

Message: After Jesus told the Pharisees, *"Thou shalt love the Lord thy God with all thy heart, and with all thy soul, and with all thy mind..."* He added *"...Thou shalt love thy neighbor as thyself" (Matthew 22:39).*

Luke 10:27 tells us that the rich young ruler could quote this verse. He knew it by heart. But he did have a question for Jesus. In verse 29, he asked, *"And who is my neighbor?"*

In answer to the question, Jesus told him the story of the Good Samaritan. I am sure this Jewish young man must have said to himself, "You are telling me that my neighbor is a Samaritan and that I am to love him as myself. How could you ask such a thing of me? You know how my people hate the Samaritans."

Herein lies Jesus' point. In Luke 6:27, Jesus said, *"But I say unto you, love your enemies; do good to them which hate you."*

So, folks, who is your neighbor whom you must love? Anyone—friend or foe—who needs your help! Our Lord commands us to love everyone, without prejudice or partiality. As a child I remember singing this little song:

> "Jesus loves the little children,
> All the children of the world
> Red and yellow, black and white,
> They are precious in His sight.
> Jesus loves the little children of the world."

The mission of this church is "inviting everyday people to experience Christ in every way." That includes "red and yellow, black and white." As you pray today, tell the Lord that you will obey the commandment to love anyone who needs your help.

OCTOBER 3   COMMANDMENT

Key Verse: *"This is my commandment, that ye love one another, as I have loved you" (John 15:12).*

Message: Jesus wanted us to get His commandment that we must love one another. He repeated it several times, in the key verse and also in John 13:34: *"A new commandment I give unto you, that ye love one another; as I have loved you, that ye also love one another."*

In his book on the Gospel of John, John Phillips describes what Jesus might have said to His disciples about loving one another: "Peter and John, I know you are so different in temperament—but love one another. Simon Zelotes and Matthew, I know you came to me from opposite backgrounds—but love one another. Daring Andrew and doubting Thomas, love one another." The message is the same for you and me and every member of the family of God. We are to love one another.

But there is more. We must look at a clause that appears in both verses: *"As I have loved you."* We are not only to love one another, but to love one another as Jesus has loved us. He loved us so much that He willingly took our place on the old rugged cross. What a sacrifice! Loving one another as our Lord loves us will demand sacrifice on our part.

Imagine a conversation that our Lord might have with you and some folks in the church body. He has the same message for us that He had for His disciples; "No matter what your differences are, you must love one another."

As you pray today, ask the Lord to teach you how to practice sacrificial love.

OCTOBER 4 COMMANDMENT
Key Verse: *"...We should love one another..." (1 John 3:23).*

Message: We have heard Jesus on this subject. Now hear John. In 1 John 3:11, he said, *"For this is the message that ye heard from the beginning, that we should love one another."* In verse 23, he said, *"And this is His commandment, that we should believe on the name of the Lord Jesus Christ, and love one another, as He gave us commandment."*

Now hear Paul. In Romans 13:8, he said, *"Owe no man anything, but to love one another."* He ended verse 9 with this command: *"... Thou shalt love thy neighbor as thyself."*

The believer always owes the debt of love for his neighbor, not just the person next door, but all people—people who need a helping hand—people who are of the family of God.

Well, how do we reveal this love? To begin with, by not doing some things! Paul lists them in Romans 13:9: *"Thou shalt not commit adultery, thou shalt not kill, thou shalt not steal, thou shalt not covet; and if there be any other commandment, it is briefly comprehended in this saying, namely, thou shalt love thy neighbor as thyself."*

The first way Paul says that we reveal love is by not doing this: *"Thou shalt not commit adultery...."* If you love your neighbor as yourself, you will never begin a relationship with another person that would cause him or her to commit adultery.

Paul's second command is. *"...Thou shalt not kill...."* Of course, you are not going to kill someone with a gun, and you surely must not kill anyone with your tongue. If you love your neighbor as yourself, you will not gossip about him.

Paul's third command is, *"...Thou shalt not steal...."* If you love your neighbor as yourself, you won't get something from him dishonestly. Then he says, *"...Thou shalt not covet...."* If you love your neighbor as yourself, you will not be jealous of who he is or what he has. Now in this verse Paul is saying that our love for our neighbor is revealed in what we do not do. He is saying that love manifests itself in our not committing adultery, not killing, not stealing, and not coveting. You can talk about love all you want to; but if you are guilty of any of these acts against your neighbor, you have no love for him.

By the way, Paul begins 13:10 with these words: *"Love does no harm to his neighbor...."* Tell the Lord that you will live this verse.

OCTOBER 5 COMMAND
Key Verse: *"Ye are my friends if..." (John 15:14).*

Message: We sing songs such as, "What a Friend We Have in Jesus," and "There's no Friend Like the Lowly Jesus." These are true songs, but they are only true for the believer if he adheres to the rest of the verse: *"...if ye do whatsoever I command you."* One command we have looked at several times is the command to love one another. Can Jesus call you friend? To be called Jesus' friend, believers must obey His commands. What about unbelievers?

In Matthew 11, Jesus listed several excuses *"this generation"* (11:16) gave for rejecting Him and John the Baptist. One excuse for rejecting Jesus is found in verse 19. He was *"a friend of publicans (tax collectors) and sinners."*

Actually, He was; but His friendship was not what they had in mind. Jesus had a purpose for being a friend of sinners. One day He walked up to a tax collector named Levi and said, *"Follow me."* He did immediately. Luke 5:29 says, *"And Levi made him a great feast in his own home and there was a great company of publicans and others (sinners) who sat down with them."* Verse 30 says that *"their* *scribes and Pharisees <u>murmured</u>"* about why Jesus would do such a thing.

Notice Jesus' answer: *"I came not to call the righteous"*—you self-righteous Pharisees— *"but sinners to repentance" (Luke 5:32).*

Jesus was a friend of sinners, and His motive for dining with them was to save their souls. Our Lord is a friend to sinners who need to be saved and a friend to believers who obey His commands. If you want Jesus to call you friend, you must be a friend to sinners in the same way that Jesus was. We are not to become best friends with them because, unfortunately, we might become like them. We must be friends for the purpose of leading them to Jesus.

Ask the Lord today to make you a friend to someone who needs Jesus and to help you to obey His commands.

OCTOBER 6 COMMAND

Key Verse: *"Ye are my friends, if ye do whatsoever I command you" (John 15:14).*

Message: Does the Word of God tell us about someone that God called *"friend"*—someone who obeyed His commands? Yes! His name is Abraham. Several times in the Word, he is called the friend of God. In his prayer for deliverance from the enemies, Jehoshaphat prayed, *"Art not thou our God, who didst drive out the inhabitants of this land before thy people Israel, and gavest it to the seed of Abraham, <u>thy friend</u> forever" (2 Chronicles 20:7)?*

In Isaiah 41:8, God said, *"But thou, Israel, art my servant, Jacob whom I have chosen, the seed of Abraham <u>my friend</u>."* In James 2:23, we read, *"Abraham believed God, and it was accounted unto him for righteousness; and he was called the <u>friend</u> of God."*

Abraham believed God, obeyed His commands, and was given the wonderful title of "friend." Need an example? How about the one that got him into the faith chapter?

"By faith Abraham, when he was called to go out into a place which he should after receive for an inheritance, obeyed; and he went out, not knowing where he was going" (Hebrews 11:8). Do you have this kind of faith?

Are you willing to obey our Lord's commands, no matter what is involved or where He leads? Abraham didn't ask questions; he just obeyed and went. If you do likewise, you can be called a friend of God. Pray that you will be a type of Abraham.

OCTOBER 7   BE
Key Verse: *Be ye kind..." (Ephesians 4:32).*

Message: In Ephesians 4, Paul is describing how a person who has new life in Christ is to live. In verse 32, he commands: *"Be ye kind one to another...."* In Colossians 3:12, he says, *"Put on therefore, as the elect of God, holy and beloved, bowels* (clothes) *of ...kindness...."*

Nothing helps your witness more than kindness; nothing hurts your witness more than unkindness. Think about the last time you were unkind. Was anger the root? Did you blurt out in anger something a Christian should not say?

Let me give you a practical word from Proverbs. Chapter 19, verse 11, from the <u>Good News Bible</u> says, *"If you are sensible, you will control your temper. When someone wrongs you, it is a great virtue to ignore it.* Chapter 16, verse 32, says, *"It is better to be patient than powerful. It is better to win control over yourself than over whole cities."*

How can you personify these verses? I know of only one way. Kindness is part of the fruit of the Spirit. If you tend toward anger, I suggest that before you begin your day, you ask the Holy Spirit to produce kindness through you all through the day.

Remember this: It is never all right for a Christian to be unkind to another Christian, and it is doubly not all right for a Christian to be unkind to an unbeliever.

Pray that the Lord will print these words indelibly on your heart.

OCTOBER 8   BE
Key Verse: *"Be ye kind...." (Ephesians 4:32).*

Message: I decided to spend another day on *"Be ye kind,"* and I particularly want to speak to the men. I don't believe it is by accident that Proverbs 19:22 is addressed to men. It says, *"What is desirable in a man is his kindness."* Men, your co-workers, particularly the women, have a desire for you to be kind.

I have observed men in the business world and men in the church world—staff people. They often walk down the hall and do not speak to a co-worker. They do not mean to be unkind, but probably are so focused on some project that they don't even see the person they pass. Sometimes they are so driven to accomplish some goal that they lash out at the one who might be holding it up. Their purpose is not to be unkind, but they have no patience with those who are not as driven as they and thus are unkind.

"Driven" is a good definition of today's man in the business world. When I thought about the businessmen we have been describing, I thought about a Person who came to earth with a goal—to go to the cross to pay for your sins and mine. But along the way, our Lord Jesus was not unkind to those whom He met. He was never so focused on His goal that He didn't stop and show kindness to those with a need. He never got in such a hurry, never was too busy for others, never was unkind to those who needed help.

Men, being driven will get you an ulcer or a heart attack; following Jesus' example will get you a *"Well done thou good and faithful servant" (Matthew 25:21).* Ask the Lord to put your drive into low gear so that kindness will not just be a desire but a reality.

By the way, ladies, Proverbs 31:26 says of the ideal woman: *"In her tongue is the law of kindness."* Kindness is to come from your mouth. This means that you do not murmur to someone else when you perceive a man to be unkind. Pray with the Psalmist: *"...I will restrain my mouth with a bridle" (39:1).*

OCTOBER 9   MURMUR NOT

Key Verse: *"I have heard thy murmurings..." (Numbers 14:27).*

Message: Quite often I ask my Sunday School class, "What is the word I hate?" They are quick to answer, "Murmur." I despise the word, but I know someone who hates it more—our Lord God.

He had such good plans for the children of Israel. He delivered them from Egypt, walked them through the dried-up Red Sea, and fed them with manna from heaven. And what did they do? They murmured! God had had enough when they rejected Moses and Aaron, their leaders, and said, *"Let us make a captain, and let us return into Egypt" (14:4).* God's response was, *"I will disinherit them" (14:12).* However, He relented when Moses intervened for the people.

But listen to God's response to Moses and Aaron: *"How long shall I bear with this evil congregation, which murmur against me? I have heard the murmurings of the children of Israel, which they murmur against me" (14:27).*

So what did their murmuring against Him and Moses and Aaron cost the congregation? It cost them their blessing and their lives. In essence God said to the people, "All of you twenty years and upward (except Joshua and Caleb) will die in the wilderness, all *"which have murmured against me" (14:29).*

You know, the murmuring of the congregation not only affected them; it also affected their children. God said in verse 33 (GN): *"And your children shall wander in the wilderness forty years, suffering for your unfaithfulness, until the last one of you dies."*

How tragic! Do you see what happened when the people murmured against their leaders? They died in the wilderness, and their children had to wander around for forty years before they could enter the land of Promise.

There is a lesson here for the local congregation. Do you murmur against your leaders? Let me say to you what Moses said to the children of Israel: *"Your murmurings are not against us, but against the Lord" (Exodus 16:8).* Let this verse sink deep into your mind.

You know, the Lord had a plan for the children of Israel. Because they murmured, He delayed His plan for forty years. He has a plan for this congregation. Will our murmuring delay His plan for us? Think what might happen to your children during the delay! Folks, don't murmur. Ask the Lord to deliver you from any murmuring that would cause Him to delay His blessing for His church.

OCTOBER 10   MURMUR NOT
Key Verse: *"Murmur not against yourselves" (John 6:43).*

Message: In one of His teaching sessions, Jesus said, *"I am the bread of Life" (John 6:34).* In verse 33, He said that He had come down from heaven. This information brought a response from the Jews.

Verse 41 says, *"The Jews then murmured about him."* I can just see them getting off to one side and murmuring because Jesus said that He had come down from heaven. They said, *"This man is Jesus, son of Joseph, isn't he? We know his father and mother. How, then, does he now say he came down from heaven?"*

These Jews probably didn't think that Jesus heard them, but He did. He hears everything. Psalm 94 tells us of some wicked people who did all kinds of evil and said in essence, "The Lord doesn't see us; He doesn't pay attention to us." To that the Psalmist replied, *"He that planted the ear, shall he not hear..." (Psalm 94:9)?* Well, Jesus who hears everything, heard these Jews and said unto them: *"Murmur not among yourselves" (John 6:43).*

You know, these Jews are typical of murmurers. They never address the one about whom they are murmuring. Instead, they get to one side or in a corner or in the hall or on the phone and murmur about someone or something they don't like. If you start to murmur, stop and hear Jesus' words: *"Murmur not among yourselves" (John 6:43).*

I'll be honest with you. I do not associate with murmurers. I'll tell you one reason why. In his little book, Jude writes about false teachers who have infiltrated the church. In verse 16, he calls them *"murmurers."* In verse 19, he said that they *"are the people who cause divisions...."* In verse 4, he said, *"For there are certain men crept in unawares (unnoticed)."*

I believe that Satan's people have infiltrated the church. One characteristic is that they are murmurers. I realize that most murmurers are not Satan's own, but I am not qualified to discern who of the murmurers are. Therefore, I stay away from them all. Ask the Lord to lead you to do likewise.

OCTOBER 11   MURMUR NOT

Key Verse: *"Do all things without murmurings and disputings (grumbling)" (Philippians 2:14).*

Message: Right after Paul said that we are to do all things without murmuring and grumbling, he gave reasons why. In verse 15, he said, *"That ye may be blameless and harmless, the sons of God, without rebuke, in the midst of a crooked and perverse nation, among whom ye shine as lights in the world."*

Paul is saying in essence, "As a child of God, you must live blamelessly in a world full of sinful people so that you can shine before the world like a star in the sky."

Jesus also commanded us to do so. In the Sermon on the Mount, He called believers *"the light of the world" (Matthew 5:14).* In verse 16, He said, *"Let your light so shine before men, that they may see your good works, and glorify your Father which is in heaven."*

We sing a little song that goes like this: "This little light of mine, I'm going to let it shine." This is what Paul and Jesus are telling us to do. The next verse says, "Hide it under a bushel, no!" I pray that this tune describes you.

But I must add this. Every time you murmur or complain, you are hiding your light under a bushel and thus the Light of the World Himself. The only way the Light of the World shines in the darkness today is through believers. Pray that you will shine *"in the midst of a crooked and perverse world."* Shine; don't murmur.

OCTOBER 12   BE

Key Verse: *"...It is written; be ye holy; for I am holy" (1 Peter 1:16).*

Message: Peter is quoting Leviticus 11:44: *"For I am the Lord your God; ye shall...be holy for I am holy...."* Truly, individuals are commanded to be holy, to be righteous. As many of you know, this is the subject that is dear to my heart and to the Lord's also.

In His Word He has much to say about corporate holiness, as well as individual holiness. In the Old Testament He addressed the congregation; in the New Testament, the church. Same message!

In Leviticus 19:2, we read, *"And the Lord spake unto Moses saying, speak unto all the congregation of the children of Israel, and say unto them, Ye shall be holy; for I the Lord your God am holy."* Psalm 93:5 says, *"...holiness becometh (adorns) thine house, O Lord...."*

What a lovely picture! Wouldn't it be wonderful if this were a portrait of every Christian congregation? Of course, we know that we cannot be free of spots and wrinkles as long as we live in a sinful world, but to avoid them should be our objective. It is our Lord's objective also. We see His ultimate purpose for us in Ephesians 5:27: *"That He might present it to Himself a glorious church, not having spot, or wrinkle, or any such thing: but that it should be holy and without blemish."*

One day we will stand before our Lord who will judge our service record and then take away all our spots and wrinkles. At that time the church will be holy indeed. I desire to live a holy life so that I will not have a whole lot of wrinkles when I stand before Jesus the Judge. How about you?

In Ephesians 2:21, Paul says that Christ Jesus is building *"a holy temple of all believers."* Can he count you in that number? Resolve today to be holy, and ask the Lord to help you to be as wrinkle-free as possible.

OCTOBER 13   REQUIRE

Key Verse: *"...And what doth the Lord require of thee..."* (Micah 6:8)?

Message: In Micah's day the home was in terrible condition. Listen to what the prophet said to the men: *"Be careful what you say even to your wife. In these times sons treat their fathers like fools, daughters oppose their mothers, and young women quarrel with their* *mothers-in-law; a man's enemies are members of his own family"* *(7:5-6 GN)*.

You might ask, "Are you sure you are describing the family in Micah's day? It sounds like America to me." I am sad to say that I have to agree with you. These verses describe many homes today. The condition is often so strained that there is no peace in the home. We put locks on doors and install alarm systems to keep criminals out but often allow war to take place within. The news is full of children who kill parents and vice versa.

Well, Micah was looking at a degenerate people who were at their wits end as to what to do—as are many today. These men began to ask questions: *"What shall I bring to the Lord, the God of heaven, when I come to worship him? Shall I bring the best calves to burn as an offering to Him? Will the Lord be pleased if I bring Him thousands of sheep or endless streams of olive oil? Shall I offer Him my first-born child to pay for my sins"* (6:6-7 GN)?

Micah's response was in essence, "None of the above!" Then what? The answer is found in 6:8: *"He hath showed thee, O man, what is good, and what doth the Lord <u>require</u> of thee, but to do justly, and to love mercy, and to walk humbly with thy God?"*

Micah's point is that what these men wanted to bring would just be band-aids. What the Lord wanted them to bring were changed lives. Micah lists three things that God requires of a man:

  (1) "But to do justly"—to be honest and true and fair in dealing with the family.
  (2) "And to love mercy"—to be merciful with the family.
  (3) "And to walk humbly with thy God"—to be the spiritual leader of the household.

In God's eyes these things are *"what is good."* Men, ask the Holy Spirit to produce love for your family through you. Do so and you will be better prepared to do *"what is required of you."*

OCTOBER 14   OBEY

Key Verse: *"But this thing commanded I them, saying, Obey my voice..." (Jeremiah 7:23).*

Message: All through the Bible, God has commanded His people to obey Him. In this verse He says, *"Obey my voice, and I will be your God, and ye shall be my people; and walk ye in all the ways that I have commanded you, that it may be well unto you."* What a wonderful appeal! In essence He said, "Obey me. Then I will be your God, and you will be my people. Obey me and things will go well with you." Surely they would obey!

"But they hearkened not, nor inclined their ear, but walked in the counsels and in the imagination (stubbornness) of their evil heart, and went backward, and not forward (7:24). These folks *"went backward, not forward."* This is always the case. You never stand still in your walk with the Lord. You either go backward or forward.

Our Lord God used another "back" word to describe His people. It is the word "backsliding." In Hosea 11:7, He said, *"And my people are bent to backsliding from me."* If you are not going forward in your walk with the Lord, you are backsliding.

Let me give you a couple of verses that describes a backslider:

- Proverbs 14:4 says, *"The backslider in heart shall be filled with his own ways...."*
- In Jeremiah 3:11, we read, *"And the Lord said unto me, the backsliding Israel hath justified herself more than treacherous Judah."*

In plain English, the backslider satisfies the big "I," does what he wants to do, and rationalizes that what he is doing is all right.

Friend, if this describes you, and you are tired of backsliding, our God says to you the same thing He said to the children of Israel: *"Turn, O backsliding children, saith the Lord..." (Jeremiah 3:14).* He also said, *"Return, ye backsliding children, and I will heal your backslidings..." (Jeremiah 3:22).*

If you are ready to get right with the Lord, you must *"turn and return."* If you are ready to come home, stop in your tracks, turn around, and return to the Lord. He will open His arms to you. Ask the Lord to guide you.

By the way, this is a good way to pray for a backsliding friend or relative about whom you are concerned.

OCTOBER 15   PRAISE AND WORSHIP

Key Verse: *"...Praise thy great and awesome name..." (Psalm 99:3).*

Message: The title of Psalm 99 is "God Has Been Faithful." Take a look at your life—the up times, the down times; the good times, the bad times. Has God been faithful to you in every situation? In gratitude to Him, live as the Psalmist directs.

In verse 3, he said, *"Let the people praise thy great and awesome name, for He is holy."* In verse 5, he said, *"Exalt ye the Lord our God, and worship at His footstool; for He is holy."* In verse 9 he said, *"Exalt the Lord our God, and worship at His holy hill; for the Lord our God is holy."*

You will notice that each verse ends with the statement that God is holy. Because He is, we are to be also. I believe we see some instructions for us in these verses. In verse 3, he says that we are to praise His holy name. Paul says in Philippians 4:4: *"Rejoice in the Lord always, and again I say rejoice."* We are to have a lifestyle of praise.

In verse 5, he says that we are to *"worship at His footstool."* We are also to have a lifestyle of worship. We have the privilege of going to the throne room of God and bowing before His throne surrounded by beautiful gem-like colors and by a rainbow of green to worship Him. We have the privilege of bowing before Jesus in all His whiteness and brightness, in all of His glory—to worship and adore Him and praise His Holy name.

After we have spent time at Jesus' feet, we will be prepared for what the Psalmist says in verse 9, that we are to *"worship at His holy hill."* This directive meant Zion for the Jews and the church for us.

If we live a life of praise, if we sit at Jesus' feet every day, we will be ready to worship in His church. The color of the carpet won't matter; the dress of the people won't matter; the style of the music won't matter. We will be ready to *"enter into His gates with thanks-giving, and into His courts with praise; be thankful unto Him and bless His name" (Psalm 100:4).*

Pray that you will be able to live a life of praise and worship so that this verse will describe you every time you enter the house of the Lord.

OCTOBER 16   SURRENDER
Key Verse: *"Submit yourselves therefore to God..." (James 4:7).*

Message: Surrender! Submit! Yield! These are not words that we would choose to live by, mainly because there is no room for the big "I" when these words are part of our lives. But, to live a life pleasing to the Lord, we must adhere to these commands.

In 2 Chronicles 30:8, Hezekiah is talking to the children of Israel, but what he said is applicable to the local church, especially to people who want the worship service to go their way. Listen to the king: *"Now be ye not stiff-necked...but yield yourselves unto the Lord, and enter into His sanctuary...."*

Are you rebellious when you enter the house of God or are you yielded? I was talking with my friend, Jack, recently and made the comment that I cannot understand how anyone could enter the worship center without anticipating the exciting time of praise and worship of Jesus that takes place there. He made this comment to me: "A person cannot really celebrate until he surrenders." That is so true. You might have personal preferences, but you must put them aside and enter into the celebration.

You know, Jesus did not like the idea that He had to go to the cross. He prayed in the Garden of Gethsemane: *"O my Father, if it be possible, let this cup pass from me" (Matthew 26:39).* But He didn't end His prayer with what He wanted: *"...Nevertheless, not as I will, but as Thou wilt" (26:39).* Jesus did as the Father bade; He did not murmur. This is what He bids us do.

We sometimes sing an invitation hymn that begins, "All to Jesus I surrender." The chorus ends with, "All to Thee my blessed Savior, I surrender all." Would you make this your prayer today? If so, you will be able to celebrate Jesus in His house.

A word of caution! If you stand in the worship service like a statue with your arms across your chest, you just might be in danger of our Lord's calling you *"stiff-necked."*

Don't be! Surrender! Submit! Yield! Celebrate!!!

OCTOBER 17   ANGER

Key Verse: *"For the anger of man does not achieve the righteousness of God" (James 1:20).*

Message: I am spending another day on the subject of anger because I want you to see how the Word of God dealt with Mr. Brown's anger.

Mr. Brown worked with me for many years. During that time I never really saw his anger and neither did his family, but I knew from others that he had it. What I heard made me realize that he exemplified Proverbs 14:17: *"People with a hot temper do foolish things."* He had not learned James 1:19: *"Let every man be swift to hear, slow to speak, slow to anger."*

Today, he is obviously a changed man. I asked him what made the change. He directed me to James 1:20: *"For the anger of man does not achieve the righteousness of God."* Then he said to me in essence, "At first, as with most people, I was in denial about having an anger problem. But one day I realized that I had the problem and that it was reaching a peak. When I read this verse, the Holy Spirit stamped it upon my heart. I realized how God is so opposed to anger, that anger is always destructive, and that it never produces *'God's righteous purpose.'"* God has delivered Mr. Brown from a lifestyle of anger.

You know, it wasn't preaching or scolding or condemning that changed him. It was the Word of God. Truly, *"The Word of God is sharper than a two-edged sword..."* (Hebrews 4:12).

If the Word of God is going to rescue you from some sin, you have to spend time in it—to know it—to let the Holy Spirit impress it upon your heart. Make it such a part of your life that you can pray: *"Thy Word have I hid in my heart, that I might not sin against Thee" (Psalm 119:11).*

OCTOBER 18 CALLED

Key Verse: *"(Our Lord) hath called us with a holy calling... according to His own purpose" (2 Timothy 1:9).*

Message: When our Lord sends someone—pastor or lay person—down here, He sends that person with a purpose. He told Jeremiah why he was sent: *"...Before thou camest forth out of the womb, I set thee apart, and I appointed thee a prophet unto the nations" (Jeremiah 1:5).* You, too, have a purpose for being here.

And God does not change His mind about why He sent you. In Romans 11:29, Paul said, *"For the gifts and calling of God are irrevocable."* In Numbers 23:19 (GN), Balaam said, *"God is not a human who changes his mind...."*

I have often said, "I have yet to see a person truly called of God uncalled." God's call never changes. A person may be disqualified by his actions, but the call never changes. When observing people who have abandoned their call, I have noticed that the "body" is often involved—adultery, pornography, crossing God's sex-lines, sex outside of marriage.

Paul knew how easy it is to stumble, so he gave this testimony: *"But I discipline my body, and bring it into subjection, lest...I myself should be disqualified" (1 Corinthians 9:27).*

Folks, don't be disqualified. Seek the Lord's call for your life and stay on course. But if you should stray, repent, and get back on track. Your assignment might change, but our gracious Lord will still use you. Pray that you will stay in the center of God's will. You do not want to be stamped "disqualified." You want to be stamped "Well done."

OCTOBER 19 REQUIRE

Key Verse: *"...what doth the Lord require of thee..." (Deuteronomy 10:12)?*

Message: When God saw that His people had made a golden calf while Moses was on the mountain, He was furious. When Moses came down and saw the calf, he broke the tablets that contained the Ten Commandments. Moses sensed God's anger and began to beg

God to forgive the people. God answered and sent Moses back up the mountain for a second printing of the Commandments. He came down with a message from God for these people, whom He had spared. Here is the word:

"And now, Israel, what doth the Lord thy God require of thee, but to fear the Lord Thy God, to walk in all His ways, and to love Him, and to serve the Lord thy God with all thy heart and with all thy soul" (Deuteronomy 10:12).

You will notice that God did not say that He would like for the people to do as He said in this verse. No! He said in essence, "This is what I <u>require</u> you to do." He had forgiven them so much. Jesus said of such people: *"...For unto whomsoever much is given, of him shall much be required..."* (Luke 12:48). We, like the children of Israel, have been forgiven so much. As a result, much is required of us also. Let's look at the requirements:

(1) *"To fear the Lord thy God"*—to have a healthy respect for—

(2) *"To walk in all His ways"*—to follow Him down the path of righteousness—

(3) *"To love Him"*—to love Him above all others—

(4) *"To serve the Lord thy God with all thy heart and with all thy soul"*—to serve our Lord with our whole being.

Folks, if you realize how much you have been forgiven, you will love the Lord with all your heart; and if you love Him with all your heart, you will serve Him and keep His commandments. Pray that you will do just that.

OCTOBER 20   FAITHFUL

Key Verse: *"...For he was a faithful man..."* (Nehemiah 7:2).

Message: When Nehemiah was serving Artaxerxes in Persia, he had a visit from Hanani and some other men from Jerusalem. Nehemiah asked them, "How are my brothers who have returned from exile doing?" The answer was, "Not good! The people are having a hard time. The walls of the city are broken down."

We next meet this man in 7:2. The wall had been rebuilt; the gates were in place; the Temple guards, the singers, and priests were in their places of service. At this point Nehemiah said, *"I put two men in charge of governing the city..." (7:2).* One was his brother Hanani—maybe literally, but probably just a Jewish brother. He had been faithful to deliver God's message to Nehemiah. As a result he was honored.

The other man put in charge of the city was Hananiah. Why was he given the honor? Chapter 7, verse 2, tells us: *"...For he was a faithful man, and feared God above many."* Nehemiah is saying that Hananiah was a faithful and God-fearing man without equal. He certainly met the requirements of being a good steward. Paul says in 1 Corinthians 4:2: *"Moreover, it is required in stewards (servants), that a man be found faithful."* Hanani and Hananiah were, and God honored them. He does the same today for faithful servants. Are you one? You just need to be faithful to do what pleases the Lord. I call these things "absolutes." Here are some of them: attending church regularly, supporting the pastors, tithing and giving, having a daily quiet time, sharing Jesus, never murmuring.

If you are faithful in these areas, our Lord has a word for you: *"Well done, good and faithful servant; thou hast been faithful over a few things; I will make you ruler over many things..." (Matthew 25:23).*

You be faithful to adhere to the "absolutes" in this life, and our Lord will give you a great place of service when He sets up His earthly kingdom. The degree of your reward will depend upon your earthly faithfulness. As you pray today, renew your vows to our Lord to be faithful in what is required of you.

OCTOBER 21   UNITED

Key Verse: *"And all the people gathered themselves together..." (Nehemiah 8:1).*

Message: If there is to be revival in the church, we must heed the message of Nehemiah 8. We must all gather together, and not just meet together, but gather together *"as one man."* These people came together in one accord to get a word from God.

Actually, the men were not the only ones who came. This was a family affair. Verses 2 and 3 tell us that men, women, and children who could comprehend all came and stood attentively for some six hours.

This worship service was so special. I do not want you to miss what happened, so I am going to quote directly from 8:5-6: *"And Ezra opened the book in the sight of all the people...and when he opened it, all the people stood up. And Ezra blessed the Lord, the great God. And all the people answered, Amen, Amen...."*

You will notice that before Ezra read the Word, he *"blessed the Lord."* He led in a praise service. Maybe he prayed Psalm 135:19-20: *"Bless the Lord O House of Israel; bless the Lord O House of Aaron; bless the Lord O House of Levi; ye that fear the Lord, bless the Lord."*

Remember, these folks *"stood together as one,"* so when Ezra blessed the Lord, they all—every person—shouted *"Amen, Amen"* as an affirmation of what Ezra prayed. But this is not all they did. They also *"lifted up their hands, and they bowed their heads, and worshiped the Lord with their faces to the ground."*

After the children of Israel lifted their hands in agreement with Ezra's prayer, they bowed their heads and worshiped the Lord face down. All the people bowed in willing submission to our Lord. When this happens, revival will come. Pray that you may experience it in your church.

OCTOBER 22 UNDERSTAND
Key Verse: *"...They...caused the people to understand..." (Nehemiah 8:7).*

Message: After Ezra read the Word of God to all the people, a group of Levites explained it to them and *"caused the people to understand."* What did they do when they understood? They wept. Verse 9 says that *"All the people wept, when they heard the words of the law."*

When these people heard the Word and understood the Word, they were convicted by it. They wept because they realized how they had violated it. They must have wept loudly because Nehemiah,

Ezra, and the Levites had to interrupt the service and say to them: *"This day is holy to our Lord. Do not mourn nor weep; for the joy of the Lord is your strength"* (8:10).

It was right for these folks to weep over their sins, but they needed to see how God forgives and blesses. They needed to celebrate because God had not destroyed them as a nation for their forsaking Him and had given them a new beginning. (He will do the same for any child of His in the far country.)

Nehemiah said, *"Go and enjoy choice food and sweet drinks, and send some to those who have nothing prepared..."* (8:10). They obeyed. You see, when you truly understand the Word of God, you will follow your leaders. Nehemiah went on to say, "You can celebrate because *'The joy of the Lord is your strength' (stronghold)."* They could have joy by understanding from God's Word that they were safe in the arms of our Lord. This knowledge caused them to rejoice.

Let me tell you this. The one who rejoices in the Lord has a strong shield that can be used to ward off the evil one. Paul says in Ephesians 6:11 that we are to put on *"the whole armor of God."* In verse 16, he says, *"Above all, taking the shield of faith, wherewith ye shall be able to quench all the fiery darts of the wicked one."*

Do you understand what Paul just said? If so, why don't you make a vow today that you will put that shield up before you leave your house each day?

OCTOBER 23   WORSHIP
Key Verse: "...Blessed be the glorious name..." (Nehemiah 9:5).

Message: Yesterday we observed the Israelites at a special worship service on the *"first day of the seventh month"* (8:2). Chapter 9 begins by noting that it was now *"the twenty-fourth day of the same month..." (9:1).* The people had come back for another service.

What did they do this time? First of all, they fasted and put on sackcloth and ashes as signs of grief over their sins. Then they began to confess their sins and the sins of their fathers. Verse 3 (GN) says that *"for about three hours the law of the Lord their God was read to them and for the next three hours they confessed their sins and worshiped the Lord their God."*

Notice the order: grief over their sins, hearing the Word, confession of their sins, worship. When they did the first three things, they were ready to worship. How did they worship? They began with prayer. Verse 4 says that a select group of Levites stood on a platform *"and cried with a loud voice unto the Lord their God."* Then a partially changed group of Levites gave a call to worship. They said, *"Stand up and praise the Lord your God; praise Him forever and ever! Let everyone praise his glorious name..." (9:5).*

When this congregation met together, they were all in one accord. They grieved over their sins, let the Word penetrate their hearts, and confessed their sins. I repeat what I said earlier. They were now ready to worship and praise the Lord.

I believe they may have ended this meeting by proclaiming, *"Blessed be the Lord God of Israel from everlasting to everlasting; and let all the people say, Amen, Amen. Praise ye the Lord" (Psalm 106:48).*

What a mighty service the people had! You can have the same experience if you do as the Israelites did. Notice that they all came in one accord. They checked their personal preferences at the door. Do likewise and you will have a wonderful time with the Lord. Do your homework before you come. That will take a special Sunday morning quiet time. Commit to it and your quality of worship will be so special.

OCTOBER 24   REMEMBER
Key Verse: *"...I remember their wickedness..." (Hosea 7:2).*

Message: Chapter 7 of Hosea begins with a message from God. In essence He says, "Every time I want to restore my people, all I see is their wickedness. They cheat; they steal; they rob. It never enters their heads that I will remember their evil ways." Jeremiah 14:10 says that God *"will remember their iniquity...."*

The people in Psalm 93 were doing evil things. They justified what they were doing by saying in verse 7: *"The Lord shall not see..."* In verse 9, the Psalmist asked, *"He that formed the eye, shall He not see?"* He does! In Psalm 11:4, David said, *"...The Lord's throne is in heaven; His eyes behold...the children of men."*

Psalm 94:11 says that *"The Lord (even) knoweth the thoughts of man...."* Nothing escapes our Lord. He sees everything; He knows everything.

Now, how long does He remember? Until we follow 1 John 1:9! Here John says, *"If we confess our sins, He is faithful and just to forgive our sins, and to cleanse us from all unrighteousness."*

And what does our Lord do with confessed sins? He remembers them no more. In Psalm 103:12, David said, *"As for as the east is from the west, so far hath He removed our transgressions from us."* In Isaiah 43:25, God says, *"I, even I, am He that blotteth out thy transgressions...and will not remember thy sins."* In Micah 7:19, God says that He will cast *"all our sins into the depths of the sea."*

I believe you can see that what God forgives, He forgets. Our part is to stay confessed up so that He will forgive and forget our sins. Folks, this will take a lot of praying. Don't let sin go unconfessed. As you pray today, lay your specific sins at Jesus' feet.

OCTOBER 25   ANGER
Key Verse: *"It was before the Lord...therefore will I play before the Lord"* (2 Samuel 6:21).

Message: David was happy that the ark was now where it belonged, in Jerusalem. Verse 12 says that he brought it there *"with gladness."* What did he do to show his happiness? He had a celebration.

He first offered an animal sacrifice. Then he danced. Verse 14 says, *"And David danced before the Lord with all his might, and David was girded with a linen ephod"* (probably a short, sleeveless tunic). To dance before the Lord, David had to take off his outer garment. He was adequately covered, maybe a bit undignified but not immodest. Anyway, he and the people had a great celebration. Verse 15 says that *"David and all the house of Israel brought up the Ark of the Lord with shouting, and with the sound of the trumpet."*

But there was one who did not join in: David's wife Michal. She looked out the window and saw *"King David leaping and dancing before the Lord, and she despised him in her heart"* (6:16).

Meanwhile, the celebration went on. David offered sacrifices. Then he *"blessed the people in the name of the Lord of Hosts"*

(6:18). Then he fed them and sent them to their homes. Then he headed for home to celebrate with his family.

But he was met at the gate by an angry Michal who said to him in essence, "You acted like a fool out there, dancing around in front of your officials and servant girls." In reply David made a very important statement about worship: *"I was dancing to honor the Lord...and I will go on dancing to honor the Lord" (6:21)*.

Michal paid a high price for criticizing David's method of praise and worship. Verse 23 says that Michal *"...had no child unto the day of her death."* Scholars believe that this means that David had nothing more to do with her. How sad!

But, folks, a negative and critical spirit is a dangerous thing. Don't be a Michal; do be a part of our Lord's worship celebration. Ask the Lord to change any "don'ts" you have to "do's" when you come to celebrate our Lord in His church.

OCTOBER 26   UNDERSTAND
Key Verse: *"Make me to understand..." (Psalm 119:27)*.

Message: The Psalmist in 119:25 was depressed. He was so down that he was on his face in the dust. His desire was to be revived. He knew there was only one way that he could get relief. Thus he prayed, *"...Revive me according to thy Word" (119:25)*. He did the right thing. Folks, you may get help from a friend or a pastor or a relative or a counselor; but you cannot be made whole apart from the Word of God.

Notice the Psalmist's next step after he prayed to be revived. In essence he said, "I have confessed my sins, so I know you have heard me. Now teach me thy statutes." Notice the progression. He asked to be revived; he confessed his sins. Then he asked to be taught, but he knew that teaching had to be coupled with understanding.

In verse 27, the Psalmist prayed, *"Make me to understand thy precepts..."* In verse 169, he prayed, *"O Lord, give me understanding according to thy Word."* He knew that any understanding must come from God's Word. He knew that it was there and there alone that he could understand how to get help in his situation.

Moses had this kind of understanding; the children of Israel did not. Psalm 103:7 says, *"He (God) made known His <u>ways</u> unto Moses, His <u>acts</u> unto the children of Israel."* Murmuring Israel knew God's acts—parting the Red Sea, manna from heaven, etc., but they couldn't see beyond, so they mumbled. Moses could. He saw God's ways. He knew that God was in every incident that happened. He knew because he knew God's ways. He knew God's ways because he talked with God, and God talked with him.

We can understand God's ways because He talks to us through His Word. Need revived? Humble yourself before the Lord; ask Him to teach you His Word; ask Him to give you understanding. When you reach this point, you will get your eyes off yourself and on to others.

The desire of the Psalmist is seen in 119:27: *"...I shall talk of thy wondrous works."* Folks, when you go from being down to being up, you are to testify as to how understanding God's Word brought you victory. Tell the Lord that you want to be revived and then follow the steps the Psalmist took.

OCTOBER 27   ANGER

Key Verse: *"...Whosoever is angry with his brother....your brother has something against you" (Matthew 5:22-23).*

Message: In this passage Jesus has a word for a person who is angry with a brother and who has someone angry with him. First, Jesus addresses the one who is angry with a brother. In verse 22, Jesus said, *"Everyone who is angry with his brother shall be guilty before the court; and whosoever shall say to his brother, Raca, shall be guilty before the supreme court; and whosoever shall say, you fool, shall be guilty enough to go into the fiery hell."*

The degree of anger determines the punishment. In Jesus' day if a person was angry, he went before the civil court. If he was angry enough to call a brother *"raca,"* meaning brainless idiot, empty head, etc., he went before the Sanhedrin, the high court that tried the more serious crimes. If he was angry enough to call his brother a fool, he would have to go to Gehenna, a garbage dump where fires burned continually (a picture of eternal fire). I believe you can see how serious the Lord takes anger—here with someone who is angry with his brother.

But He also takes it very seriously when someone is angry with you. In 5:23, He gives this stern command: *"If therefore you are presenting your offering at the altar, and there remember that your brother has something against you, leave your offering there before the altar, and go your way; first be reconciled to your brother, and then come and present your offering."*

Our Lord is saying that before you give your offering, you need to deal with anger—anger with a brother that you can do something about or anger directed toward you that you can try to do something about. You offer an apology. It is up to that person to accept.

Now when we think of offering, we usually think of money. It certainly is included. But I believe it covers so much more. It includes whatever your service is: teaching, preaching, singing, playing an instrument, serving as a deacon, etc. I suggest that you leave your offering at the altar until you have done your best to deal with anger against someone or anger toward you. You may have to stay on your knees for a while, but it will be worth it. God accepts no offering if it has anger attached to it. Pray!

OCTOBER 28   DESIRE

Key Verse: *"What I desire from you is plain and clear..."* *(Hosea 6:6 GN).*

Message: The title of Chapter 6 in the Good News Bible is, "The People's Insincere Repentance." I am reminded of a story that a friend of mine told me recently. His five-year-old grandson lives with him and his wife. When it came time to visit his biological father, he didn't want to go. He said, "I don't like him. He's not my daddy."

To this my friend replied, "Yes, he is your daddy, and you have to be nice to him." The child replied, "I'll pretend to like him. I'll be nice to him, and God will honor that." This brought a chuckle, but God doesn't honor pretense. He didn't with the children of Israel who were guilty of all sorts of sins.

Oh, it seemed as if they were sincere. They said the right words. In 6:1, they said, *"Come, let us return unto the Lord...."* In verse 3, they said, *"Let us acknowledge the Lord...."* This was exactly what the Lord had been calling on them to do. But, folks, there is something missing from their confession. There is no acknowledgment of their sin. As a result God did not accept their prayer. He knew their hearts. In 7:14, He said, *"They do not cry out to me with their hearts."*

In 6:4, the Lord asked a question that many parents ask: *"Israel and Judah, what am I going to do with you? Your love for me disappears as quickly as morning mist...."* He went on to say in essence, "That is the reason that I have sent my prophets to you to speak of your coming judgment."

Then our Lord said something to the children of Israel that brought sadness to my heart. He said, *"What I want from you is plain and clear: I want your constant love, not your animal sacrifices. I would rather have my people know me than have them burn offerings to me"* (6:6).

The children of Israel wanted God's blessings on their terms. He only grants blessings on His terms. They missed God's best because they did not confess their sins and then do as He desired. His desire was that they love Him and know Him. That is His desire for us also. If we do as He desires, He will bless us. Need to confess sin? Do so right now.

OCTOBER 29   SUPPORT
Key Verse: *"...He cheered me up many times"* (2 Timothy 1:16 GN).

Message: When Paul wrote his second letter to Timothy, he was in chains in a dark, dank prison in Rome. In the epistle Paul mentioned some of their mutual acquaintances, many of whom he had led to Christ and nurtured.

By what Paul said to Timothy, we see how some of these people reacted to Paul's being in prison. Some turned away from him. In 2 Timothy 1:16, Paul said in essence, "Timothy, you know that everyone in Asia has turned away from me, including Phygellus and Hermogenes." So sad! This is the only mention of these two men in the Bible, and the only thing said about them is that they had deserted their spiritual leader. Paul had been there when they needed him, but they were no place to be found when he needed them. Unfortunately, this could be said about many church members today. They tend to jump ship when times are tough for their leaders, rather than stay around and support them, and supporting them brings reward. We see this in the next person whom Paul mentioned. His name is Onesiphorus.

Before Paul said anything about this man, he said in essence, "May the Lord bless his family." Then he told why. There are several reasons. One is found in verse 16: *"...For he often refreshed me."* The Good News puts it this way: *"...because he cheered me up many times."* He was a breath of fresh air to Paul.

The second reason is also found in verse 16: *"(He) was not ashamed of my chains."* Paul was chained to a Roman soldier twenty-four hours a day. Onesiphorus could have just stayed in Ephesus, but he didn't. He came to Rome and cheered Paul up.

The third reason is that *"when he was in Rome, he sought me out very diligently and found me" (1:17).* This verse seems to indicate that Onesiphorus had trouble finding Paul but kept looking until he found him; and when he did, he refreshed him.

What Onesiphorus did for Paul in Rome and Ephesus will bring him reward at the Judgment Seat of Christ. Paul said in verse 18: *"The Lord grant unto him that he find mercy of the Lord in that day...."* Onesiphorus is mentioned in these verses and in 4:19. There Paul told Timothy to *"salute...the household of Onesiphorus."*

The only thing we know about this man is that he stuck by this great preacher through thick and thin and cheered him up many times. What a blessing to the man of God is a person who supports him and encourages him! The church needs many people like Onesiphorus. Won't you be one? Tell the Lord that you will.

OCTOBER 30   HEAR

Key Verse: *"If any man has ears, let him hear" (Mark 4:23).*

Message: Jesus had just asked the people, including His disciples: *"Do you bring in a lamp to put it under a bowl or a bed? Instead, don't you put it on a stand" (4:21)?* Here Jesus is making a logical point. You don't hide light; you get it out into the open.

Then He goes on to say, *"For there is nothing hidden which will not be revealed, nor has any thing been kept secret but that it should come to light."* In the Old Testament something is hidden, the church. In the New Testament nothing is hidden. It is possible to understand God's Word. How?

First, by hearing! In verse 23, Jesus said, *"If anyone has ears, let him hear."* In verse 24, He said, *"Pay attention to what you hear."* You see, if you want to know God's Word, you can't just hear it with your ears. You have to hear it with your heart also. This requires your hearing the Word taught and preached and studying it on your own in your daily quiet time.

Now notice what Jesus said in verses 24 and 25: *"...The measure you give will be the measure you get, and still more will be given you."* Jesus' point is that the amount of time you spend hearing and studying Scripture will determine how much of God's Word you understand. The more you listen and study, the more insight you will be given!

Ever said something like this: "I've read that verse many times, but today I saw something I had not seen before"? Why was that true? The key is in the "many times." Stay in the Word, and you will be given more and more insight.

I like the footnote in my King James Study Bible about this verse: "This may be paraphrased: 'Give careful attention to what you hear. For according to the proportion of study given God's Word, a corresponding amount of knowledge will be given you, and generously multiplied at that.' The point is that God's truth, instead of being divinely hidden from man, will be understood in proportion to one's attention to and study of it."

Want more insight? Stay in the Word. Commit to the Lord that you will do just that.

OCTOBER 31   FOLLOW
Key Verse: *"...But I wholly followed the Lord"* (Joshua 14:8).

Message: As we see in Joshua 14, the children of Israel were in the Promised Land, and it was now time for Joshua to divide the land among the tribes. Caleb came and made his request. He began by reminding Joshua, "You remember that when I was forty years old, Moses sent me to spy out the land. I came back and said that we could take it. The people rejected what I said *"...but I wholly followed the Lord" (Joshua 14:8).*

What was his reward for having done so? Well, while the original children of Israel were dying in the wilderness, God kept him alive. He was now eighty-five years old. Was he old and decrepit? Not so! God rewarded him with strength. In verse 11, Caleb said, *"I am as strong this day as I was in the day that Moses sent me...."*

Now Caleb was ready to make his request. What land did he choose? In verse 12, he said, *"Give me this mountain...."* You know, he did not ask for a nice rich valley or some city already built or a retirement home. Instead, he asked for a mountain where the enemy still lived. He said to Joshua, *"...If so be the Lord will be with me, then I shall be able to drive them out..." (14:12).* Request granted! Verse 14 says, *"Hebron therefore became the inheritance of Caleb... because he wholly followed the Lord."* The Lord was with Caleb, and he was able to drive the enemy off the mountain.

Caleb is an example to us all. He was rewarded for one reason: *"...because he wholly followed the Lord."* As you journey through this world, you will encounter some mountains along the way. You can choose to run from them or climb them in the power of the Lord. If you choose to follow the Lord, you will get to the top. Obedience brings blessing!

Now that you have read these words, are you ready to let them influence your life? I pray that you will take them with you as you travel down *"the path of righteousness."* What will matter when you stand before Jesus the Judge at the Bema Seat (Judgment Seat) of Christ one day is this: Did you wholly follow the Lord?

November

PROMISES WHEN YOU_____

I n Psalm 5:8, David prayed, *"Lead me O Lord, in thy righteous-ness;...Make thy way straight before my face."* In Hebrews 12:13, we hear this prayer: *"Make straight paths for your feet...."* In Proverbs 4:25 and 27, we read, *"Let thine eyes look right on, and let thine eyelids look straight before thee. Turn not to thy right hand nor to the left...."*

I am sure that these verses contain the desires of our hearts. We want to walk down the road of righteousness right straight toward Jesus. We don't want to stumble or waiver or get off course; but because of our old sin nature, there will be times when we will need encouragement in order to stay the course. Where do we go for help? To the Word! There we find promises for anything that might cause us to veer to the left or to the right or even backwards.

I am calling this month "Promises When You _____." Each day we will fill in the blanks with a word of encouragement.

NOVEMBER 1   ARE DEPRESSED

Key Verse: *"I will never forget you "(Isaiah 49:15 GN).*

Message: The people of Jerusalem were at a low point. They said, *"The Lord hath forsaken me, and my Lord hath forgotten me" (Isaiah 49:14).* Ever felt this way? Ever been so down that you wondered if you had been forsaken by God?

Take heart, my friend; He hasn't left you. Listen to the promise He made to His people: *"Can a woman forget her own baby and not love the child she bore? Even if a mother should forget her child, I will never forget you" (49:15 GN).*

When Moses commissioned Joshua to take his place to lead the children of Israel to the Promised Land, he gave the same promise: *"The Lord himself will lead you and be with you. He will not fail you or abandon you..." (Deuteronomy 31:8).* We see the same promise in Hebrews 13:5: *For he hath said, I will never leave thee nor forsake thee."*

So, when you are down, force yourself, as an act of your will, to claim this promise: *"I will never forget you."* Read all of these verses out loud as a prayer. If you are so down that you cannot pray, just hold on to the hem of His garment and repeat His name: "Jesus! Jesus! Jesus! Jesus! You are Lord." As you call out to Him, our Lord will hear you and whisper in your ear, *"I will never forget you."*

NOVEMBER 2   ARE IMPATIENT

Key Verse: *"...after he had patiently endured, he obtained the promise" (Hebrews 6:15).*

Message: We live in an impatient society. We want what we want when we want it. We want God to act on our timetable. We want God's blessings on our timetable.

Impatience robs a person of blessing. It did Moses. In Numbers 20:8, God told Moses: *"Take the rod, and gather thou the assembly together...and speak ye unto the rock before their eyes, and thou shalt bring forth to them water out of the rock...."*

Well, Moses gathered the people together, but he had lost patience with them. He called them *"rebels."* Then he lifted up that rod and *"smote the rock twice" (20:11)*. Oh, the water came out all right; in fact, it came out in abundance. However, Moses' impatience caused him to miss God's blessing. In his impatience he hit the rock, a violation of God's command. As a result God said, *"...ye shall not bring this congregation into the land which I have given them" (20:12)*. What a blessing Moses missed because of his impatience!

On the other hand, there is Abraham. I want to read to you Hebrews 6, verses 14 and 15, from the <u>Good News Bible</u>: *"God said, I promise you that I will bless you and give you many descendants. Abraham was patient, and so he received what God had promised."* The <u>King James Bible</u> puts it this way: *"...after he had patiently endured, he obtained the promise."* There was no impatience on Abraham's part, and he received God's blessing. It didn't come all at once; but he waited, he endured, and it came.

There is a blessing promised for all who wait on the Lord. It is found in Isaiah 40:31: *"But they that wait upon the Lord shall renew their strength; they shall mount up with wings as eagles they shall run and not be weary; and they shall walk, and not faint."*

Folks, "impatience" must give way to "wait" if you want great blessings of the Lord. Don't get ahead of God. Don't make impulsive changes. Don't change jobs, schools, churches, etc. until you get a peace from God. Wait until you do. The Psalmist has good advice: *"Wait on the Lord...Wait, I say, on the Lord..." (Psalm 27:14)*. Ask the Lord to help you do just that.

NOVEMBER 3   WANT TO QUIT

Key Verse: *"Blessed is the man that endureth trials..." (James 1:12)*.

Message: Has there been a period in your life when nothing went right? When others prospered and you could barely make ends meet? When you just wanted to quit?

The Psalmist in Psalm 73 was at that point. In verses 2 and 3 (GN), he said, *"...my faith was almost gone because I was jealous of the proud when I saw that things go well for the wicked."* But he didn't quit. He went to God's house where his faith was restored. (The best place to go!)

275

I thought about the two blind men in Matthew 9. One day as Jesus was walking along the way, two blind men followed Him crying, *"Thou Son of David, have mercy on us" (Matthew 9:27).* They probably yelled this plea several times, but Jesus didn't answer them. He just kept walking.

Verse 28 tells us that Jesus went into a house. Did the blind men give up and go to their regular begging place? No! They followed Jesus into the house. They probably stumbled over the furniture, but they were determined to get to Jesus. It would have been easier to quit, but they didn't, and their persistence brought their healing.

Jesus asked them: *"...Believe ye that I am able to do this? They said unto Him, Yea, Lord. Then touched he their eyes saying, According to your faith be it unto you" (Matthew 9: 28-29).* Because they showed faith and didn't give up, they were blessed.

Now if you are like the Psalmist before he went to God's house and want to be like the blind men, there is a promise for you. It is found in James 1:12: *"Blessed is the man that endureth temptations (trial)s: for when he is tried* (has his service record approved at the Judgment Seat of Christ), *he shall receive the crown of life, which the Lord hath promised to them that love him."*

Folks, trials will come. Don't quit! Endure! Earn a crown to lay at the feet of the One who saved you by His matchless grace. The last stanza of the hymn, "Yield Not to Temptation" goes like this: "To him that o'ercometh, God giveth a crown. Thro' faith we shall conquer, Tho' often cast down. He who is our Savior, Our strength will renew. Look ever to Jesus, He'll carry you through."

Why not sing this in your quiet time today? Then get up resolved never to quit, but to endure and thus earn a crown.

NOVEMBER 4   NEED PEACE

Key Verse: *"Great peace have they..." (Psalm 119:165).*

Message: In this message I am going to talk about the promise to believers who need peace, but I am going to show how our actions can bring peace in the church. Unfortunately, many churches resemble war instead of peace. This is not our Lord's plan.

Are you helping to create peace in the body? Check yourself on these instructions from God's Word. In 1 Thessalonians 5:12-13, Paul exhorts the brethren. He says, *"And we beseech you, brethren, to know them which labor among you, and are over you in the Lord, and admonish (instruct) you. And to esteem them very highly in* <u>love</u> *for their work's sake...."* If there is to be peace in the church, the body must respect the pastors for their labor of love and follow them where God leads. If a person were to murmur to me, I would simply say, "If my pastor says that the Lord is leading us to go in a certain direction, I will go. 'I don't like' is not part of my vocabulary."

Paul's next instruction is found at the end of verse 13: *"...and be at peace among yourselves."* What a formula for a great church— follow the leaders and be at peace with one another!

The big "I" sometimes keeps us from following these instructions. How can we obey? I found some good advice in Psalm 119. It seems that the Psalmist was having trouble. In verse 161, he said that powerful men were after him. Notice how he handled the enemy. He got in the Word. In verse 162, he said, *"I rejoice at thy word."* Then he got into praising. In verse 164, he said, *"Seven times a day do I praise thee...."* The enemy didn't bother this man because he spent a lot of time praising the Lord and feasting on His Word. What a lifestyle!

We have an enemy that does not want peace in the church. He is after us; but he won't get to us if we follow our leaders, get along with one another, praise the Lord all day, and stay in His Word. Staying in His Word has a great promise: *"Great peace have they which love thy law, and nothing causes them to stumble" (Psalm 119:165).*

Why not offer this song to the Lord today? "This is my story; this is my song, praising my Savior all the day long." Then get into the Word. You will find peace individually and thus contribute to peace in the body.

NOVEMBER 5 NEED REMINDING

Key Verse: *"...happy is that people, whose God is the Lord"* (*Psalm 144:15*).

Message: David was able to pen this promise after he reminded himself of who man is and who God is. Sometimes we get so caught up in the here and now that we act as if this life is all there is. We spend our days trying to make it in this world. Self sits on the throne. The promise in verse 15—*"...happy is that people, whose God is the Lord"*—cannot be applied to these folks.

Then, to whom can it apply? It can apply to the person who allows God to sit on the throne of his life. He is the one who knows what our Lord is to him and lives accordingly. Listen to who David says He is. In Psalm 144:1, he says that the Lord is his *"strength."* In verse 2, he says, *"My goodness (my loving kindness), and my fortress; my high tower, and my deliverer; my shield, and he in whom I trust (take refuge)...."*

If you remind yourself of who you are when self is on the throne— *"a shadow that passeth away"*; and if you remind yourself of who you are when the Lord is on the throne of your life—when you acknowledge Him as your strength, your fortress, your deliverer, your shield—you can become David's promise: *"...happy is that people, whose God is the Lord."*

Why not tell the Lord that you realize who you are—nothing— and that you realize who He is—everything—and tell Him that you will live accordingly.

NOVEMBER 6 ARE UP AGAINST AN ARMY

Key Verse: *"...be not afraid..."* (*Joshua 11:6*).

Message: Joshua and his army marched through the land promised to the children of Israel, winning victories along the way *"...because the Lord God of Israel fought for Israel"* (*Joshua 10:42*). They defeated five Amorite kings and took strategic cities far to the south and west of Jerusalem. Then Joshua *"returned, and all Israel with him, unto the camp to Gilgal"* (*10:43*).

Well, when this news of Israel's victories reached King Jabin of Hazor, he got concerned; so he sent for help from too many kings to count to come to do battle with Joshua and Israel.

They came. In verses 4 and 5 in the Good News Bible we read, *"They came with all their soldiers—an army with as many men as there are grains of sand on the seashore. They also had many horses and chariots. All these kings joined forces and came together and set up camp...to fight Israel."* What a picture! Little Israel against a gigantic army! When those Israelites saw all of those soldiers and horses and chariots ready to come against them, they must have felt that they could not win.

They were about to find out that soldiers and horses and chariots are powerless when God steps in. In 11:6, He made this promise to Joshua: *"...be not afraid because of them; for tomorrow about this time will I deliver them up all slain before Israel...."*

This was one of those times when Israel was united in obeying the Lord. This in itself brought the enemy armies against them. But you see, a people united in obedience to God has no need to fear the enemy. Today, the church has an enemy. He is using his army from without and from within to try to destroy the church. Can he succeed? Unfortunately, in many cases he can and does.

Can he be stopped? Absolutely! How? By our doing what the first church did in that upper room as they waited for Jesus to appear! Acts 1:14 says, *"These* (the apostles, the women and Jesus' half brothers) *all continued with one accord in prayer and supplication...."*

A key to victory over the enemy? Being in one accord! Practically, what does that mean? To me it means we first realize that the church is not about us. It is about Jesus. It is His church. He gives direction to the pastor; we follow.

I believe your pastor would say the same thing to the congregation that Paul said to the Philippians: *"I urge you to make me completely happy by having the same thoughts, sharing the same love, and being one in soul and mind" (Philippians 2:2 GN).* When we as a church live this verse, we can receive God's promise to Joshua.

A second key to victory over the enemy? Praying! The upper room church prayed as they waited for Jesus. Folks, the real battles are won, not by armies and horses and chariots, but by an army of the Lord—His church—on knees united in one accord for the purpose of building His church that the gates of hell cannot prevail against. Pray, folks! Pray as individuals, as the staff, as Bible class members, as a congregation! If you do so, there is no telling what God might do!

NOVEMBER 7 — ARE PRONE TO BE DOUBLEMINDED

Key Verse: *"Draw nigh to God, and he will draw nigh to you..."* *(James 4:8).*

Message: James makes this promise; then he begins to set forth conditions. It is interesting to note that he gives them to the *"double-minded" (4:8).* The doubleminded person is one who claims one thing but lives another. Sad to say, there are doubleminded people in the church.

On the one hand, they profess that the church belongs to Jesus. It does! These folks know Scriptures that confirm this: *"And He (Jesus) is the head of the body, the church..." (Colossians 1:18).* They know that Jesus told Peter the conditions on which He would build His church (Matthew 16:18).

On the other hand, they act as if the church belongs to them. "I don't like" rolls so easily off their tongues or "I don't think we should do this" or "I don't like these changes,"—etc. Test yourself. Think back over the last few days. Did any of these statements come out of your mouth? Be careful! You just might be doubleminded.

In verses 4 through 9, James tells what we must do in order to be able to *"draw night to God...."* In essence he says, "Wash your hands; purify your hearts; cry and weep; humble yourselves before the Lord." When you do these things, you become a singleminded person—one who realizes that the church is not about you and all about Jesus. When you realize this and act accordingly, there is another promise for you the end of 4:9: *"...and he shall lift you up."*

You can *"draw nigh to God"* in your prayer time today and have Him *"draw nigh to you"* if you allow Him to be the Head of His church.

NOVEMBER 8   OBEY

Key Verse: *"...ye shall possess their land, as the Lord your God hath promised unto you" (Joshua 23:5).*

Message: Joshua 23 begins by saying that the *"Lord had given rest unto Israel from all their enemies."* At this time Joshua was very old. He knew his time was short, so he called all Israel to come and stand before him. He said to them in essence, "God has fought for you and will continue to do so, and you will possess all the land *'the Lord your God hath promised unto you'"*(23:5).

Then Joshua began to list conditions that must be met if this promise were to come true. Let me list some of them:

1. *"...keep and do all that is written in the book of the law of Moses..." (23:6).*
2. *"Cleave unto the Lord your God..." (23:8).*
3. *"Take diligent heed therefore unto yourselves that ye love the Lord your God" (23:11).*

Then Joshua said to them in essence, "If you don't obey these commands, you will not possess your land." You know, I believe that every church has a certain territory God intends for it to possess. To do so, the church must meet the same conditions laid down by Joshua: adhere to God's Word, cleave to the Lord, and love Him above all others.

The church that meets these conditions will be able to claim its promised territory. Will your church succeed? It all depends on the believing members. Will you do your part? Tell the Lord that you will.

NOVEMBER 9   FEEL GUILTY

Key Verse: *"...for he will abundantly pardon" (Isaiah 55:7).*

Message: The Psalmist in Psalm 73 was jealous of the rich people who had everything while he had nothing—until he got right with God. Then he felt so guilty and so sorry that he had doubted. When he went to bed, he was sure that the Lord would desert him; but he woke up the next morning able to declare: *"Nevertheless I am* *continually with thee..."* (73:23). The guilt was gone. His life became a life of praise. Then there was David.

If anyone ever felt guilty about his sin, it was David. He couldn't get over how he had sinned against God with Bathsheba. In Psalm 51:3, he said, *"...my sin is ever before me."* Also, if anyone ever felt sorry for his sin, it was David. He prayed: *"Purge me with hyssop, and I shall be clean; wash me, and I shall be whiter than snow"* (51:7). In verse 10, he prayed, *"Create in me a clean heart, O God; and renew a right (steadfast) spirit within me."* God did and went on to use David in a mighty way.

I don't know where you are today. I don't know if you are carrying guilt around with you. You don't have to. But if you are, Isaiah 55:7 tells you what to do and also what God will do: *"Let the wicked forsake his way, and the unrighteous man his thoughts; and let him return unto the Lord, and he will have mercy upon him; and to our God, for he will abundantly pardon."* If your guilt is making you feel *"wicked"* and *"unrighteous,"* just *"return unto the Lord, and...he will abundantly pardon."*

I leave you today with some wonderful promises found in the first three lines of the first three stanzas of the hymn, "Though Your Sins Be as Scarlet":

> Tho' your sins be as scarlet, they
> shall be as white as snow;
> Hear the voice that entreats you,
> O return ye unto God!
> He'll forgive your transgressions,
> And remember them no more.

This is the God we serve. Let Him remove any guilt you carry and praise Him for delivering you.

NOVEMBER 10   ARE BOUND

Key Verse: *"...and the opening of the prison to them that are bound"* *(Isaiah 61:1).*

Message: Chapter 61 of Isaiah tells what Jesus would do when He came to earth. One of the things He would do would be to *"open the prison to them that are bound."* In Luke 4:18, Jesus said the same thing, in slightly different words. He said, *"The Spirit of the Lord is upon me...to preach deliverance to the captives."*

Are you bound by an enemy or a habit or another sin? I recall one occasion when Samson was. Out of anger he burned the fields and orchards of the Philistines — an act that caused the Philistines to come after Judah, who asked, "Why are you after us?" And they answered, *"...to bind Samson...to do to him as he hath done to us"* *(Judges 15:10).*

The people of Judah approached Samson and said in essence, "What were you thinking? Don't you realize that they have rule over us? We are going to bind you up and give you over to the Philistines." This they did: *"They bound him with two new cords..."* *(15:14).* Then they gave him over to the Philistines.

There he stood, bound! He was a strong man, but he did not escape in his own strength. When the enemy was about to take him, *"...the Spirit of the Lord came mightily upon him, and the cords that were upon his arms became as flax that was burnt with fire, and his bands broke loose from off his hands"* *(15:14).* You know the rest of the story. Samson was able to slay a thousand men with the jawbone of an ass. Samson was able to break free of his bonds and slay his enemies because the Spirit of the Lord was upon him.

I asked you earlier if you were bound by an enemy or a habit or another sin. If so, you cannot escape on your own. You might have tried many times, only to fail. The only way you can be free is to appeal to our Lord and ask Him to use the Holy Spirit within you to release your bonds and set you free. Stay in the Word and on your knees until He does.

NOVEMBER 11   FAIL

Key Verse: *"...whoso confesseth (his sins) and forsaketh them shall have mercy" (Proverbs 28:13).*

Message: It took Sampson a long time to get to the point where this verse could apply to his life. You see, he entered into a relationship with a wicked woman named Delilah. For about five thousand dollars, she agreed to trick Samson into revealing the source of his strength so that the Philistines could capture him.

She went to Samson and said, *"Please tell me what makes you so strong. If someone wanted to tie you up and make you helpless, how could he do it" (Judges 16:4 GN)?* Samson played along with her and gave her three false ways. Then verse 16 says, *"She kept on asking him day after day. He got so sick and tired of her bothering him about it that he finally told her the truth" (16:16 GN).* Samson dabbled in sin until he fell.

Verse 21 says, *"The Philistines captured him and put his eyes out. They took him to Gaza, chained him with bronze chains, and put him to work grinding at the mill in the prison."* Here we see that Samson was a total failure.

But, God had not abandoned him. Verse 22 says, *"However, the hair on his head began to grow again after it was shaved off."* Even in Samson's failure, God was working to restore him. I truly believe that Samson confessed his sins, forsook them, and received mercy. I believe this because he is listed in the faith chapter. One thing Hebrews 11:24 tells us about Samson and several others is this: *"They were weak, but became strong."*

And Samson surely personified this verse. In his weakened condition, he asked the Lord to give him strength one more time so that he could defeat the Philistines. God granted the request, and Samson died with them. Verse 30 says, *"Samson killed more Philistines in his death than he had killed during his life."* God used him after he was restored more than He had before the fall.

You may know what it is to fail as Samson did. You may have fallen under temptation. But let me tell you that the hair can grow back again. Know that if you confess your sins and forsake them, our Lord will be merciful to you and will use you again. Now is a good time to get on your face before the Lord and accept His mercy and forgiveness. There is a bumper sticker that reads: "Christians aren't perfect; they're forgiven." Praise the Lord!

NOVEMBER 12   MESS UP
Key Verse: *"I will instruct thee..." (Psalm 32:8).*

Message: We all mess up. How do you feel when you do? Awful? I do. I feel awful when I hurt someone's feelings, when I say something I shouldn't, when I don't do what I know I am to do, etc. But I really feel awful when I disappoint my Lord by my self-will or my apathy or my disobedience—when I really mess up.

I once heard someone say, "God doesn't concentrate on your messes; He concentrates on your destiny." In other words, He concentrates on how you are doing what He sent you down here to do. Every one of us was sent here with a commission.

Jeremiah is a good example. In Jeremiah 1:5, God said to him: *"Before I formed thee in the womb I knew thee; and before thou camest forth out of the womb I sanctified thee, and I ordained thee a prophet unto the nations."*

You were sent here with a mission, just as Jeremiah was. Have you ever messed up and gotten off course? David did. What can we learn from him?

Well, he was sent here to be God's king, but he really messed up. I'll just mention "Bathsheba," and you will know how greatly he sinned. But what he did haunted him day and night. Finally, he prayed, *"I acknowledged my sin unto thee, and mine iniquity have I not hid. I said, I will confess my transgressions unto the Lord, and thou forgavest the iniquity of my sin" (Psalm 32:5).*

When David confessed his sin, something wonderful happened. He got a word from God: *"I will instruct thee and teach thee in the way thou shalt go..." (32:8).*

If you have messed up, repent and get right with God. When you do, He will instruct you and teach you step by step. Just start walking in the direction He leads. Ask the Lord to reveal His will by closing a door or opening it wider. Keep walking!

NOVEMBER 13   BEHOLD HIS EYES

Key Verse: *"...I will guide thee with mine eye" (Psalm 32:8).*

Message: Right after our Lord said to David, *"I will instruct thee and teach thee in the way which thou shalt go,"* He added, *"I will guide thee with mine eye."*

I don't mean to be facetious, but I can tell you that my mother personified this verse. When she had that certain look in her eye, she guided me to stop what I was doing. When I started teaching school, I soon found that staring at a student did a lot more good than yelling. I used my eyes to get the attention of many students.

My mother's eyes and my eyes were convicting eyes, but ours in no way can compare to the convicting eyes of our Lord Jesus. Remember Peter? He swore that he would never deny Jesus, but he did. *"The cock crew" (Luke 22:60).* Notice what happened next: *"And the Lord turned and <u>looked</u> upon Peter, and Peter remembered the word of the Lord, how he had said unto him, before the cock crow, thou shalt deny me thrice" (22:61).* What did Peter do when his eyes met the convicting eyes of our Lord Jesus? He repented. He *"went out and wept bitterly" (22:62).*

Now, I have good news concerning those eyes of Jesus for anyone walking down the path of righteousness. He says to you what He said to David: *"I will guide thee with mine eye" (Psalm 32:8).* That is good news. Let's look at another promise found in 2 Chronicles 16:9: *"For the eyes of the Lord run to and fro throughout the whole earth, to show himself strong in the behalf of them whose heart is perfect (loyal) toward him."*

If your heart is right with our Lord, His eyes will behold you and give you strength in your journey. The eyes of the Lord will always see you. Will He see you with convicting eyes or guiding eyes? The choice is yours. Ask the Lord to guide you with His eyes as you begin each day.

NOVEMBER 14   FACE REBELLION
Key Verse: *"Those that be planted..." (Psalm 92:13).*

Message: Micah wrote in a day when Israel was in total disobedience, far away from God. His lament was, *"The good man is perished out of the earth..." (Micah 7:2).* He went on to say, *"The son dishonoreth the father, and the daughter riseth up against the mother" (7:6).* This sounds so much like America today. Children are rebelling against their parents.

Let's think for a moment about rebellious children. Parents, you reach a point in which talking or lecturing does no good. At that point, you really can do nothing but pray. Maybe you need to think about how you are praying.

One day as I was driving from Dallas to Jackson, I heard a preacher on the radio say, "If you have a rebellious child in the far country, pick out a promise of God and pray this prayer every day:

'In the name of the Lord Jesus Christ and by the power of His shed blood, I claim Proverbs 22:6: *'Train up a child in the way he should go; and when he is old, he will not depart from it.'* Lord, I did the best I knew how to follow this command. Now I ask you to visit my child in rebellion land, bind Satan in his life, and draw him back to you and to our family.'"

Parents, there are three things to remember when you pray this kind of prayer:

1. You must quit lecturing your child.
2. You should not tell your child that you are praying this prayer. Just pray it every day and watch your child and <u>you</u> change.
3. You need to be living where God answers prayer.

Your child may be in the pig pen of the world; but if you have planted him in God's house, there is a promise for you: *"Those that be planted in the house of our Lord shall flourish in the courts of our God. They shall still bring forth fruit in old age" (Psalm 92:13-14).* Your child may go away for a season; but if he is really saved, I believe he will be back.

Make no mistake! The home is in serious trouble today. The family is God's building block of any nation; and when the bricks crumble, the entire nation falls. Plant your children in God's house and plant God's Word in their hearts. Then pray and pray and pray!

NOVEMBER 15   ARE BETRAYED
Key Verse: *"...love your enemies..." (Matthew 5:44).*

Message: David's son Absalom became his father's enemy. He went behind the king's back and stole the hearts of the people. Then he put into place a plan to overthrow his father. 2 Samuel 15:12 says, *"The plot against the king gained strength, and Absalom's followers grew in number."* Brokenhearted, David fled from his son.

The day came when David sent out his troops to face Absalom. He sent them with this message: *"For my sake don't harm the young man Absalom" (18:5).* But they did. And with Absalom's death, David's foes—his people who had followed Absalom—were defeated.

Joab allowed a slave and Ahimaaz to go tell the news to the king. Ahimaaz arrived first with the news: *"Praise the Lord your God, who has given you victory over the men who rebelled against you" (18:28).* Notice David's reply: *"Is the young man Absalom all right" (18:29)?* The slave arrived with the same message. David's response? *"Is the young man Absalom all right" (18:32)?*

You know, at this time David's concern for Absalom far outweighed his desire to hear of victory. Absalom had looked at his father as his enemy, but David had looked at Absalom as his son. He just waited too late to show it.

Dad, let me say this to you. The love of a sensitive father carries a quality more profound than any victory can match. Be that sensitive parent. David's son slipped away from him. He was so busy being king that he neglected being a father. Don't let this happen to you. Don't be so busy being a businessman that you neglect being a father.

Father, be sensitive to your child's needs. Be there for him. Be loving when he isn't loving you back. Don't let him slip away. Keep the lines of communication open. Encourage him. Spend time with him. Stay on your knees for him. Start right now.

NOVEMBER 16   NEED WISDOM
Key Verse: *"...ask of God..." (James 1:5).*

Message: James 1:5 begins, *"If any of you lack wisdom, let him ask of God...."* Of course, the first place and the best place to go for counseling is to our Lord. However, sometimes we need human counseling as well. Proverbs 12:15 says, *"...he that hearkeneth unto counsel is wise."*

We see something about wise human counseling at the time God was ready to call Saul to be king. Kish said to his son, Saul, "Son, some of our donkeys have wandered away from home. Take one of the servants and go look for them." Off they went. They traveled far but could not find the donkeys.

Saul finally said to the servant, *"Let's go back home, or my father might stop thinking about the donkeys and start worrying about us" (1Samuel 9:5 GN).* The servant gave wise counsel at this point. He said in essence, "I hear there is a man of God in this town. Let's go see him. Maybe he can tell us where the donkeys are." Do you see what he did?

He didn't give counsel he wasn't qualified to give, but he knew where to send Saul—to a godly counselor, Samuel, who had the answer: *"As far as the donkeys that were lost three days ago, don't worry about them; they have already been found" (9:20).*

Then Samuel proceeded to tell the real reason Saul had come to see him—to be told he would be king. But you see, Samuel wasn't qualified to give this counsel. Several times in this account we read, *"The Lord had told Samuel....The Lord said to him" (9:15, 17).*

Here is the point I want to make. The servant knew he wasn't qualified to counsel Saul, but he knew someone who was, Samuel. Samuel wasn't qualified to counsel Saul, but he knew someone who was, the Lord.

Folks, don't try to counsel someone if you are not qualified. Send the person to a counselor who counsels based on the Word of God. If you need counsel yourself, go to God's Word and to a godly counselor. Ask the Lord to lead you to the right person.

NOVEMBER 17   FOLLOW THE LEADER

Key Verse: *"Whoever welcomes God's messenger because he is God's messenger will share in his reward" (Matthew 10:41 GN).*

Message: According to 1 Peter 5, the God-called pastor who feeds the flock and is an example before the people will *"when the chief Shepherd shall appear...receive a crown of glory that fadeth not away" (5:4).* If you support your pastor because he is God's messenger, you will share in his reward.

It seems that many people do not claim this promise. They seem to think that they know, better than the pastor, the direction the church should go. Instead of supporting and following, they murmur and complain. They seem to have a "Korah" complex. Numbers 16:1 (GN) says that he *"had the audacity to rebel against Moses,"* and he persuaded 250 men to stand with him and say in essence, "All of us belong to the Lord, and He is with us all. Why do you set yourself above us all?" They were on dangerous ground. In fact, the ground opened up and swallowed them and their families and their possessions.

When we think we have as much right as the pastor to say where God is leading the church, and when we influence others to join us, we are on dangerous ground.

There is a valuable lesson for us to learn from God's Word. In our Sunday School, we have recently studied the book of Hebrews. As I was discussing the first lesson with my friend Jack Jackson, he called my attention to four very important words found in chapter 1, verses 1 and 2: *"God spoke....God speaks,"* and then he made this statement: "In the Bible God always spoke His message for His people to their leader." Then he pointed me to an example found in Joshua 5. We'll go there tomorrow, but for today, why don't you tell the Lord that you will follow your spiritual leader?

NOVEMBER 18   GOD SPEAKS

Key Verse: *"...God spoke....God speaks..." (Hebrews 1:2-3).*

Message: Yesterday we looked at a statement that Jack made to me: "In the Bible God always spoke His message to the leaders." Then he pointed me to an example in the book of Joshua. Here we see that God had a word for His people. The Israelite army stood at the gates of Jericho, but they couldn't attack it. They couldn't get in. Chapter 6 (GN) begins, *"The gates of Jericho were kept shut and guarded to keep the Israelites out. No one could enter or leave the city."* A perplexed Joshua stood before Jericho. Suddenly, *"He saw a man standing in front of him, holding a sword" (5:13).* Joshua asked Him, "Are you one of our soldiers, or an enemy?"

Notice the answer: *"Neither....I am here as the commander of the Lord's army" (5:14 GN).* Joshua found himself face to face with the preincarnate Jesus Christ. He came with a message of how the Israelites were to take the city.

Please note that our Lord did not appear to the people. He appeared to the leader. And you know, He gave some unusual instructions to Joshua. He said in essence, "Joshua, I am going to tell you exactly how the city is to be taken."

You know the story of the marches around the city. I'm sure some of the soldiers thought the plan was foolish—certainly not a military strategy. March around the city behind priests blowing trumpets???—but they obeyed. On the seventh day of the marches, *"The priests blew the trumpets. As soon as the men heard it, they gave a loud shout, and the walls collapsed" (6:20 GN).*

When our current pastor came to this church, he had a vision for the church that he received from the Lord. He has not wavered from that vision. The way has not been easy. Some people have thought the direction the church has been going as foolish. But our leader hasn't. Under the direction of the *"commander of the Lord's army,"* he has marched on.

I truly believe we have seen the walls begin to come tumbling down. I believe we are now in a position to take our Jerusalem because the pastor has stuck to his vision, and key leaders and most members have marched around the city with him. Praise God that we have a pastor to whom the Lord speaks, and praise God for people who listen and follow. If you belong to a church, you have a "Joshua." Thank the Lord for him and follow his leadership.

NOVEMBER 19   WHEN YOU NEED TO FORGIVE

Key Verse: *"For if ye forgive men their trespasses, your heavenly Father will forgive you" (Matthew 6:14).*

Message: There were five children in my family, four girls and one boy. (My brother has passed away.) I can honestly say that since we have been grown, we have never had a cross word, never had an argument, never had a falling out. So, it amazes me how often I speak with people who are estranged from a family member. I often talk with ladies who have a broken relationship with a grown child. The reason usually involves the lifestyle of the child.

When a lady with this problem sits before me, she usually begins the conversation with, "I know the Bible says I am to forgive my child, but I am having a hard time doing so." I reply, "You have to forgive." Jesus said, '*And when ye stand praying, forgive, if ye have anything against any...*' *(Mark 11:25)*. Let's talk about how to get there."

I begin by asking this question: "Do you want to have a relationship with your child?" If the answer is yes, I often make this suggestion: "Put some distance between you. Don't call; don't shame; don't condemn. Just be silent for a while."

Here is my reasoning. Forgiveness is a process. It takes time, and it must be sincere. You stay away and spend much time in prayer. I believe you will find that the Lord has gradually changed you. When this happens, you will be ready to forgive and restore your relationship.

A friend who followed this suggestion, said to me, "In the silent time the Lord changed me, and I was able to restore my relationship with my daughter. She still isn't doing all I know she should be doing, but we have a good relationship. And besides, if we hadn't mended our differences, I would not be able to know my wonderful grandson." I love this testimony. If you are estranged from a grown child, put some space between you, pray, and watch God change you. Remember His promise: *"For if ye forgive men their trespasses, your heavenly Father will also forgive you."*

By the way, try this suggestion when you are estranged from another family member or a friend or a neighbor or even a fellow church member. You just might be surprised how God will change you in the silent time.

NOVEMBER 20   NEED HELP

Key Verse: *"...He (Jesus Christ) ever liveth to make intercession for us" (Hebrews 7:25).*

Message: Hebrews 1:3 tells us that *"When he (Jesus) had by himself purged our sins, sat down on the right hand of the majesty on high."* When Jesus had shed His blood to pay for our sins, His work on earth was complete. There was nothing more for Him to do. He returned to heaven and sat down on the right hand of our Father. What is He doing today?

One of the things He is doing is praying for us. *"He ever liveth to make intercession for us."* What do you need? Do you need strength? Do you need help? Do you need hope? Do you need comfort? Whatever you need, go to Him for it.

Actually, we often go many places before we go to Him. We focus on our need. We talk to others. I am reminded of a time that Mr. Brown brought five-year-old Austin to my house. I knew he liked jelly beans, so after a while I asked, "Austin, do you want some jelly beans?" He looked at me, rolled those brown eyes, and replied, "I thought you would never ask."

We chuckle, but I believe our Lord just might say that to us when we finally get around to taking our need to Him. He wants to help, but bear this in mind. Whatever we ask, He will answer according to His will, not ours.

Here is a point that has been driven home to me lately. Prayer is not getting God to do what we want Him to do. Prayer is getting us in line with His plan for our lives.

I firmly believe that each of us is sent here for a purpose. I believe that Jesus prays for us to do His will as we walk down the path of righteousness. I believe He prays even more earnestly when we veer to the left or the right that we will get back on the right track. Folks, when you mess up and get off-center, remember that Jesus is praying for you that you will get back in line. Why don't you keep this in mind and go to Him and His Word before you camp out on your need or go to someone else? *"He ever liveth to make intercession for you."*

NOVEMBER 21   ARE PERSECUTED

Key Verse: *"...persecuted but not forsaken"* (2 Corinthians 4:9).

Message: In our key verse Paul is saying that the one who walks with the Lord may be persecuted, but never forsaken. Hebrews 13:5 says, *"...for he hath said, I will never leave thee, nor forsake thee."* These are promises that are absolutely true.

Since these promises are true, why do we have to suffer persecution? I believe one reason is for our Lord to test us—to see how we walk in the midst of our trial.

I am reminded of the relationship between Saul and David. A change happened in their relationship when the women sang, *"Saul hath slain his thousands, and David his ten thousands"* (1 Samuel 18:7).

Saul was furious. Twice he tried to kill David with a javelin. He missed. He sent David on a seemingly impossible task to face the Philistines, with this purpose: *"But Saul thought to make David fall by the hand of the Philistines."* David won; Saul lost.

Every time Saul tried to get rid of David, he failed. How did David react to this persecution? Did he seek revenge? No! He just did what the king told him to do. Chapter 18, verse 5 tells us that *"David went out withersoever Saul sent him...."* Now hear these important words: *"...and behaved himself wisely...."* 18:14 says, *"And David behaved himself wisely in all his ways; and the Lord was with him."* In the midst of persecution, David obeyed, and the Lord was with him.

Now, I firmly believe that the blessing after the persecution depends on how we walk during the trial. Look in 2 Samuel 5:10: *"And David went on, and grew great, and the Lord God of Hosts was with him"*—and he became king of Israel. Great was his reward!

Remember Job? What happened to him on the other side of his persecution? Job 42:12 says, *"So the Lord blessed the latter end of Job more than his beginning...."*

Are you being persecuted? Perhaps our Lord is testing you. Keep these two things in mind:

- You may be persecuted, but you will never be forsaken.
- Staying faithful in the trial will bring reward on the other side.

Ask the Lord to help you behave wisely, no matter what your circumstances are. He will be there for you. That's a promise.

NOVEMBER 22   NEED STRENGTH

Key Verse: *"...to them that have no might he increaseth strength"* *(Isaiah 40:29).*

Message: David claimed this promise many times in the Psalms. In 28:7, he said, *"The Lord is my strength...."* In 29:11, he said, *"The Lord will give strength unto his people...."* In 31:4, he said, *"...for thou art my strength."*

I am going to share with you my personal testimony about physical strength. I am sometimes asked, "How are you able to do so much at your age?" (At the time of this writing, I was seventy-six years old.) I usually reply, "It's the Lord," and it is. I know He is my strength, but at one time I wasn't sure how to get that strength into my body.

One day I was reading Psalm 71, a prayer for help in old age. In verse 16, the Psalmist said, *"I will go in the strength of the Lord."* I told the Lord that I would do just that, but I still needed help in knowing just how to do this.

Here is how He directed me. He led me to Psalm 133:2. This is the picture that caught my attention. Here David is talking about *"the precious oil that ran down upon the beard, even Aaron's beard that went down to the edge of his garments."*

This picture led me to the prayer I pray every time before I teach God's Word. Here it is: "Lord, Aaron was the high priest in his day; You are ours in this day. I believe there is oil in the hem of your garment. Right now I take hold of your hem, and I ask you to release that oil and let it flow from the top of my head to the bottom of my feet for strength for today." He has been gracious to do so. If you need that oil, no matter your age, pray this prayer. He wants to be your strength.

NOVEMBER 23   YOU ARE DESPERATE

Key Verse: *"...the Lord will not suffer the soul of the righteous to famish..." (Proverbs 10:3).*

Message: After a time of desperation, the Psalmist understood this promise. How did he get there? I believe it is important to see how he came to understand that God would not forsake him. He was in a desperate condition. He said, *"I am so troubled that I cannot speak" (77:4).*

At that point he began to question God. In essence he asked, "Will the Lord always reject me? Will He never again be pleased with me? Has He stopped loving me? Do His promises no longer stand? Has he forgotten to be merciful" (77:7-9)? Ever had any of these questions? What did you do? If you are there now, what are you doing?

Let's see what the Psalmist did. In 77:11-12, he said, *"I will remember thy wonders of old. I will meditate also of all thy work, and talk of thy doings."*

Look where his thoughts went. To his problem? No! He remembered how God had worked wonders in the past; he meditated on all that God was doing in the present; he talked about both to other people.

How can what the Psalmist did apply to you in your desperation? You can remember how God was faithful to you in the past; you can meditate on what He is doing in the present; you can talk about both to other people.

Notice that the Psalmist did the right things. As a result he came to this conclusion: *"...who is so great a God as our God" (77:13)?* Follow the Psalmist's example and you can give the same testimony. Just in the day of your trouble, seek the Lord. Remember, He will not let the soul of the righteous famish. Be righteous! Ask the Lord to lead you down that path.

NOVEMBER 24   NEED SPIRITUAL POWER

Key Verse: *"...be filled with the Spirit" (Ephesians 5:18).*

Message: Recently, a lady in my class asked me, "Are all Christians Spirit-filled?" I answered that all believers have the Holy Spirit living in them. Jesus Himself said so in John 14:17: *"...ye know him (the Holy Spirit) for he dwelleth with you, and shall be in you."*

I believe the Bible teaches one baptism. Paul says in Ephesians 4:5 that there is *"one Lord, one faith, one baptism, one God and Father...."* I believe that the Bible teaches one baptism but many fillings. In our key verse Paul says, *"Be filled with the Spirit."* This means "to be continually filled."

Therefore, the individual himself determines how filled he is. As you know, I never get out of bed without having put on the whole armor of God. One prayer I pray every day is this: "Lord, I ask to be so filled with your Holy Spirit that I can't hear that old sin nature talking." I truly want to be continually filled.

You know, one thing I have noticed in God's Word is that the people who had power with God had this said about them: "They were filled with the Holy Spirit." Let's take Stephen, for example. He was filled with the Spirit when we first saw him, and he was filled with the Holy Spirit when we last saw him.

When the apostles were looking for men *"full of the Holy Spirit"* to take over the ministry needs so that they could pray and preach, one of the men they chose was Stephen. Acts 6:5 says, *"...and they chose Stephen, a man full of faith and the Holy Ghost."* Thus the first time we saw Stephen, he was filled with the Holy Spirit.

Now let's look at the last time we saw him. He was receiving brutal treatment by the Jews. How was he able to bear it? Acts 7:55 says that he was *"full of the Holy Ghost....,"* and because he was, he was able to say as they were stoning him: *"Lord, lay not this sin to their charge" (7:60).* What a testimony of one who was obviously "continually filled"!

Here is a point I want to make. The only way to have spiritual power is to be continually filled with the Holy Spirit. The greater the filling, the greater the power! The people God uses the most are the ones who are continually filled with the Holy Spirit. You can be one of these people. Just be right with the Lord and ask to be filled — every day!

NOVEMBER 25   NEED SPIRITUAL POWER

Key Verse: *"...be filled with the Spirit"* *(Ephesians 5:18).*

Message: We will now continue with the message of yesterday. I made the statement that the only way to have spiritual power is to be filled with the Holy Spirit. Today I will address what Paul says that a person does as a result of being filled with the Holy Spirit.

Right after Paul says *"...be filled...,"* he says, *"speaking to one another in psalms and hymns and spiritual songs..."* (5:19).

"Speaking," as used here, is an interesting word. It means to make a sound. Dr. John MacArthur says this in his commentary on Ephesians: "Speaking here includes any sound offered to God from a Spirit-filled heart. The music from an organ or a choir is no more acceptable to God than the sound of a guitar or a home-made flute. The sound that pleases Him is the sound that comes as a result of a heart submissive to His Spirit and that sings or plays to His glory." Ponder this!

Now look at what Paul says the Spirit-filled person sings: *"psalms and hymns and spiritual songs."* He sings *"psalms."* These are psalms set to music. Many of the contemporary songs we sing are the psalms. When you are singing them, pay attention to the words. They magnify our Lord. David had such a wonderful invitation for us in Psalm 34:3: *"O magnify the Lord with me, and let us exalt his name <u>together</u>."*

The Spirit-filled person also sings hymns. Many of us grew up singing hymns of the faith. Nothing moves me any more than singing "Amazing Grace" or "The Old Rugged Cross." Hymns are wonderful, and many people think they are the only songs to be sung in the church. Folks, that is not Scriptural. Paul says we are to sing *"psalms and hymns and spiritual songs."* To me, *"spiritual songs"* are songs that often give a personal testimony, such as "I'd Rather Have Jesus."

Paul teaches us here that the Spirit-filled church sings a variety of songs. Whether *"psalms or hymns or spiritual songs,"* we are to sing from a Spirit-filled heart that seeks to glorify our Lord and Him only. Do you need to get right with the Lord concerning music? Why don't you do so right now?

NOVEMBER 26   NEED SPIRITUAL POWER
Key Verse: *"...be filled with the Spirit"* (Ephesians 5:18).

Message: Today we will continue with the statement I made that the only way to have spiritual power is to be filled with the Holy Spirit. Yesterday, we said that the Spirit-filled person sings *"psalms and hymns and spiritual songs"* to the glory of the Lord.

Now in verse 20, Paul says that the Spirit-filled person is *"always giving thanks for all things in the name of our Lord Jesus Christ to God, even the Father."* It is hard to get past *"all things."* Are we to give thanks when we hurt? When things go wrong? When we are ill? When a child goes to the far country? Paul said so. In 1 Thessalonians 5:18, he said, *"In everything give thanks; for this is the will of God in Christ Jesus concerning you."* The Spirit-filled Christian gives thanks in everything—not for everything—but in everything for the good that will come out of it.

Daniel is such a good example. King Darius was talked into signing a decree that said that if any person bowed to any god or man for thirty days, except the king, he would be cast into the den of lions. Daniel heard about the decree. What did he do? *"He went into his house; and his windows being open in his chamber toward Jerusalem, He kneeled three times that day and prayed, and gave thanks before his God, as he had been doing before this"* (Daniel 6:10).

Daniel thanked God for who He is, even though his life was in danger. The Spirit-filled believer is to thank our Lord for who He is, even though he is in the midst of a storm. Can you do this? If so, He will bring you to the other side. He did Daniel. Ask Him to do so for you.

NOVEMBER 27   HAVE UNANSWERED PRAYER

Key Verse: *"And they continued steadfastly...in prayers"* (Acts 2:42).

Message: When Peter preached at Pentecost, about three thousand souls were saved. What was the next thing they did? *"They continued steadfastly...in prayers."* What was one thing the apostles said they would do when seven men were elected to do the ministry of the church? They said, *"We will give ourselves continually to prayer..."* (Acts 6:4). The words *"continued"* and *"continual"* are of the essence when it comes to prayer. Even if you feel your prayer will never be answered, keep praying continually. Don't give up.

Let me give you an example. About two or three years ago, a precious lady came to see me in tears. She had in her hand a letter—a mean letter—from a sister who had refused to have any contact with her for a long time. In the letter the sister went back to their childhood and accused my friend of all sorts of things. Even though she was not guilty of those accusations, she wrote a letter of apology, but received no response.

Now on the day my friend came to see me, she had been praying about their relationship for a long time. I asked her to continue—and may I say that it is hard to pray for someone who attacks you unfairly—but she did.

On the day she came to see me, I told her that one of the main verses I pray for someone in her situation is Proverbs 16:5: *"When a man's ways please the Lord, he makes even his enemies to be at peace with him."* I told this dear lady that I would pray every day that her ways would be so pleasing to the Lord that He would cause her sister to be at peace with her, and I asked her to do likewise. We prayed this prayer every day for between two and three years.

One day the telephone call came. The sister called and said in essence that she had recently started praying about their relationship and that all animosity was gone and she wanted them to be sisters and friends again. The answer to our prayers was a long time coming, but it came.

If you have an unresolved relationship and you have done your best to reconcile and have prayed and prayed, listen to the second stanza of this hymn: "Have faith in God when your prayers are unanswered. Your earnest plea He will never forget; Wait on the Lord, trust His Word and be patient. Have faith in God, He'll answer yet." If you have a strained relationship, pray *"continually."* Don't give up. Begin right now.

NOVEMBER 28   WHEN TRIALS COME

Key Verse: *"He sent hardships on you to test you, so that in the end he could bless you..." (Deuteronomy 8:16 GN).*

Message: Trials come to all of us. They come for various reasons. One reason is that God wants to test us and then bless us if we pass the test.

God tested the children of Israel in the wilderness. Why? *"...to do them good at the latter end" (8:16)!* What was their *"latter end"?* The Promised Land! Did they pass the test? No! Their disobedience kept them from possessing all of the Promised Land. They still have not passed the test. They are still disobedient. They still occupy only a small portion of the Promised Land.

Then there is Joseph! We know that he was put in prison for a crime he did not commit. Psalm 105:19 says that the *"word of the Lord tried (tested) him."* Did he pass God's test in prison? Yes, he did! He was a model prisoner; thus he received God's blessings through Pharaoh. Verse 21 says that Pharaoh *"made him lord of his house, and ruler of all his substance (possessions)."* Obedience in the midst of a test brings blessings.

It would be good if we didn't have to have trials. We certainly do not want them. They are no fun, but there is a special blessing for those who endure and stay faithful in the midst of the trial. James 1:12 says, *"Blessed is the man that endureth trials; for when he is tested, he shall receive the crown of life, which the Lord hath promised to them that love him."*

Folks, be faithful in the test. If you are, our Lord will exchange your trial for a crown. If you are in a trial, as you pray today, tell the Lord that you will hold on until victory comes.

NOVEMBER 29   YOU STAND BEFORE JESUS

Key Verse: *"For God is not unjust so as to forget your work and the love which you have shown toward his name, in having ministered and in still ministering to the saints" (Hebrews 6:10).*

Message: When you stand before Jesus the Judge at the Judgment Seat of Christ, He will consider your work and your labor of love in ministering in His name to the saints, not to determine your salvation, but to determine your reward.

Your salvation was settled forever when you accepted Jesus as your personal Savior. Hebrews 5:9 says that Jesus *"became the source of eternal salvation...."* Jesus Himself said in John 10:27-28: *"My sheep hear my voice, and I know them, and they follow me; and I give unto them eternal life."*

At the Judgment Seat of Christ, your rewards will be settled. Jesus will look at your service record. Works that you have done because you love Jesus and obey Him by ministering to the saints in His name will go with you to heaven as rewards. Paul says in 1 Corinthians 3:14: *"If any man's work abide...he shall receive a reward."*

Works that you have done for any reason other than your love of Christ and your obedience to him by ministering in His name to the saints will not go to heaven with you as rewards. In verse 15, Paul says, *"If any man's work shall be burned, he shall suffer loss (of rewards), but he himself shall be saved, yet so as by fire."* He will go in with his coattails smoking. He will go in, but he will suffer loss of rewards. Folks, don't be in this group.

Serve the Lord! Serve His people! Be faithful to do what He put you down here to do. If you do, He promises that when you stand before Him, He will not *"forget your work and labor of love...."* Check your motive for serving. Ask the Lord to reveal to you what your service is to be.

NOVEMBER 30   GOD IS SILENT

Key Verse: *"I call to you, O God, but you never answer; and when I pray, you pay no attention" (Job 30:20 GN).*

Message: One day my friend Jack Jackson was discussing a Sunday School lesson with me. He made the statement: "We are to live on God's promises, not on His explanations." That hit a chord with me, and I asked him if I could use this and more of his material to conclude this month. He agreed.

He began his lesson by saying, "Here is one way to align our lives with God when He is silent on the specifics of our lives: Live on God's promises, not on explanations." Job was having a hard time. He tried to reach God, but he couldn't. In Job 23:4, he said that if he could reach God, he would *"state my case before Him and present all the arguments in my favor."* Job wanted an explanation as to why he was having such a hard time. We are so like him. We should not be. We are to trust Him and not test Him by expecting Him to reveal all things to us. He will reveal just enough for us to see what will happen if we follow Him.

The Word of God never promises us that the Lord is going to give us the answer to everything that happens to us here on earth. It does tell us that we can depend on His promises. Take Abraham, for example.

In Genesis 12:1, the Lord told him to leave his country and his family and go to *"a land that I will show thee."* You will notice that God did not tell him where he was to go, but He did make Abraham a promise: *"I will make thee a great nation..."* (12:2). He didn't know where he was going, but verse 4 says, *"Abraham departed as the Lord had spoken unto him...."* It took a while, but God kept His promise to Abraham. He had to be patient, and so must we. We must trust our Lord and be patient as He works out His promises in our lives. Some promises may be fulfilled immediately; some may come later. We are to persevere and wait on the Lord.

The best advice with which I can leave you is found in Proverbs 3:5-6: *"Trust in the Lord with all thine heart; and lean not unto thine own understanding. In all thy ways acknowledge him, and he shall direct thy path."* Make this your prayer.

December

LESSONS LEARNED AS I STUDIED GOD'S WORD
ON MY BLUE COUCH

The first eleven months had a theme. As I thought about the twelfth and last month in this series, I decided not to have a theme. Rather, I chose to share with you what the Lord is teaching me from His Word in my quiet time, which I have <u>every</u> morning.

I have been asked how I study the Word of God. A typical morning goes like this. I begin on Monday and study every day in preparation for my Sunday School class. I also read a chapter or two or three from a selected Old Testament or New Testament book, a Proverb, and a Psalm. Sometimes I share what I am studying and get insight from a friend.

This month will be a compilation of what the Lord taught me from His Word as I sat on my blue couch.

DECEMBER 1 GOD'S WORD

Key Verse: *"...Daniel, from the first day that thou didst set thine heart to understand...thy words were heard, and I am come for thy words" (Daniel 10:12).*

Message: On the first day that Daniel prayed, an angel was sent from God with the answer. However, he was not high enough in rank-to get past the demon in charge of Persia. He had to go back to heaven to get help from the highest ranking angel, Michael. As a result, it took three weeks for the answer to come.

As I studied this event, the thought struck me that Satan will do his best to keep God's Word from getting to you. He will have his demon present at the quiet time hour. He will try to convince you that you will be late for work, that you can study later, that you don't feel like studying. He will interrupt you any way he can. Someone will come into the room; the phone will ring; a child will have a need, etc.

Satan will also have his demon do his best to keep you from hearing the Word taught and preached. He will whisper in your ear that it is all right to miss because you are tired, because you need to do work around the house, because your child has a ball game, because you have company, etc.

You get the idea. If you succumb to these excuses, you can rest assured that the Lord Jesus did not lead you to do so. If not, then they must come from the devil through his demons. Folks, don't give in. How can you keep from doing so? As an act of your will, make your individual and corporate Bible study "absolutes" in your life.

Remember! Satan's objective is to keep the lost lost and the saved defeated. He does so by keeping the Word of God out of people's hands. Don't let this happen to you. Pray hard that it will not.

DECEMBER 2 STUDY

Key Verse: *"Study to show thyself approved unto God, a workman that needeth not to be ashamed, rightly dividing the word of truth"* *(2 Timothy 2:15).*

Message: I am often asked how I prepare to teach God's Word. I will share with you how I prepare to teach my Sunday School class.

On Monday morning I begin by reading the Scripture passage for that Sunday's lesson. Often I read and get no clear message of what I am to teach. I keep reading. I have to ask the Lord to reveal to me what He wants me and my class members to learn, and I beg Him not to let me teach anything that cannot be supported by His Word. I truly want to *"rightly divide the word of truth."*

So, I study. On Monday through Wednesday, I read the Scriptures and commentaries by people I respect. As I read, the Holy Spirit begins to point out a point here and a point there that I am to share. By Thursday evening I have the lesson down on paper, and I study the rest of the week. I go on Sunday morning ready to teach this message.

Does it ever change? Yes, it does, I'll tell you how. Sunday morning is the most important quiet time I have each week. After I read over my notes, I always pray this way:

"Lord Jesus, I have no message. Please do not let me try to teach. I know that if I do, no learning will take place, and no life will be changed.

"Lord Jesus, I know you have a message for me and for the students. I know you have given it to the Holy Spirit in me.

"Now, Holy Spirit, please occupy my whole house and have the freedom to teach me and through me what my Lord wants taught.

"Lord Jesus, I give you praise for what we learn today from your Word and for how we apply it to our lives. Dear Jesus, in your name I pray. Amen."

As I said earlier, I believe Sunday morning quiet time is the most important of all days. I once had a young man say to me, "I have a quiet time every day but Sunday." I'm afraid he voiced the pattern of many teachers. It seems that the devil does his best to keep us from having a Sunday morning quiet time. Something always seems to interfere. Don't let it. Make it an act of your will to spend time alone with the Lord every day, and especially on Sunday. You will be amazed at how much more effective your ministry will be if you do so.

This message has been for teachers; but, students, let me say this to you. Have your quiet time every day, and especially on Sunday. Pray for your teacher. Ask the Lord to speak to your heart through him/her. You will be amazed at how much more effective your ministry will be, whatever it is, if you do so.

DECEMBER 3 PROVIDENCE OF GOD

Key Verse: *"And we know that all things work together for good to them that love God..."*
(Romans 8:28).

Message: The footnote in my <u>King James Study Bible</u> reads like this: "God is working all things together for good, but those who love God are best able to appreciate that fact because they love Him no matter what." I hope that this describes you.

However, for this message I will concentrate on the first part of the quotation: "God is working all things together for good." Truly, He is always at work. Our God, the unseen power, controls everything for His purpose. This is what we call the providence of God.

The best example I can think of is found in the book of Esther. God is not mentioned in the book. No prayer! No worship! No sacrifices! There is no reference to Esther in the New Testament. Why not? I believe the reason is that the Jews in this book were outside the will of God. They should have gone home to Judah when Cyrus the Persian king gave them permission to do so, but they did not. Thus, they were outside the will of God.

However, God as the unseen power took control of every event in the book. Step by step He worked out every detail to move a beautiful Jewish orphan girl to become queen of the land and ultimately to save God's people—her people—from being exterminated.

Can you recall a time when you were outside the will of God? When you were restored, did you look back and see that God was working then? I think of my friend, Mr. Brown. Many years ago he got on his motorcycle and headed west, moving away (or so he thought) from the hand of God.

When he came back and got right with the Lord, he said to me in essence, "You know, when I was in the far country, I did many things I should not have done. However, I could never take drugs, and I had plenty of opportunities to do so. That, I believe, was the providence of God at work in my life."

You might have a similar testimony. If so, I'm glad that you have been restored, but you do not have to take a trip outside the will of God. Remember that the unseen hand of God is ever at work in your life. Tell Him that you want to live for Him and ask Him to work out everything in your life for your good and His glory.

DECEMBER 4   PROVIDENCE OF GOD

Key Verse: *"And we know that all things work together for good to them that love God..." (Romans 8:28).*

Message: Today we will continue talking about the providence of God which means that His is the unseen hand that is ever at work in a believer's life.

Truly, His hand is always at work, even when the situation seems hopeless. My friend Gretchen gave me an example that illustrates the providence of God in a seemingly impossible situation.

Her brother was saved but was living in the far country. He passed away at the age of forty-seven. He left behind a wife, who was into drugs, and a young daughter. The family was so concerned about what would happen to the child. Well, Gretchen's sister-in-law and her daughter went to live with the grandmother. This mother got off drugs, and she and her daughter are now saved and bound for heaven.

Gretchen made this comment to me, "I don't believe this would have happened if my brother had lived."

We see here an example of the providence of God. He is at work, in His own way, when things seem impossible. He, and He alone, knows how to work all things together for good. No matter what your situation, trust our Lord and tell Him that you know He works all things for your good and His glory.

DECEMBER 5   PROVIDENCE OF GOD

Key Verse: *"And we know that all things work together for good to them that love God..." (Romans 8:28).*

Message: Once again we will continue talking about the providence of God which means that He is the unseen hand that is ever at work in a believer's life.

Here is another example of the hand of God at work in a seemingly impossible situation. My friends Steve and Julia had a rocky marriage. They loved the Lord, but Steve kept slipping back into old habits that hurt the family emotionally, spiritually, and financially. Many times divorce entered Julia's mind, but on more than one occasion she said to me, "God won't let me leave him." That was the providence of God at work. Our Lord was the unseen hand at work in Julia's life when Steve was in the far country. He was the unseen hand at work in Steve's life when he was in the far country.

How do I know this? I know because Steve has been set free, and their marriage has been restored. Steve said to me, "It isn't perfect, but we are working on it." Today, they are faithfully serving the Lord in the local church. The providence of God!

Here is another point I want to make. Throughout this whole ordeal, Julia was faithful to stay in the Word and on her knees. She prayed; God worked. If you are in a seemingly impossible situation, you pray while God works.

Hear the words of this song: "Are there any rivers that seem to be uncrossable? Are there any mountains you cannot tunnel through? God specializes in things that seem impossible. He knows a thousand ways to make a way for you."

He does! Stay in the Word and on your knees. He will work out all things for your good and His glory—in His way and in His time.

DECEMBER 6   FOR ALL THE SAINTS

Key Verse: *"...Pray always for all God's people..." (Ephesians 6:18 GN).*

Message: Right after Paul listed the pieces of the armor, he added that we are to pray in the Spirit and *"for all God's people."*

I personally believe that prayer is part of the armor. Recently, I was teaching a class on putting on the whole armor of God. I told the folks that I pray for people the Lord lays on my heart—also before I get out of bed.

I remarked that I pray every day for the guys I know named Daniel because they have such a difficult name to live up to. Daniel was a young man who *"purposed in his heart that he would not defile himself..." (Daniel 1:8).* And he did not! He lived out his commitment throughout his entire life.

I have to pause to tell you what awaited me when I got to class the next evening. Thanks to the wit of my friend Gretchen, all forty-one people wore a name tag that read, "My name is Daniel." We all had a good chuckle.

You know, I wish I could pray for every one of them every day; but if I did, I would never get off my blue couch each morning. Now here is a point I want to make. When we have our quiet time, we usually have certain people for whom we pray; i.e., spouses, church staff, children, lost people. We should pray for these folks, but our verse says that we are to pray *"for all God's people."*

I am reminded of one part of the prayer of Jabez: *"Oh, that thou wouldest bless me indeed, and enlarge my coast..." (1 Chronicles 4:10).* I believe that one coast that needs to be enlarged is our prayer list. Ask the Lord to lay those on your heart for whom you need to pray. When someone's name pops into your head, even in the middle of the night, lift up a prayer for that person. We are always to be ready to pray. I believe this is what Paul meant when he said, *"Pray without ceasing" (1 Thessalonians 5:17).* Again I say, always be ready to pray.

DECEMBER 7   DISCIPLINE

Key Verse: *"He that spareth his rod hateth his son, but he that loveth him chasteneth him betimes" (Proverbs 13:24).*

Message: I read a Proverb every day. I cannot begin to tell you how many times I have read this verse, but it took on new meaning one morning when I looked in the margin to see what *"betimes"* means. It means "promptly."

This Proverb says that if you love your child, you must discipline him. Proverbs 19:18 says, *"Chasten thy son while there is hope."* To me, the message is that you are to discipline your children promptly and to start when they are young. The greatest deterrent to your having to discipline your children is to let them know when they are young that your "yes" always means "yes" and your "no" always means "no." No discussion!

So many times parents let their children argue with them, and soon the children get out of control.

Let me tell you what happened in Eli's home. He was a priest, but he did not discipline his sons. They got out of control. 1 Samuel 2:12 says that they were *"scoundrels."* They did evil things. Verse 22 says that *"they were even sleeping with the women who worked at the entrance to the tabernacle."*

Eli approached his sons and asked, "Why are you doing these things? Everybody is telling me about your evil ways." In verse 24, he said, *"Stop it, my sons!"* Sad words followed: *"But they would not listen to their father..." (2:25).*

He was so busy being a priest that he neglected to be a father. Other people had to tell him about his sons' evil deeds. Because he did not discipline his sons early and promptly, he lost them and also his priesthood.

When Paul listed the qualifications for the pastor, he said that the pastor was to have *"his children in subjection" (1 Timothy 3:4).* When he listed the qualifications for the deacons, he said that deacons were to *"rule their children and their houses well" (3:12).*

I believe these requirements not only apply to pastors and deacons, but also to every Christian man who is the head of his household. Discipline early and promptly and consistently. Will this be hard? Yes! Ask the Lord to guide you.

DECEMBER 8   JOY
Key Verse: *"...the joy of the Lord is your strength"* *(Nehemiah 8:10).*

Message: One day I was teaching the words that Ezra spoke to the Jews when the building of the wall had been completed under Nehemiah's supervision. Those words are *"...the joy of the Lord is your strength" (8:10).*

What is this joy? It is the joy we have because we have been forgiven of our sins through Jesus' blood. It is the joy we have when we obey Paul's command to *"rejoice in the Lord always, and again I say rejoice" (Philippians 4:4).* It is the joy we have no matter our circumstances.

We must realize that nothing can touch us unless the Lord allows it, and He will. I have to tell you that trials will come into your life at some time. When you realize this fact, you can still have the joy of the Lord in your heart.

This does not mean, of course, that a Christian is always happy, for happiness depends on what happens. But it does mean that even in the midst of heartbreak, deep down in your heart, there is a joy that nothing on earth can take away.

My friends Sam and Dottie were in the class I was teaching. Some time ago they lost their wonderful son in a tragic accident. This family is one of the godliest families in our church, and they were so even in this terrible time. I said to them, "You were an example to all of us at that time. We saw that '...the joy of the Lord is your strength.'" Sam very matter of factly said, "You either believe it, or you don't." How profound were these words! They believed, and we saw.

Folks, let your song be, "The joy of the Lord is my strength,"—no matter your circumstances. Sing it! Believe it! Live it! Ask our Lord for strength to do so.

DECEMBER 9   WONDERFULLY MADE

Key Verse: *"...for I am fearfully and wonderfully made..." (Psalm 139:14).*

Message: My friend Macy was invited to a baby shower and was asked to bring a letter to the baby. I thought that the contents of this letter would be good for a parent or grandparent to share with a special baby. Therefore, with Macy's permission, I will now share the message with you:

"Dear Baby from Heaven,

"David talked about you in Psalm 139. There he gives you some wonderful words to speak to our Lord when you are able to talk to Him.

"Here are some of the things you can say: *'You created every part of me; You put me together in my mother's womb....When my bones were being formed, carefully put together in my mother's womb, when I was growing there in secret, you knew I was there—you saw me before I was born...' (Psalm 139:13, 15-16a GN).*

"Our Father in heaven knew everything about you before you were placed in your mother's womb. He wrote your name in His book before your parents wrote it on the birth certificate. He made you for a purpose. You are like no other person; you are individually different.

"When you realize how special you are, you can say to our Lord: *'I will praise thee; for I am fearfully and wonderfully made...'"* *(Psalm 139:14).*

As you pray today, tell the Lord that you know how special this baby is to you and thank Him for sending this bundle of joy into your life.

DECEMBER 10   TRUST

Key Verse: *"It is better to <u>trust</u> in the Lord than to put confidence in man" (Psalm 118:8).*

Message: Psalm 117 is the shortest chapter in the Bible. Its theme is praise. Psalm 119 is the longest. Its theme is the Word of God. To me, this placement emphasizes how important it is for believers to praise our Lord and to love and live His Word.

Now in between these two Psalms is Psalm 118. It contains the middle verse in the Bible: *"It is better to trust in the Lord than to put confidence in man" (118:8)*. This verse sets the theme of the entire Bible. Its teaching is the major point of all Scripture.

Let's look at some of the people in the Bible who put their trust in God. David is one. Saul became jealous of David and tried to have him killed. On one occasion when God delivered him out of the hands of Saul and the rest of his enemies, David said, *"The Lord is my rock....in him will I trust..." (2 Samuel 22:3)*. Is He your rock?

David says in Psalm 2:12: *"...Blessed are they that put their trust in him."* He says in 40:4: *"Blessed is that man that maketh the Lord his trust...."* Need a blessing? Trust!

Nahum said, *"The Lord is good, a stronghold in the day of trouble, and he knoweth them that trust in him" (1:7)*. Does this include you?

Then there is Job. He is the epitome of one who trusted the Lord. There came a time in his life when it seemed that God had turned His back on him. Yet, he said, *"Though he slay me, yet will I trust in him..." (Job 13:15)*. And he got a blessing. He went through the fire, but God brought him through. Job 42:12 says, *"So the Lord blessed the latter end of Job more than his beginning."*

See what happens when you are faithful, when you trust God in the midst of the fiery furnace, when you hold on to the hem of His garment, no matter what! Just trust Him. Man will fail you; our Lord will not. When you trust Him, no matter what happens, He has a blessing waiting for you. Pray for strength to trust day by day.

DECEMBER 11   DESIRES

Key Verse: *"Delight thyself also in the Lord, and he shall give you the desires of your heart" (Psalm 37:4)*.

Message: If you are a believer, Satan cannot possess you. Jesus said in John 10:28: *"I give unto them* (His sheep) *eternal life; and they shall never perish, neither shall any man pluck them out of my* *hand."* Satan cannot possess you, but he can get a stronghold on your life, maybe without your even realizing it.

How can he do this? One way is to work on a person's unfulfilled desires. What are some of them? "I want to get married."—"I want a baby."—"I want to make a lot of money."—"I want to be popular." You get the idea. If you identify with any of these, be careful. If you dwell on your desire, it will become a stronghold on your life. Satan will use it to lead you to choose to be unequally yoked when you are wanting a mate. He will lead you to be bitter when you can't have a baby. He will lead you to commit adultery when you don't feel loved at home. He will lead you to work long hours and cut corners when you are seeking to make a lot of money. He will lead you to lower your standards when you want to be popular.

How often do you let Satan influence you to dwell on your unfulfilled desires? Too many times, very often! If so, you have a stronghold that is hindering your walk with the Lord. You are in a spiritual battle. Paul says in 2 Corinthians 10:4: *"For the weapons of our warfare are not carnal* (of the flesh), *but mighty through God to the pulling down of strongholds."*

We can only pull them down with the help of our Lord. Paul said in 2 Corinthians 10:5 GN) that we are to *"take every thought captive and make it obey Christ.".* We must, as an act of our will, turn our eyes on Jesus when Satan throws a stronghold against us.

Now let's concentrate on the key verse: *"Delight thyself in the Lord...."* When you are occupied with your unfulfilled desires, you won't. You will be depressed. You must force yourself to get your eyes back on the Lord.

When you do, *"he shall give you the desires of your heart,"* but your desire will become His will, and you will be content with the outcome. Satan will no longer have a stronghold over you. Ask the Lord to help you with the process.

DECEMBER 12   CAST YOUR BURDEN

Key Verse: *"Cast your burden upon the Lord..." (Psalm 56:22).*

Message: You probably do a better job of quoting this verse than you do of practicing it, particularly when you have a spouse or a grown child or another family member for whom you are concerned.

You probably have talked with him about his relationship to the Lord, about his lifestyle, about specific sins in his life. You have probably put him on a guilt trip, even resorted to playing the Holy Spirit in his life. Yet, to no avail! So, what do you do?

Here is what I suggest. Get the responsibility off of you and onto the Lord Jesus. *"Cast your burden upon the Lord...."* Simply tell our Lord, "I've done all I know to do. Nothing has worked. Therefore, I am placing him in your hands. Please do whatever you need to do in order to accomplish your will in his life. I take hands off."

Tell the person involved that you are through trying to change him and will no longer attempt to do so. Then tell him that you will be praying only one prayer for him, and this is it: "Lord, please do whatever you need to do in order to accomplish your will in _____'s life."

Will this be hard to do? Yes! Will you always succeed? No! But should you keep praying this prayer? Yes!

You see, in the final analysis, no matter what you do, you cannot change anyone. The best you can do will probably end up putting the one about whom you are concerned on a guilt trip or turning him off. The best our Lord can do has no limits. He loves you and wants to give you your heart's desire. Make 1 Peter 5:7 a life verse: *"Casting all your care upon him, for he careth for you."*

As you pray your new prayer each day, be sure to follow it. Do not let your resolve break down in practice.

DECEMBER 13   GOOD CONSCIENCE

Key Verse: *"Having a good conscience..." (1 Peter 3:16).*

Message: In chapter 3, Peter is talking about the way a believer is to live. One thing he said is that a Christian is to have a good conscience. Let's define a good conscience. It is that moral regulator in your heart of what is right or wrong. A Christian should be careful not to do anything that will bother the conscience. We all know what it is to have our consciences bother us. So what should we do?

In his commentary on 1 Peter, Warren Wiersbe says this: "Conscience may be compared to a window that lets in the light of God's truth." This is a good analogy.

Think of your conscience as a window. When you do something that bothers your conscience, a little dirt gets on your window. Right then get the glass cleaner out and clean that window.

Let's take an example. One of God's truths is found in Hebrews 10:25. There the writer says that we are not to *"forsake the assembling of ourselves together...."* You obey. You go to church on Sunday. You miss once because you are tired. Your conscience bothers you. You get a little dirt on your window. If you don't go the next Sunday, your conscience will still bother you, and you will add more dirt to your window. If you keep missing, you will get so much dirt on your window that the light of your conscience cannot shine through. Paul says that when you get to this point, *"your conscience is defiled" (Titus 1:15).*

Do not let this happen to you. The first time you feel guilty, get the glass cleaner out and clean off that dirt. I once heard a friend say that she prays that if her child does something wrong, he gets caught the first time he errs. A good practice!

Why don't you ask the Lord to prick your conscience the first time you get a little dirt on your window? If you do, you can sing with Jiminy Cricket, "Always let your conscience be your guide."

DECEMBER 14   YOUR FEET

Key Verse: *"I have refrained my feet from every evil way, that I might keep thy word"*
(Psalm 119:101).

Message: What do you say about your feet? "My feet hurt because I have been on them too long."—"These shoes are hurting my feet."—"This corn is killing me."

Do you ever stop to think that your feet can lead you into trouble? You might think about meeting someone else's spouse, but your feet have to start moving in order for you to get there. You might think about going some place a Christian should not go, but your feet have to start moving in order for you to get there. It is so easy for you to let your feet take you into sin. So what are you to do?

I suggest that you consider your feet in a spiritual way. We are to avoid obstacles that will spiritually trip us up. Listen to the advice given in Proverbs 4:26-27: *"Ponder the path of thy feet….turn not to the right hand nor to the left; remove thy foot from evil."* Also listen to Hebrews 12:13: *"Make straight paths for your feet…."* When you do this, you will refrain your feet "from every evil way." You will have spiritual feet.

When I think of spiritual feet, I think of Arthur Blessitt, the man who has carried a cross all over the world. I heard him speak one time. In the midst of his talk, he took off his shoes and socks, held up a foot, and said to us in essence, "See, my feet are soft. I have no corns or callouses. Do you know why?" Then he quoted Romans 10:15 to us: *"How beautiful are the feet of them that preach the gospel of peace, and bring glad tidings of good things!"*

You might not have beautiful physical feet, but you can have beautiful spiritual feet if you take up your cross and point your feet down the path of righteousness.

Can you pray with the Psalmist: *"I have refrained my feet from every evil way…."*? I pray that you can; but if not, tell our Lord that you will begin today to do so.

DECEMBER 15   STAND

Key Verse: *"Your adversary the devil, as a roaring lion, walketh about, seeking whom he may devour"* (1 Peter 5:8).

Message: Satan works through lost people to accomplish his goal. This fact was made very clear to me as I read in the "Georgia Christian Index" a testimony of a pastor who had at one time been a Satanist.

When he was a Satanist, he met up with a witch at his office. They were a powerful combination. He said, "If we had a run-in with someone, we would cast a spell of sickness, marital strife, or financial loss on them. We would throw all sorts of things at them to cause them harm, and we saw the results very clearly."

Notice what he said about their power over Christians: "The power over Christians was less effective, but those without a strong commitment to Christ were more vulnerable."

He worked with one of those sold-out believers. This man loved to persecute Christians. He worked with one lady that he wanted to get rid of because she witnessed to him on several occasions. He said that he did everything he could to get rid of her. Here are his words: "I could never touch her. There was such a hedge of protection around her that I could never penetrate." And God used this lady to play a great part in this man's conversion.

I hope you noticed that because this lady was a living testimony for the Lord, the Satanist and the witch could not get through her protective hedge to harm her. I pray that this is your testimony.

Folks, there is a "hedge" that you must wear daily in order to keep the roaring lion away from you. Paul tells what it is in Ephesians 6:11: *"Put on the whole armor of God that ye may be able to stand against the wiles (schemes) of the devil."* Don't leave home without this armor, and don't leave home without asking the Lord for strength to stand.

DECEMBER 16   NO OTHER GOD
Key Verse: *"Thou shalt have none other gods before (beside) me"* *(Deuteronomy 5:7).*

Message: The pastor I mentioned yesterday had another god in his home before he got saved: Satan! The man's wife and children had left him (they were reunited later); he was the only one in the house, and Satan was enthroned there, and so were his tools: a Satanic bible, literature, candles, and books on how to cast spells.

When this man got saved, he knew that he had to get this Satanic material out of his house, but he had a hard time doing so. Satan did all he could to keep his hold on his former follower.

Listen to what happened when he started to get rid of the Satanic materials: "I went over to the Satanic bible and picked it up, and I was hit by a force like I had felt only once before when I had been electrocuted." (He had been hit by 860 volts of electricity while in the military.) He went on to say, "That's when I got a broom and mop, and holding them by the straw and cloth ends, picked up the Satanic bible by the wooden handles like giant chopsticks and took it outside to the trash can."

Satan will do everything he can to keep his own serving him and God's own from serving Him. Do you know how this man got into Satanism? He said, "In 1994, power and money were my gods."

In 1 Timothy 6:10, Paul warns: *"For the love of money is the root of all evil, which...some coveted after...."* In 1994, this man personified this verse. Paul is saying that the love of money is the source of all evil. "Coveted after" means that some people have "striven after" money as the goal of their lives.

Of course, you cannot be taken over by Satan if you are saved, but you can be influenced to follow his ways. If you see yourself in any way in the previous paragraph, run for your life and ask the Lord to put money in the right perspective in your life.

DECEMBER 17 NO OTHER GOD
Key Verse: *"Thou shalt have none other gods before (beside) me"* *(Deuteronomy 5:7).*

Message: Satan will do anything he can to keep you from getting rid of something that honors him, even if it is a picture of Buddha. That is what my friend Terri had in her house. After she got saved, having that picture in her house bothered her. She and I talked about what she should do with this fine painting.

One morning as I was sitting on my blue couch, a Scripture passage came to my mind. I called Terri and asked her to read Deuteronomy 5:7-9 and to meditate on these words from the passage: *"Thou shalt have none other gods before (beside) me....I the Lord thy God am a jealous God...."*

She did and felt convicted to get that picture out of her house and burn it, but Satan did not make it easy. Terri took it into the back yard and tried to set it on fire. She used a whole box of matches, except one, but the picture would not catch on fire.

She still had a whole picture, but only one match. I believe the Holy Spirit took over at this point. She felt led to put the painting into a sack. She did and struck her last match. It worked! The picture began to burn. Terri stood there and watched, but she said that the sound that comes from that bag was not like the sound of a normal fire. I believe that Satan was trying to keep that Buddha from burning, right down to the last minute.

Folks, don't let anything that honors Satan abide in your home. The longer you do, the harder it will be to get rid of it. Ask the Lord to point out to you anything in your home that honors Satan. When He does so, get out the matches!

DECEMBER 18   EVERLASTING
Key Verse: *"...Every one that seeth the Son, and believeth on him may have everlasting life" (John 6:40).*

Message: "Everlasting" is a comforting word for believers in Jesus. Think of the promise made in the key verse. Think of the promise made in John 3:16: *"For God so loved the world, that he gave his only begotten Son, that whosoever believeth in him should not perish, but have everlasting life."* The word our Lord had for Israel is the same word He has for us: *"...I have loved thee with an everlasting love..." (Jeremiah 31:3).*

Don't you just love this word, "everlasting"? Our Lord's love for us is everlasting. Our Lord's plan for us is everlasting life with Him.

Well, the word "everlasting" took on a new meaning to me one day as I was talking to Mr. Brown and my five-year-old friend, Austin. When they started to walk away from me, Mr. Brown told him to give me an everlasting hug. I had a quizzical look on my face as he hugged me, because I did not know what an everlasting hug was; but I soon found out. As they walked away, Austin turned around, looked at me, and said, "It's still there." What a precious thought! The hug stays after the hugger is gone.

That is a thought for us to remember when we need a word of comfort or cheer. Here is another. Moses said, *"God's eternal (ever-lasting) arms are your support..." (Deuteronomy 33:27).* Truly, they are. His arms always hold us up. Why not sing to Him today, "What have I to dread, what have I to fear, Leaning on the everlasting arms? I have blessed peace with my Lord so near, Leaning on the everlasting arms." His arms will always embrace us. When you cannot seem to feel His hug, remember, it is always there.

DECEMBER 19 GOD'S UNDERSHEPHERD
Key Verse: *"...Ye shall receive a crown of glory..." (1 Peter 5:4).*

Message: I realize that I write a lot about the God-called pastor, the undershepherd of the church. I just believe it is so crucial that we understand what the Bible says about him.

In 1 Peter 5:2 and 3, we see some very important qualifications for the pastor: *"Feed the flock of God which is among you, taking the oversight thereof, not by constraint, but willingly; not for filthy lucre, but of a ready mind. Neither as being lords over God's heritage, but being examples to the flock."*

Let's look at what the pastor is not supposed to do. He is not to take the office unwillingly; he is not to work for money, although we should pay him well; he is not to be a dictator. Let's look at what he is supposed to do. He is to feed the flock; he is to shepherd the flock; he is to be an example to the people.

What happens when the pastor meets these qualifications? In 5:4 (GN) Peter says, *"And when the chief Shepherd shall appear, ye shall receive a crown of glory that fadeth not away (that will never lose its brightness.*

I did some thinking about the last part of verse 4: *"Ye shall receive a crown of glory that will never lose its brightness."* Peter has been talking about suffering all through this book. I can tell you that no servant of God suffers as much as the pastor does. He is under constant scrutiny. People just seem to think that it is all right to criticize him.

I believe Peter is saying that the God-called, God-serving pastor will receive a very bright and shining crown that will be a badge of honor for eternity. We will lay our crowns at Jesus' feet, but I believe the faithful pastor will have a special crown for faithful service and faithful suffering.

I may be going a little far, but I have to add this. From time to time a pastor falls. We are quick to put all the blame on him. I wonder if the church might need to bear some of the responsibility. What might happen if we spent as much time supporting the pastor as we do criticizing him? What might happen if we said as many encouraging words as we say discouraging words? Today, why don't you tell the Lord how thankful you are for your pastor, and then tell him. You will be glad you did.

DECEMBER 20   GROW

Key Verse: *"But grow in grace, and in the knowledge of our Lord and Savior Jesus Christ..." (2 Peter 2:18).*

Message: In his second epistle, Peter emphasizes that after our salvation, we are to *"...grow in grace, and in the knowledge of our Lord and Savior Jesus Christ..." (2:18).* In verses five through seven, he lists several things that must characterize our lives in order for us to grow.

One is the word "virtue." This is a word that has changed. To us it means a person who has a good character. That was not the meaning when Peter wrote this epistle. Virtue here means moral energy. Be sure your faith is an energetic faith. How excited are you about your faith? How energetic are you about sharing it? I am reminded of a story that my friend Doris told me.

On an Easter Sunday afternoon, Doris was watching her four-year-old grandson play with the toys from her toy box. He took out two toy men. He picked up one and said, "This is a good man. He loves Jesus."

Never missing an opportunity to teach her grandchildren, Doris asked, "Ethan, did you know that Jesus died for us?" He looked at her in wide-eyed wonder and asked, "Grandma, is Jesus dead?" Quickly Doris replied, "Oh no! He died, but He is alive now and living for us." Ethan gave a sigh of relief and said, "I'm so glad."

Ethan often gives this message to people with whom he comes in contact. With all the vigor he can muster, he proclaims, "Jesus died for us, but He ain't dead now. He is living again!"

I can think of no better message for us to share than this word from the lips of a child. Just thank the Lord that "He ain't dead," and then get the word to those who need to hear it. To do so is a sign of your growth.

DECEMBER 21   PRAISE
Key Verse: *"Praise ye the Lord..." (Psalm 149:1).*

Message: In the last few years, I have come to realize how important it is for us to praise the Lord through music. Listen to these words from the Psalmist: *"Praise ye the Lord. Sing unto the Lord a new song, and his praise in the congregation of saints....Let them praise his name in the dance; let them sing praises unto him with the timbrel (drum) and harp" (Psalm 149:1,3).*

Now notice what the Psalmist says right after he says to praise the Lord by singing and dancing and playing the drum and the harp: *"For the Lord taketh pleasure in his people..." (149:4).* Our Lord takes pleasure in praise worship when we gather as a congregation.

I also believe He takes pleasure in praise worship when we are alone in our quiet time. Let's look at David. He gave us a wonderful promise in Psalm 9:9-10. Here he gives us another reason to sing: *"The Lord also will be a refuge for the oppressed, a refuge in times of trouble. And they that know thy name will put their trust in thee...."*

David is saying that if you are a believer, you will put your trust in the Lord, and He will be your stronghold when you are down and a refuge when a trial comes. This is your "blessed assurance."

Do you know what David said to do when you have this assurance? He said, *"Sing praises to the Lord..." (Psalm 9:11).*

Make music, folks. If you play an instrument, play as unto the Lord. If you sing, sing as unto the Lord. No matter the situation, in a down time or an up time, sing. Why don't you sing a praise song to our Lord in your quiet time today?

DECEMBER 22

THE CHURCH AND THE PASTOR

Key Verse: *"...And to esteem them very highly in love" (1 Thessalonians 5:13).*

Message: I know that I have written a lot about the church and the pastor, but I must continue to do so because I believe the church is not operating with the power our Lord intended. When this is true, we look for reasons in all the wrong places: lack of money, lack of new members, lack of baptisms, lack of facilities, lack of workers, etc. I believe the greatest reason is that the congregation does not respect and love and follow the leadership of the pastor.

Of course we need money and new members and baptisms and facilities and workers, and I believe the church would have all of these things if the relationship between the pastor and the congregation ever became what our Lord intended it to be.

Now in this message, I am going to concentrate on what would make this happen by asking some questions and answering them with scripture.

1. To whom does the church belong? Not to the congregation, as some people seem to think! In Acts 20:28, Paul calls it *"the church of God."* 1 Peter 5:2 calls the church *"the flock of God."* God has put over it the One who *"loved the church and gave himself for it."* –our Lord Jesus Christ!

2. Who calls the pastor to a church? Not the congregation, as some people seem to think! Not even the pastor-search committee! I have served on three, and our desire each time was to find God's man; we had no agenda. So who calls the pastor? Paul tells us in Acts 20:28: *"Take heed therefore unto yourselves, and to all the flock, over the which the <u>Holy Ghost</u> <u>hath</u> <u>made</u> <u>you</u> <u>overseer</u>...."* The Holy Spirit leads God's man to the church and the church to God's man.

3. How is the flock to treat the pastor? Not by telling him how to run the church and criticizing him when he doesn't fall in line! Then how? In 1 Timothy 5:17, Paul says that pastors who rule well are to be *"counted worthy of double honor,"* which means "respect" or "regard." In 1 Thessalonians 5:13,

Paul says to *"esteem them (pastors) very highly in love for their work's sake...."* The flock is to love the undershepherd and give him double respect.

4. How is the congregation to respond to the pastor? Hebrews 13:17 gives the perfect answer: *"Obey them that have the rule over you, and submit yourselves...."* Obey and submit. It's just that simple.

I can only imagine what our Lord could do in a church in which the flock and the undershepherd carried out His plan for them. As you pray today, tell the Lord that you will do your part to make the church where you worship the Lord's church.

DECEMBER 23   BUILD
Key Verse: *"...Consider your ways" (Haggai 1:5).*

Message: Every growing church will probably at one time or another need to enter into a building program. It is amazing to see how the people respond. Some might react the way Israel did in Haggai's day.

Haggai was called by God to be a prophet to the Jews who returned from exile in Babylon. At that time the foundation of the new temple had been laid. However, the work had been stopped because of opposition from enemy neighbors and apathy of the people. God called Haggai to rouse the people to get back to building the temple.

I want you to notice what God said to the people through Haggai in verse 2: *"This people say, 'The time is not come...that the Lord's house should be built.'"* What were they doing when they said this? God lets us know by asking this question: *"Is it time for you, O ye, to dwell in your ceiled houses, and this house lie waste?"* Here our God is pointing out the selfishness of these people. They were only interested in their houses, not God's house.

Do you see today's church here? To a great extent, it is a selfish church, more interested in building their own houses than the house of God.

Now in verse 5 and in four more verses in this prophecy, our Lord gave these folks some sound advice: *"Consider your ways."* He is appealing to these folks to take note of what they were doing and change their ways.

And with this admonition, the Lord said in essence, "Get to work." Did they? Verse 14 tells us that the people *"came and did work in the house of the Lord of hosts, their God."* The <u>Good News</u> puts it this way: *"Zerubbabel, the governor of Judah; Joshua, the High Priest, and all the people who had returned from exile."* All!

I believe the call to the church about to enter a building program is, *"Consider your ways."* How about your ways? Are they selfish? Are you more interested in your house than God's house? If you are, would you be willing to let the Holy Spirit lead you to put God's house above yours? Why not give your answer to the Lord today?

DECEMBER 24   SAY THE NAME

Key Verse: *"...The Lord my God will enlighten my darkness"* *(Psalm18:28).*

Message: Recently, the choir at the church I attend sang a beautiful song called, "Say the Name." Of course, that name is Jesus.

These words from that song stuck in my mind: "When you can't find the words to say, and you don't even know how to pray, When you can't make it one more day, Just say the name of Jesus."

As I listened to these words, I thought of the sobbing women who have sat in my living room and said to me, "I am hurting so badly that I cannot even pray." I have said to them, "When you cannot bring yourself to pray, just say the name of Jesus over and over. He will accept His name as a prayer. And He will do more."

Another line of the song says, "He's gonna make a way when you say Jesus." And He truly will. Consider David. Saul was after him; many enemies were after him. He was in a dark period, but he knew that there was hope. In Psalm 18:28, he said, *"For thou wilt light my candle; the Lord my God will enlighten my darkness."* And He did! He will do it for you also. Just keep saying the name of Jesus when you can say nothing else. "Jesus! Jesus! Jesus!" When you do, there will come a time when the Lord will turn your darkness into light. Keep praying this one-word prayer: Jesus!

DECEMBER 25   OBEY THE LAW

Key Verse: *"Submit yourselves to every ordinance (institution) of man for the Lord's sake..." (1 Peter 2:13).*

Message: Now let me say first of all that we are to obey the law of the land unless it contradicts the law of God. Under no circumstance does our verse tell us to submit to any law that violates God's commands.

However, to obey God is to obey legitimate civil authority. We should make a commitment to being the best citizens possible *"for the Lord's sake"* as a witness of His.

Now I am sure you submit in most ways. You pay your taxes; you build your house according to the building code; you do not park in a handicapped space; you pay your bills; generally, you obey the law. Obey the law!!! Let me talk to you about this.

Being a law-abiding citizen often stops when you get behind the wheel of your car. The speed limit says 70 miles per hour. You abide by the law; but your foot gets a little heavier as you rationalize that you have to speed because you are in a hurry to get home or to a meeting or to a game or to any other destination. You might even brag that you made the trip in a shorter time than the law allows. Do you ever consciously acknowledge that you have broken the law? Do you ever consciously realize that you might have hurt your witness?

Let me tell you a little story I once heard. The story goes that when a Christian gets behind the wheel, an angel rides on each of the four corners of the car, but that they all fall off when he exceeds the speed limit. This may be fiction, but there is a lesson here. Obey the law as if it is a law of God. Actually, it really is. In Romans 13:1 (GN), Paul says, *"Everyone must obey state authorities because no authority exists without God's permission, and the existing authorities have been put there by God."*

If you have taken speeding lightly, tell the Lord that you will obey the speed limit *"for his sake"* and for your witness. I have to add to this. If you read this, grin sheepishly, plead guilty, and keep right on speeding, beware! Remember Psalm 33:13: *"The Lord looketh from heaven; he beholdeth all the sons of men."*

DECEMBER 26   GOD'S WILL
Key Verse: *"Concerning the words of men, by the word of thy lips I have kept me from the paths of the destroyer" (Psalm 17:4).*

Message: Recently my pastor, Brother Mark, preached on how a person can know the will of God. One point he made was that we must discern Biblical standards versus cultural norms. The cultural norms come by *"the words of men."* Biblical standards come from *"the words of thy lips."*

Brother Mark made it clear that we must know the words that come from the lips of God. He then gave us some passages to study and learn and follow. They are as follows:

1. The Ten Commandments (Exodus 20:1-17)— These are practical guides for everyday living. The first one says, *"Thou shalt have no other gods before me" (20:3).* Remember! Anything you put before our Lord is a god.

2. The Sermon on the Mount (Matthew 5-7) Verses 3-11— all begin with *"Blessed,"* which means "happy, happy." Strive to follow each one. Then in the Sermon Jesus teaches on many subjects that believers face; for example, anger, adultery, divorce, love for enemies, giving, fasting, etc. We must know and practice what Jesus says in His Sermon.

3. The Parables (Matthew, Mark, and Luke)— Most of us understand that a parable is an earthly story with a heavenly meaning. Jesus used the parables to convey spiritual truth through earthly comparison. There are many parables. A section in the back of my King James Study Bible lists thirty-nine of them. They will speak to you if you study them, learn the meaning of them, and follow them.

We have just seen how a growing believer is to learn the Word and follow it in a world in the hands of Satan. I always tell a new believer to begin by studying the book of John. It begins, *"In the* beginning was the Word...." Then it goes on to tell us all about our wonderful Lord, the Son of God, and what He has done for us.

Tell the Lord that you will follow Paul's advice in 2 Timothy 2:15: *"Study to show thyself approved unto God...."*

DECEMBER 27   GOD'S WILL

Key Verse: *"For I know the plans I have for you..."(Jeremiah 29:11).*

Message: One of the things that I teach over and over is that when God sends a person down here, He sends him with a recorded life plan. In Psalm 139:6, David prayed, *"...in thy book all my members were written...."* In the Good News he prayed, *"You saw me before I was born."* God said to Jeremiah, *"For I know the plans I have for you..."* *(Jeremiah 29:11)* God also said to him: *"Before I formed thee in the womb, I knew thee,...and I ordained thee as a prophet..."* *(Jeremiah 1:5).* These verses apply to us also.

Our entire planned lives are recorded in God's book. If we are saved, our Lord will reward us on how well we followed that plan. In Revelation 22:12, our Lord said, *"And, behold, I come quickly; and my reward is with me, to give every man according as his work shall be."*

Now I believe there is one way to tell if you are following God's plan. If you are, He will have other believers encourage you. They will tell you that you have helped them or blessed them or taught them or encouraged them. Of course, you do not go around seeking confirmation from anyone that you are in God's will. If you are, confirmation will come.

Now I must add this. Every person is listed in God's book of life. However, the person who refuses to be saved will have his name blotted out. Revelation 20:15 says, *"And whosoever was not found written in the book of life was (will be) cast into the lake of fire."* I wish I didn't have to write this. I want everyone to be saved by the blood of Jesus and rewarded at His coming. As you pray today, tell the Lord that you want to be in His perfect will, not His permissive will. You be a blessing to someone today.

DECEMBER 28   KNOW AND GROW
Key Verse: *"But grow...in the knowledge of our Lord and Savior Jesus Christ..." (2 Peter 3:18).*

Message: When you study the two epistles of Peter, you will see that the overall theme is that we are to know Jesus Christ as Savior and to grow to be like Him.

If you are a believer, you are to grow. Paul said in Ephesians 4:15 (GN): *"...we must grow up in every way to Christ...."* We must grow up in everything, in every respect to conform to Christ—to be like Him in every way.

Our key verse says, *"But grow...in the knowledge of our Lord and Savior Jesus Christ...."* We must know Him in every respect in order to grow to be like Him.

And in order to grow to be like Jesus, we must heed Peter's words: *"As newborn babes, desire the sincere (pure) milk of the word, that ye may grow thereby" (1 Peter 2:2).* If you are growing, you will have a craving for God's Word just as a baby does for milk. And when you have this craving that leads you to stay in God's Word, you will *"grow like a cedar in Lebanon" (Psalm 92:12).*

You know, the cedar is an interesting tree. It grows in snow and in storms. Its roots reach down and wrap around the rocks. Get the picture! If you are growing like a cedar, you will make it through the snows and storms of life because your roots will wrap around the *"...rock that is higher than I" (Psalm 61:2).*

There is a little song that goes like this: "To be like Jesus, to be like Jesus, all I ask to be like Him. All through life's journey from earth to glory, all I ask, to be like Him." Why don't you sing this to the Lord today? Why don't you make it your theme song? Know: grow!!!

DECEMBER 29   MOUTH
Key Verse: *"...so is he that singeth songs to a heavy heart" (Proverbs 25:20).*

Message: In 2005 Hurricanes Katrina and Rita destroyed much of the coasts of Mississippi, Louisiana, and Texas. Many people had lost all they had worked for all of their lives. Let's say that you have the opportunity to minister to some of your Christian brothers. What should you say to them? First let me tell you what not to say: *"As he that taketh away a garment in cold weather, and as vinegar upon nitre (soda), so is he that singeth songs to a heavy heart" (Proverbs 25:20).* Don't tell these folks that time will heal—that everything will work out all right—that they just have to trust. At this point they probably do not even want you to quote Scripture.

They do not want you to tell them about tomorrow. They need help right now. They just need to know that you care, and they need to see you extend Jesus' hand. Sometimes they just want you to sit with them and say nothing or listen to them. They need for you to pray in your quiet time that Romans 8:28 will become a life verse for this season.

We have talked about what you can do to help your brothers. Now what can these folks who have lost much do? They can become devastated and grow bitter, or they can initially be devastated and grow better. The choice is up to them. May I say this to you? Becoming better is a process. Don't try to rush these folks. Just pray that they will walk toward recovery, clinging to Romans 8:28: *"All things work together for good to them that love the Lord...."*

DECEMBER 30   BENEFITS
Key Verse: *"...and forget not all his benefits" (Psalm 103:2).*

Message: David began Psalm 103 with a praise: *"Bless the Lord, O my soul, and all that is within me, bless his holy name."* Then he added in verse 2: *"...and forget not all his benefits."*

Usually when we think of benefits, we think in worldly terms; for example, when a person is applying for a job, he wants to know the benefits: salary, insurance, vacation time, etc. However, David is talking about spiritual or soul benefits: *"Bless the Lord, O my soul...."* What are these benefits? Let me list a few of them.

1. *"Who forgiveth all thine iniquities..."(103:3a).* The idea here is that our Lord takes away confessed sins and puts them somewhere else. In verse 12, David says where our Lord

puts them: *"As far as the east is from the west, so far hath he removed our transgressions from us."* What a benefit!

2. *"...who healeth all our diseases" (103:3b).* Now our Lord does heal physical diseases, on earth or in heaven; but David is talking about disease of the soul. These all abide in your old nature. I am sure you are quite familiar with them: greed, guilt, hate, jealousy, depression, anger, etc. If you confess these soul diseases and forsake them, the Holy Spirit will fill you with the fruit Jesus gave him for you: *"...love, joy, peace, long-suffering, kindness, goodness, faithfulness, gentleness, self-control..." (Galatians 5:22-23 NKJ).* What a benefit!

3. *"Who satisfieth thy mouth with good things; so that thy youth is renewed like the eagle's" (103:5).* I am going to quote from John Phillips' Exploring the Psalms: "Rotherham tells us that the word translated mouth can be rendered old age. 'He satisfieth their old age with good things so that their youth is renewed like the eagle's.' How wonderful to be one of God's happy old people." I can praise the Lord because, like David, I am one of God's happy old people. What a benefit!

Read the rest of Psalm 103 and thank the Lord for all His benefits.

DECEMBER 31 BLESSED TO BLESS

Key Verse: *"...show how great things God hath done unto thee..." (Luke 8:39).*

Message: As you know by now, I teach that God honors righteousness. Proverbs 10:6 says, *"Blessings are upon the head of the just...."* Proverbs 28:20 says, *"A faithful man shall abound with blessings...."* When these blessings come, we praise the Lord and thank Him for them. We stop there, but we are to take another step. I believe we are blessed in order to be a blessing to someone else. My friend Julia shared with our Sunday School class that she stresses this in her home. Jesus taught this principle.

Remember the man of Gadara? Jesus cleansed him of a whole lot of demons. He begged to travel with Jesus, *"...but Jesus sent him away, saying, 'Return to thine own house, and show how great things God hath done unto thee....'"(Luke 8:38-39).* In other words, Jesus said, "You have been blessed; now go home and pass that blessing on to other people." He did so. *"And he went his way, and published (proclaimed) throughout the whole city how great things Jesus had done unto him" (Luke 8:39b).* This man was blessed, and he blessed others.

Never let a blessing stop with you. I am one who is truly blessed. I cannot begin to tell you what the Lord does for me through other people. I have a personal policy. When someone blesses me, I, in some way bless someone else that the Lord lays on my heart. It is rather amazing that the recipient is seldom the person who has blessed me. I challenge you. When you are blessed, bless someone else. Ask the Lord to reveal the one you are to bless. Your life will change if you do so.

I close this book by saying to you that if the Lord has taught you anything that has blessed you, pass it on. God bless!

Bibliography

Alcorn, Randy, <u>The Treasure Principle</u>. Sisters, Oregon: Multinomah Publishers, Inc., 2001.

Bentley, Michael, <u>Saving a Fallen World</u>. Darlington, Co. Durham, DLI IRQ, England: Evangelical Press, 1992.

DeHaan, R.R., <u>Revelation</u>. Grand Rapids, Michigan: Zondervan Publishing House, 1980.

Harris, J. Gerald, <u>Pardoned to be Priests</u>. Nashville, Tennessee: Broadman Press, page 59, 1988.

<u>King James Study Bible</u>. Nashville, Tennessee: Thomas Nelson Publishers, 1981.

Lloyd-Jones, D Martin, <u>Darkness and Light</u>. Grand Rapids, Michigan: Baker Books, 2000.

MacArthur, John, <u>Ephesians</u>: Chicago, Illinois: Moody Press, page 258, 1986.

MacArthur, John, <u>Galatians</u>: Chicago, Illinois: Moody Press, 1987.

MacArthur, John, <u>Hebrews</u>. Chicago, Illinois: Moody Press, 1983.

McGee, J. Vernon, Ezra, Nehemiah & Esther. LaVerne, California: El Camino Press, 1977.

McGee, J. Vernon, I & II Kings, LaVerne, California: El Camino Press, 1976.

Patterson, John, Watchman Prayer Guide. Jackson, Mississippi: Colonial Heights Baptist Church, 2007.

Phillips, John, John. Neptune, New Jersey: Loizeaux Brothers, page 260, 1988.

Phillips, John, Exploring the Psalms, Volume I. Neptune, New Jersey: Loizeaux Brothers, 1988.

Phillips, John, Exploring the Psalms, Volume II. Neptune, New Jersey: Loizeaux Brothers, Page 126, 1988.

Strauss, Lehman, Devotional Studies in Galatians and Ephesians. Neptune, New Jersey: Loizeaux Brothers, 1981.

Strauss, Lehman, Revelation. Neptune, New Jersey: Loizeaux Brothers, 1982.

Wiersbe, Warren, Be Hopeful. Wheaton, Illinois: Victor Brothers, page 85, 1994.

Printed in the United States
122689LV00004B/7-30/P